SOULCRAFT

How God Shapes Us Through Relationships

Douglas D. Webster

InterVarsity Press
Downers Grove, Illinois

InterVarsity Press
P.O. Box 1400, Downers Grove, IL 60515
World Wide Web: www.ivpress.com
E-mail: mail@ivpress.com

InterVarsity Press® is the book-publishing division of InterVarsity Christian Fellowship/USA®, a student movement active on campus at hundreds of universities, colleges and schools of nursing in the United States of America, and a member movement of the International Fellowship of Evangelical Students. For information about local and regional activities, write Public Relations Dept., InterVarsity Christian Fellowship/USA, 6400 Schroeder Rd., P.O. Box 7895, Madison, WI 53707-7895.

All Scripture quotations, unless otherwise indicated, are taken from the Holy Bible, New International Version®. NIV®. *Copyright ©1973, 1978, 1984 by International Bible Society. Used by permission of Zondervan Publishing House. All rights reserved.*

The letters on pages 167-68, 183, 202 and 220 are used by permission. Joanne Blackford's testimony on pages 144-46 is used by permission. Beth Brewer McCartney's testimony on pages 215-17 is used by permission. The quotes on pages 68-70 from The Hiding Place *©1971 are used by permission of Chosen Books, Inc.*

Cover photograph: Daniel Aubry/The Stock Market

ISBN 0-8308-2253-4

Printed in the United States of America ∞

Library of Congress Cataloging-in-Publication Data

Webster, Douglas D.
  Soulcraft: how God shapes us through relationships/Douglas D. Webster.
    p. cm.
  Includes bibliographical references.
  ISBN 0-8308-2253-4 (pbk.: alk. paper)
    1. Interpersonal relations—Religious aspects—Christianity. I. Title.

BV4597.52.W43 1999
248.4—dc21   *99-048676*

23 22 21 20 19 18 17 16 15 14 13 12 11 10 9 8 7 6 5 4 3 2

18 17 16 15 14 13 12 11 10 09 08 07 06 05 04 03 02 01 00

For Ginny, with love,
a true friend and soulmate
on whose love and wisdom I depend,
and without whom this book would never
have been written.

CONTENTS

1
SOULCRAFT

The law of the LORD is perfect,
reviving the soul.
The statutes of the LORD are trustworthy,
making wise the simple.

P S A L M   1 9 : 7

S OULCRAFT, IF NOT A LOST ART, IS A HIDDEN ART IN NEED OF RECOV-
ery, and there is no better place to begin than with friendship, singleness, marriage and family. Relationships have become the
proving ground for the gospel, impacting the authenticity of worship, ministry and witness. Soulcraft engages relational concerns
and endeavors to relate the gospel of Christ to their full spectrum of
needs and challenges. There is no program or technique for the
recovery of soulcraft, but there is a path for renewal. This path
involves earnest prayer for loving discernment, insight into God's
Word, and the cultivation of the spiritual discipline of humility.
Nothing pragmatic is practical enough to restore soulcraft, but there
is a course of action that will nurture the gifts and abilities essential
to becoming faithful soulcrafters.

Soulcraft may seem like an unusual term at first, but when you live with the concept awhile and allow its meaning to grow, it underscores the true work of the follower of Jesus. If I were writing on carpentry I might begin by offering a simple definition, such as: "Carpentry is the art of cutting, working, and joining timber into structures" and then get into the subject of wood and tools and buildings.[1] This is what I would like to do with soulcraft. Simply said, soulcraft is the art of discerning, applying and enjoying the wisdom of God in every aspect of life.

Most books on spirituality dwell on our communion with God. They focus on our daily walk with God, the character of our worship and the centrality of Christ in the experience of life. The dimension of spiritual formation that I aim to pursue in this book is the impact of our relation to God on our self-understanding, friendships, marriages and parenting styles. To do this I will address the biblical perspective on life in God's creation ("Rhythms of Grace") and what it means to be human ("The Soulful Self"). From there I discuss the relationship between single-hearted devotion to God and singleness ("Wholeness"), and the relationship between loving God and loving one another ("Friendship" and "Two Loves").

The next two chapters deal with what the Word of God has to say about sex. We will look at the beauty and wisdom of human sexuality, in contrast to sexual aversion produced by distorted spirituality ("Body and Soul") and in opposition to the sexual immersion promoted in culture ("East of Eden"). The final five chapters apply Christ-centered spirituality to homosexuality ("Conviction and Compassion"), marriage ("Soulmates"), parenting ("A Little Seminary"), divorce ("Brokenness") and grief ("From Everlasting to Everlasting").

The purpose of this book is to explore what it means to love the Lord our God with all our heart, mind, strength and soul in the ordinary relationships of life. I believe the reason for this book is obvious. The proving ground for the soul has become friendship, singleness, marriage and family. I believe sexuality and all of its related concerns has become our number one challenge. This is where our spirituality is being tested and Christian discipleship is being challenged.

The church is showing that it is having a very hard time living east of Eden. We are confused about what it means to follow Christ into friendships and marriage. We are becoming increasingly aware of the battle for the soul being waged in our midst. Straightforward biblical admonitions such as the apostle Peter's, "Dear friends, I urge you, as aliens and strangers in the world, to abstain from sinful desires, which war against your soul," seem to have about the same moral power among Christians as the warning label on a pack of cigarettes has for smokers (1 Pet 2:11). Our spiritual workmanship in the area of sexuality has become sloppy. Soulcraft engages these concerns and endeavors to relate the gospel of Christ to the full spectrum of relational needs and challenges.

Soul

A good Christian friend asked me what I meant by *soul*.

"It is the essence of who you are," was my response. "The soul is not a part of you like your brain or your liver, it's *you*. You won't find the soul in the cerebral cortex or in DNA, anymore than you'll see the Lord God in space. The soul is not a 'what' but a 'who.'"

"When blacks speak of the soul," he responded, "they mean emotion, passion, rhythm and dance."

Soul describes who we are in the depth of our being. By virtue of being in Christ we experience an inherent emotion, passion and rhythm to life. In a profound sense we are emotionally, ethically and spiritually distinct and set apart from those who are outside of Christ. In Christ we have soul, and the meaning of that soul is nurtured and cultivated in humility.

At the core of our being, in the center of our soul, there is a defining principle that is basic to Christian spirituality. "You are not your own," writes the apostle Paul, "you were bought at a price. Therefore honor God with your body" (1 Cor 6:19-20). If God has your soul he has you lock, stock and barrel, to use an old expression. We can't give our souls to God and keep our bodies. It is a package deal. We are neither bodyless souls nor soulless bodies but bodies and souls in community.[2]

Another friend of mine teaches history at Point Loma University, a Southern California school with a reputation for being one of the best surfing schools in the country. In their spare time, students attend classes and discuss such matters as the soul. In my friend's "High Thinking on Right Living" class, students are taught the Hebrew meaning and Greek tradition behind the early Christian understanding of the soul. They learn that the soul is the immaterial essence that gives to the body life and individuality. Christians have always had a great time debating the distinctions between the soul and the spirit or between the heart and the mind, while through the ages philosophers have been impressed with their own theories on constitutional parts of the person. Some thinkers prefer to divide human beings up three ways—body, soul and spirit (trichotomists); some make a two-way division—body and soul/spirit (dichoto-mists); and some insist that we should view the person simply as a self without distinctions (monists).

I like the way one of my former professors describes the nature of the person: "Man is a unified being, but his being is profoundly cre-ative and complex. This profoundness about man's being can only be understood by the use of the whole set of terms; hence various dimensions of his being are pictured by such terms as 'soul,' 'spirit,' 'heart,' and 'mind.' Of these terms, 'soul' seems to be the most basic."[3] The soul is the vital, living being of the person, and the cen-ter of emotion, desire, intelligence, memory and passions. The soul is the thinking-feeling-loving self, which is at one with the body, yet distinct from the body.

The Bible does not leave the impression, nor should we foster it, that the spirit is limited to spiritual concerns and the soul is focused on relational issues. It is important that spiritual and relational mat-ters are not compartmentalized. For academic purposes colleges separate theology and psychology, and many professors seem to insist on keeping these two departments clearly distinct. Biblical realism suggests that this is both artificial and impossible. We sim-ply cannot divorce internal self-perceptions and relational dynamics from the experience of knowing and loving God. To do so would be as foolish as insisting that soccer players must only make offensive moves or that a baseball manager should emphasize only hitting or pitching.

Spirituality is to psychology what biology is to medicine or what politics is to government. We cannot talk effectively about self-esteem apart from true spirituality, nor can we consider interpersonal relationships apart from our communion with God. The Bible concentrates on both our relationship with God and our relationships with one another, and it does not engage in esoteric speculation about the nature of the person.

I have endeavored to apply Christian theology within the matrix of spirituality and relationships. The lines between psychology, theology and spirituality are blurred. Those who feel they need visas to cross these borders may be confused at first, but my hope is that we will see God's wonderful provision for deep spirituality in the midst of ordinary life. To center our lives in Christ is to center our relationships in the most meaningful way possible.

Followers of Jesus know that it doesn't take a rocket scientist or a high-powered theologian to get us started in the basic work of soulcraft. We don't need to make a mystery of this work or wait for someone special to come along to teach us a secret, foolproof method. The basic skills are elementary. They are to soulcraft what swinging a hammer is to a carpenter or plowing is to the farmer. These basic skills are not only our starting point, but they become essential to our daily practice of soulcraft. They are to the art of soulcraft what listening to the patient is to the art of medicine or working with primary colors is to the artist. The basic skill-set for soulcrafters begins with praying for discernment, knowing the mind of Jesus and cultivating a spirit of humility. If we get these basics down we will be engaged constructively in soulcraft.

Prayer
Soulcraft begins with prayer. There is not a day that goes by in which we don't face a pressing need for discernment. We cannot

spend too much time either by ourselves or with others before we feel compelled to pray. The human community provokes within us a personal sense of the need for wisdom. In ourselves we feel deeply inadequate. Our ability to discern and our capacity to love do not meet the complexities and needs of the human situation. If you never feel this way, just try being a pastor or a counselor for a day or so. Better yet, try being a parent or a friend. Love requires discernment and the source for this discernment is not in ourselves but is the Lord God, our Creator and Redeemer. Community compels authentic communion with God—not pious prayers, rote prayers, list-prayers or glib prayers but an earnest and honest seeking after God's will.

Prayer is to soulcraft what measuring is to carpentry. Carpenters are always measuring and then double-checking to make sure the measurements are accurate. They are always reaching for their tape measures and marking off lines with bold lead. Carpenters are not skilled in guessing, nor do they rely on appearances; their work is exact. Just as carpenters rely on their measurements as a prerequisite to building, soulcrafters rely on prayer, our communion with God. Prayer is where the work begins.

Prayer is not the "spiritual" thing to do; it is the sensible, practical thing to do. Doing soulcraft apart from the Master is foolhardy, impertinent and egotistical. We are often tempted to do our own thing and go it alone, resulting in snap judgments and sloppy workmanship. It seems that we often conclude that our problems are beyond the scope of God's comfort and solution. We turn to psychologists and physicians before turning to the Lord in prayer, tacitly tacitly assuming that modern life has eclipsed the provision of the Lord God. This is not true, however, and our neglect of prayer has been at the expense of our physical, emotional and mental health.

The solution is not to take a course, read a book or consult an expert. True apprenticeship begins with soul-searching prayer, prayer on the order of the psalms. Praying the psalms invariably places human matters in the context of God's sovereign power and purposes. Take for example the psalm we all know so well, the psalm that is so often recited but seldom prayed. If we began with Psalm 23 the way a carpenter begins with a tape measure, how would we measure a given situation? It has fallen out of style to be as God-centered with our personal dilemmas as the psalmist was, but it is imperative.

How would it be if we began our prayers with an affirmation of confidence in God—"The LORD is my shepherd, I shall lack nothing"—rather than an account of our troubles? Why has it become so acceptable to dwell on our pain rather than rely on the provision of God? To ask this question is not to minimize the provision of the psalms themselves for empathizing with human pain. The psalms are an invaluable spiritual guide to the full range of self-expression. There is no better direction for praying out anguish and pain than that found in the psalms. But confidence in the Lord God remains the overall theme of psalms, and praying them nurtures this soul-craft discipline. In spite of the pain, the psalmist declares, "I will fear no evil, for you are with me." There are certain "controls" in place that curb self-pity and transcend worst-case scenarios. "Even though I walk through the valley of the shadow of death," I will not be overwhelmed, because you are my strength and protection. This kind of confidence is seldom heard today and is in critical need of restoration.

The preeminent source of pain in this culture is broken relationships. The only war many people experience firsthand is the war going on inside their homes and within themselves. This is the war that rages between husband and wife, parents and children, and soul and spirit. This is where we feel the spiritual famine, the emotional drought and the physical drain. It is in our friendships, our marriages, our families and in our very selves that we feel this leanness of soul—this humiliation. It is against such soul-impacting pain that we pray the psalms in confidence, because to pray the psalms is to declare that there is a relationship that takes precedence over all other relationships. Prayer declares that our most significant Other, bar none, is God and God alone. Apart from the surety of this relationship, life is like a tightrope walk over the abyss of loneliness.

Psalm 23 celebrates the power of our personal relationship with God by depicting the Lord as the good shepherd and the gracious host. The provision, rest, guidance and fellowship that we truly need are found in this primary relationship. This is how the needs of the soul are to be met: "He makes me lie down in green pastures, he leads me beside quiet waters, he restores my soul. He guides me in paths of righteousness for his name's sake." Implied in these verbs is the submission of the true self—the real you—to the provision, purpose and plan of the Lord. As we pray the psalms we become increasingly aware that solutions, satisfactions and securities are found not in ourselves but in God. The table fellowship that we are most in need of is the Lord's. Praying the psalms is like meeting the Lord for lunch or getting together with our Master for dinner. I mean this in no sacrilegious sense but as an example of holy fellowship. For who among us, who profess to follow Jesus, could despise the intimacy and comfort of such a time with the Lord? Would not such a fellowship put our concerns in perspective and strengthen our confidence? Who wouldn't rejoice in such an opportunity to seek direction and discernment?

The apostle Paul gives us a great example of soulcraft in the way he prayed for the believers at Philippi:

> This is my prayer: that your love may abound more and more in knowledge and depth of insight, so that you may be able to discern what is best and may be pure and blameless until the day of Christ, filled with the fruit of righteousness that comes through Jesus Christ—to the glory and praise of God. (Phil 1:9-11)

True craftsmanship knows no substitute for quality. It discerns what is best. The original meaning of the word *craft* carried the idea of strength, force, power and virtue. In English the word came to be associated with artistic skill and quality workmanship. It may have been an occupational precursor to our word *professional* but *craft* retains its emphasis on ability rather than title. We don't think of a craftsman as an executive so much as we picture a hands-on, skilled laborer. Craftsmen leave the paperwork and the cushy jobs to others so they can concentrate on their craft. Proficiency requires discernment, discipline and diligence. These qualities are standard, not optional. Soulcraft does not belong to professionals and experts but to those engaged in crafting life according to the Master's specifications. This work requires discernment. It is a practical, hands-on, roll-up-your-sleeves labor of love, and it begins with prayer.

The most striking aspect of Paul's prayer for the Philippian believers is its insistence on uniting what we have often unwittingly separated, namely love and knowledge. May "your love abound more and more in knowledge and depth of insight." The apostle's prayer is for discerning love, insightful love, righteous love. To the apostle, love minus regard for God's will is really not love at all. Love abstracted from the knowledge of the holy is mere sentiment and opinion. For many people, love is distinct from biblical love and is divorced from knowing and doing the will of God. Even in the church, love has become synonymous with acceptance, an excuse for moral compromise. The loving thing to do, we are told, is to lay aside our "prejudice" and accept and affirm people regardless of their actions. There appears to be little room, in today's emphasis, for honoring God's law. Talk of morality is looked down upon as moralistic. It is becoming increasingly difficult for many to distinguish between "living by grace" and "everyone doing what is right in their own eyes." This tragic situation develops when love is divorced from knowledge.

Paul prays for true love, love that seeks to discern what is best and to practice what is pure and blameless. Such discerning love, provided by God, demonstrates wisdom and results in righteousness. Love is to soulcraft what color is to the artist and music is to the musician. Each practitioner exhibits an inherent respect, understanding and love for the nature of one's chosen medium. Therefore love and understanding are not divorced. The carpenter loves working with oak because he understands and appreciates the qualities inherent in oak. A musician loves jazz because she appreciates the complexity of rhythms and tempos intrinsic to jazz. Love is tied to insight; the greater the insight, the greater the love. That is why Paul prayed that the Philippian believers' love would "abound more and more in knowledge and depth of insight," so that they would be "pure and blameless until the day of Christ, filled with the fruit of righteousness."

We commonly distinguish between love and infatuation for the sake of a strong marriage, and between loving your child and spoiling your child for the sake of good parenting. Likewise, the apostle Paul understood that to love others in Christ is to insist that they walk in a manner worthy of the gospel of Christ, that they do nothing out of selfish ambition or vain conceit, and that they stand firm in the Lord. Anything less, even if it is promoted in the name of love, is not loving!

Discernment is to soulcraft's labor of love what trust is to marriage and sacrifice is to parenting. Purity, blamelessness and righteousness are as basic to soulcraft-love as the use of light is to a painter or as timing is to the musician. To take this a step further, the most loving thing a surgeon can do for his patient is to operate skillfully. A caring bedside manner is, of course, better than a gruff demeanor, but the real test of love comes in the operating room. A surgeon who does not love surgery enough to perform with diligent care and expert skill needs to stop operating. This is just as true, if not more so, when it comes to soulcraft. If soulcrafters begin to substitute pleasing people for discerning God's will through prayer, then everything is reduced to cut flowers and mere bedside manner. Following advice from the amazingly popular book *Chicken Soup for the Soul* may be okay if you suffer from a common cold, but it is positively deadly if you suffer from a malignancy.

The Word of God
Soulcraft also begins with a prayerful comprehension of the wisdom of God revealed in the Bible. The prayer for discernment finds its answer in the admonition, "let the same mind be in you that was in Christ Jesus" (Phil 2:5 NRSV). The desire to engage in soulcraft quickly leads us to Jesus and his Word. Throughout the Bible God has provided a very unique way of guiding us in our relationships,

but for many this way is hidden and for the most part undiscovered. The Bible is actually more intriguing and exciting than we give it credit for, and of far greater practical help than most ever realize. Many people seldom benefit from its distinctive and comprehensive approach because their Bibles have become too thin. They have selectively edited, abridged and reduced the Bible to a *Reader's Digest* of religious stories and sayings, thinking that it may be good for some things but that for practical, personal matters it is better to turn elsewhere.

I'm not referring here to people who have written the Bible off as an ancient work of religious mythology but of Christians who revere the Bible as the inspired Word of God. The issue is not the doctrine of Scripture but the discernment of Scripture; not the authority of Scripture but the authoritative use of Scripture. We hold to the apostle's affirmation, "All Scripture is God-breathed and is useful for teaching, rebuking, correcting and training in righteousness" (2 Tim 3:16), but we often do not allow the Word of the Lord to address our personal dilemmas and family situations. We lament the lack of guidance and we turn elsewhere.

Over lunch, Gary, a talented man in his mid-forties, shared with me his frustration with being single. He had a good job with a good income and a nice house but no wife to share his life with. He didn't feel our church was helping him very much, too few possible "prospects" and not enough social events. "Frankly," he said, "I'm getting more out of John Gray's book *Men Are from Mars, Women Are from Venus* than the Bible." Gary had the honesty to say what many Christians are thinking. The easy-reading, self-help books on relationships seem to them more practical and helpful than the Bible. Such books may offer what we think we want, but do they give us what we need? They are relationally "lite," cleverly written, highly anecdotal and usually simplistic. The subtitle of *Men Are from Mars, Women Are from Venus* captures the ethos of today's relational quest: *A Practical Guide for Improving Communications and Getting What You Want in Your Relationships.* Does that advertised promise come close to capturing the meaning and purpose of relationships that please God?

If you had a choice between receiving counseling from John Gray or receiving it from Jesus, whom would you choose? It is a question worth considering. Are we ready to be led, problems and all, into a more serious course of discipleship? Are we willing to surrender our wills to the will of Christ as it is revealed in his Word? This may sound old-fashioned, and the talk of surrendering our will may seem pietistic. But until the call of discipleship is responded to, most of what Jesus has to say about relationships will continue to be written off as "religious" material, irrelevant to how a person develops friendships and interacts with family. The very counsel that we need, of the kind that we find in the beatitudes, is reduced to clever, practical pieces of relational common sense, like "don't talk behind other people's backs," or "make time for family." We skip over Jesus' words on "mourning" and "meekness" in favor of planning fun outings and enjoying each other's company. Instead of affirming, "As for me and my household, we will serve the LORD" (Josh 24:15), we prefer to choose for ourselves and do our own thing.

Instead of bringing the Word of God to bear on our personal lives we tend to compartmentalize the Bible. We have artificially narrowed the biblical focus to "religious" issues, without applying the full scope of the Bible to all relationships. Ironically, we have trusted the Bible on salvation but tend to ignore the Bible on sanctification. We need the Bible as a devotional guide and relational guide. It is not a matter of trying to make the Bible relevant but of allowing the Bible's relevance to impact our personal lives.

Our sources for relational guidance run the gamut from step-by-step, relational-success formulas to modern novels that offer blow-by-blow descriptions of dysfunctional family life. At one end we have simplistic approaches promising virtually overnight relational cures, and at the other end we have a nearly universal picture of hopelessly complex, self-destructive relationships. Between the pragmatism and pathos of today's sexual and spiritual dilemma there is an insight gap that begs for wisdom. I am convinced that the Bible can fill that need for wisdom in a far deeper way than many have ever experienced or imagined. It is time for Christians to

---

return to their biblical roots and learn the true nature and depth of meaning intended by God for our relationships.

Studying the Bible for practical discernment is less complicated than you might expect. We have been blessed with an invaluable resource that, when used wisely, guides us in ways that truly strengthen the soul, lift the spirit, and yield positive, productive relationships (Ps 19:7-11). The mind of Jesus and the Word of God are one and the same. If it helps you to liken reading the Bible to sitting down with Jesus in a counseling situation, I encourage you to do that. Bring all of the issues of your life to Jesus, the living Word of God. We believe that the Spirit of Christ, the Holy Spirit, illuminates the Scriptures, revealing God's truth to us. Having affirmed the doctrine of Scripture, we pray for discernment, that we might hear and understand the Word of God, and know the mind of Jesus.

Through the Word, Jesus is our instructor. He who is the way, the truth and the life guides and persuades us in the path that leads to freedom (Jn 14:6; 8:31-32). His counsel is practical, not theoretical, and it is designed to strengthen the soul and lead us to obedience. We should not think that our first duty is to master the biblical text, as if being wise rests on *our* wisdom. Well-informed exegesis of the Word of God is important, but it is secondary to the humility necessary to listen carefully to God's Word. Wisdom and obedience are advanced far more effectively by responding to Jesus our Master, than by mastering the biblical text.

A prerequisite for soulcraft is allowing the Word of God to shape our souls. Remember the old Nike tagline, "Just do it"? Well, apply that to reading God's Word. I have a friend who often spends an hour or so at Starbucks reading God's Word and jotting down observations and questions in a notebook. My impression is that he has just enough distractions in that coffee shop to keep his mind focused on the Word of God.

I have vivid childhood memories of specific times when God's Word broke into our family life and shaped the course of our lives. Like the time we were earnestly praying about a move to Wisconsin from New York. I don't remember the exact text, but I remember my dad, a typical Englishman when it came to emotions, closing his Bible and beginning to cry. Believe me, I can count on one hand the times my father cried, but that night the counsel of God's Word was so definite and clear for the future of our family that he wept. It's not the method or the technique that's important when it comes to reading the Bible. What's important is that you do it! You will find a time and place that fits for you. As we prayerfully explore the truth of God and see ourselves and others in its light, we will be better equipped for deeper, more mature relationships.

Humility

Soulcraft also begins with humility. As we pray for discernment and obey the Word of God, we are led to this third essential element in soulmaking—the learned discipline of humility. It is a learned discipline because humility does not come to us naturally. It is not bestowed on us as a gift, nor is it a feature of personality. Humility is a discipline, an intentional commitment of the will in relationship to God and others. It is a chosen and cultivated quality of character that matures and deepens with experience in Christ. Paul's counsel—"Let the same mind be in you that was in Christ Jesus"—leads to intentional and resolute self-emptying (Phil 2:5-8 NRSV). Humility is a surrender of our will to the commands of God and the needs of others.

If our Lord Jesus "did not consider equality with God something to be grasped" (Phil 2:6), how can *we* sit in judgment on the Word of God? How can *we* vie with God for authority? The challenge before us is to not repeat again and again the sin of Adam and Eve, who were beguiled by Satan's ego temptation, "and you will be like God" (Gen 3:5). If Jesus "made himself nothing," how can we do anything less. If Jesus "humbled himself," how much more should we? If Jesus "became obedient to death—even death on a cross," we need to look at obedience and faithfulness more seriously (Phil 2:7-8).

I suppose that at this point I should say that many people don't think very highly of humility. They write humility off as a less-than-cool, churchy topic that only serves to decrease people's already dangerously low sense of self-esteem. "In this put-down world of ours, where we are brow beaten by bully bosses and thoughtless spouses," they protest, "don't talk about humility, talk about grace. We've had enough of gloomy piety, doormat theology, and self-flagellation. Give us hope, not humility!" I can empathize with people's spiritual paranoia and share their criticism of false piety, but genuine, honest-to-goodness humility is not part of the problem; it is the solution. Humility before God is not the opposite of hope and grace, it is the foundation of God's blessing.

Far from being an optional feature of personality, humility is an essential quality for excellence in soulcraft. From God's perspective, humility is being obedient to his Word. It is a virtue received and nurtured by grace. It involves submitting our minds and lives to the Lordship of Jesus Christ. Humility is the moment-by-moment, act-of-the-will decision to center life on Christ rather than self. Humility is basic to our self-understanding, moral perception and emotional strength. Think of humility as both our starting point and the bottom line.

> He has showed you, O man, what is good.
>   And what does the LORD require of you?
> To act justly and to love mercy
>   and to walk humbly with your God. (Mic 6:8)

The apostle Peter considered humility to be imperative: "Humble yourselves, therefore, under God's mighty hand, that he may lift you up in due time. Cast all your anxiety on him because he cares for you" (1 Pet 5:6-7).

The first thing that humility does is to work within us a vivid sense of our own personal sinfulness. We understand why it was necessary for Jesus to go to the cross on our behalf. We are sinners saved by grace and not by works. This awareness powerfully affects the way we practice soulcraft. Humility before God is born out of an acute realization of sin *and* a grateful acceptance of God's grace in Christ. If these two foundational truths are missing, the counsel we will accept is reduced to self-help strategies, idealistic platitudes and superficial solutions. Unless the systemic depravity of the human condition is addressed there will be no long-term, productive results. The last thing we need to be told is to believe in ourselves. After we strain for brilliance and self-recognition, we come down to the necessity of respecting this simple fact: we are sinners in need of the mercy of God.

The realization of one's own sinfulness can be painful, especially when our culture persistently emphasizes the need to have high self-esteem. This is one reason why the Christian approach to relationships is so radically different from the patterns of the world. Instead of being helped along the way with a few relational pointers and some practical paradigms, we are told that we are sinners on the verge of death. The problem is actually much more serious than we imagined it to be. We want a little solace and support, but what we need is radical surgery.

On the surface we are resistant to this verdict: "for the wages of sin is death" (Rom 6:23). It sounds melodramatic to modern ears, but deep down there is an inherent human awareness of sinfulness. What we want is affirmation and approval; what we need is deliverance. Scaled-down forms of salvation will not work. The last thing we need is to be told we are okay, that all we are suffering from is a problem of self-esteem or boredom.

There is a true humanness about admitting our sinfulness and dependence upon God that is humbling, not humiliating. What could be more human than honestly confessing our need? In the absence of humility, there is an ever-present fear of humiliation.

A college teacher performs an experiment every semester designed to give his graduate students an ego shock. He administers a standard I.Q. test to his class. After he evaluates the tests he writes a fictitious range of scores on the board from the lowest to the highest. When he returns the test scores he doesn't tell the students that he has given everyone in the class the lowest score. He sits back and watches as the stunned students grapple with their low scores. Some instinctively cover up their test papers so no one can see them. Others blush with embarrassment or anger. In the discussion that follows some hotly condemn the test as unfair and biased, others make excuses rationalizing why they did such a poor job on that particular day. Before the class figures out the professor's experiment, he informs them that what they are feeling is how students feel when they consistently score poorly on exams. He has given them all the same low score so that they could appreciate the feelings of a failing student.

In a far more profound sense, we too need an ego shock, not so that we can empathize with the feelings of others but so that we can be honest about our own spiritual need. Instead of trusting in ourselves we need to depend upon the mercy of God. We can say that the guilt we feel is false, imposed upon us by our emotions or by the moralism of others, or we can be honest with ourselves and face up to our real guilt. It comes down to two choices: humiliation or humility. It is only one or the other. No matter how outwardly successful or physically attractive or brilliantly smart we may be, if we haven't experienced humility before God, we are hounded by the fear of humiliation. As long as we are impressed with ourselves and seek to impress others the fear of humiliation keeps the grace of humility at bay. The Lord declares,

Let not the wise man boast of his wisdom
  or the strong man boast of his strength
  or the rich man boast of his riches,
but let him who boasts boast about this:
  that he understands and knows me,
that I am the LORD, who exercises kindness,
  justice and righteousness on earth,
  for in these I delight. (Jer 9:23-24)

The humiliation of failure is something that we naturally understand. It is the humiliation of success that surprises us. Garrison Keillor, in his novel *Wobegon Boy*, captures this humiliation well in the main character John Tollefson's reflections:

When I look back on my thirties, I am stunned by the shallowness— how easy life was! . . . The newspaper landed on the front step, I read it, none of it had the slightest reality to me. What was most real was something missing from my life that was intimated in great music. I would look up from my desk to hear Jussi Bjoerling sing "Nessun dorma" from *Turandot* and suddenly know that my life lacked nobility and purpose. I was sleepwalking. People sat around my dining room table and actually discussed the merits of different brands of blenders, coffee beans, cheeses. They flew off to foreign lands and nothing happened; they came back and described their hotel rooms and the dinners they ate and how crowded the Louvre was. My thirties were a foreign country where there was no crisis, no suffering, nothing wondrous or noble, just nice people and a wonderful vinaigrette dressing.[4]

The writer of Ecclesiastes would have agreed with Garrison Keillor's character. He suffered the same emptiness, the same feelings of humiliation. He was successful beyond his wildest imagination and terribly empty.

> I denied myself nothing my eyes desired;
>   I refused my heart no pleasure.
> My heart took delight in all my work,
>   and this was the reward for all my labor.
> Yet when I surveyed all that my hands had done
>   and what I had toiled to achieve,
> everything was meaningless, a chasing after the wind;
>   nothing was gained under the sun. (Eccles 2:10-11)

Sounding like a typical person steeped in selfism, Solomon sums up the humiliation of his success. "So I hated life, because the work that is done under the sun was grievous to me. All of it is meaningless, a chasing after the wind. I hated all the things I had toiled for under the sun, because I must leave them to the one who comes after me" (Eccles 2:17-18).

Humiliation—the feeling of shame, inadequacy and disappointment that fills the soul in spite of outstanding success—warns us against trusting in ourselves. Humiliation is to the soul what pain is to the body. Shame and pain are warning systems calling us to seek help and healing. The absence of pain because of nerve damage is a serious problem and can lead to unintentional bodily damage. Likewise, the absence of shame because of a hardened, insensitive conscience, can lead to soul damage. Humility is not humiliation; in fact it is just the opposite. Humility bows the knee to God; humiliation results from rejecting God. Humility receives God's Word; humiliation denies God's Word. Humility leads to hope; humiliation leads to despair.

Humility frees us from the often subtle, manipulative and destructive powers of humiliation. Humiliation describes well the feeling of personal inadequacy and shame that runs so deep in the human psyche. Its obvious symptoms, however, distract us from its primary source. Ultimately, humiliation has little to do with feeling inferior about our bodies or insecure about our personalities. Poor parenting, sexual addiction, spousal abuse, divorce, same-gender sex—are all symptoms of a deeper problem, a malignancy of the soul. Sin, not sex, is at the root of it all. Humiliation is our enemy, we feel it in our soul; but humility is our friend, whether we know it or not. For there is no other way to deal with humiliation, than with humility.

True humility not only shapes our self-understanding, but it strengthens our appreciation of God's authority and our commitment to God's will. Humility and authority are not mutually exclusive. Rather, they are inseparable. True confidence depends upon humility, not upon a strong ego. "What we suffer from today," G. K. Chesterton wrote, "is humility in the wrong place."

> A man was meant to be doubtful about himself, but undoubting about the truth; this has been exactly reversed. Nowadays the part of a man that a man does assert is exactly the part he ought not to assert—himself. The part he doubts is exactly the part he ought not to doubt—the Divine Reason.[5]

Spiritual authority is the natural corollary to Christlike humility. People who submit to God reflect discernment and wisdom.

Jesus-style humility is affirmed in his Beatitudes (Mt 5:3-11). To be *poor in spirit* is to know in our heart of hearts that we really need

God. To *mourn* is to grieve deeply for our own guilt and to sorrow for our sinfulness. Wisely understood, these first two beatitudes are neither idealistic nor platitudinous. They are simple, profound truths that, when acknowledged personally and practically, help us to live life the way it should be lived in dependence upon God. The strategy of Jesus for living in the real world begins with humility, not pride; repentance, not pity.

The third beatitude, about *meekness*, has more to do with how we view the world and our role in it than it does with a personality type. It is a mindset, not a mood. Meekness is belief in the truth about how we are to relate to the world; it is not a temperament determining how we feel about the world. In no way do meekness and humility suggest weakness or softness; meekness does not mean being laid-back, easygoing, tolerant or laissez-faire. On the contrary, it requires conviction and strength. There is nothing superficial about the meekness blessed by Jesus. Meekness is an intentional reliance upon God to accomplish his will and his work in his way. It is an openness to see God in the big picture of life and the recognition that "in all things God works for the good of those who love him, who have been called according to his purpose" (Rom 8:28). Humility is the spiritual discipline that overcomes the world—beginning by overcoming humiliation.

The humiliation that has become so much a part of today's experience of family life and interpersonal relationships does have a grace-filled solution. There is a way out of the brokenness and confusion and malaise that is the shared experience of so many. By the grace of God the Spirit of Christ promises a way out of our humiliation through humility. This humility causes us to embrace the mercy of God in Christ and enables us to accept the truth of God's word with confidence.

The Big Rocks
Soulcraft begins with praying for discernment, depending on the word of Jesus and cultivating humility. This is the basic skill-set necessary for soulmaking in the family. These three come first in devel-

oping self-understanding, good friendships, solid marriages and effective parenting.

Stephen Covey, author of *The 7 Habits of Highly Effective Families*, offers a useful illustration to demonstrate the importance of first things. He takes a large glass jar and fills it with several big rocks. He then asks his audience if the jar is filled. They immediately say yes. Next, he adds pebbles to the jar, filling it to the top. "Now is the jar filled?" he asks. Again the audience agrees that it is filled. Then he adds sand, again filling the jar to the top. "Surely, the jar is filled now," he declares and everyone agrees. But to the surprise of the audience he is still able to pour in a couple of pints of water. "Now that the jar is finally filled with rocks, pebbles, sand and water, what's my point?" Covey asks. Invariably the audience responds, "You can always pack more things in. Even when something is full you can squeeze more in." Covey politely disagrees. "No, the point of this object lesson is that if you don't fit the big rocks in first, you'll never get them in."[6]

Covey's point that we need to keep first things first is important, and the illustration is effective, but what are the first things? What are the big rocks that we want to make sure we put in place first? The illustration is clear, but what is the truth behind the illustration? Are the big rocks family bonding time, creating a family mission statement, prioritizing your home life, listening to others empathetically, and cooperating together as a family to solve problems? These are positive, practical relational disciplines, but do they qualify as the big rocks that need to be put in the jar first?

My concern is that much of what captivates our attention on the subject of relationships misses the essential truths fundamental to self-understanding and the building of relationships. It is like discussing the floor plan and decor of your future house without knowing in what state you're going to live. It reminds me of the person planning how he is going to spend his money before he has trained for an occupation.

So much of the popular relational advice amounts to little more than pebbles and sand, purposefully avoiding the big rocks that represent our relationship to God and the meaning and purpose of life. Much of today's advice simply ignores human depravity and the sin problem. The fact that there is biblical guidance on relationships and sexuality remains unsaid. In fact, a person reading most of today's Christian how-to books on relationships could conclude that Jesus and the cross have nothing to do with the subject of friendship and family.

Soulmaking requires a different set of "first things" than is found in the marketplace of popular advice. While we can be thankful that the easy-reading common sense of practical authors is often an expression of God's common grace, we need to go deeper if our souls are going to be redeemed and empowered. We can be thankful that secular authors tap into the relational wisdom of God, but invariably their insights depend on foundational truths which they ignore. Our chief end is not to have a great marriage and happy family but to glorify God and enjoy him forever. For that we need communion with God, the mind of Christ and humility. With these cornerstones, let the work of soulcraft begin.

2

RHYTHMS
OF GRACE

*By faith we understand that the universe was formed at God's command,
so that what is seen was not made out of what was visible.*

H E B R E W S   11 : 3

O UT OF THE CHAOS GOD CREATED ORDER AND RHYTHM, BEAUTY
and purpose, rest and work. These gifts are foundational to developing and experiencing relationships. There is by design no divorce
between the physical self and the spiritual self, between the material
world and the spiritual world, between sexuality and spirituality.
Body and soul, heaven and earth are created to embrace. Soulcraft
restores the rhythm to life by calling us back to God's "Let there be
. . ." His voice separates the light from the darkness and establishes
meaning and purpose.

All relationships were designed to be God-centered. We were
meant to begin with God rather than with our relational disillusionment and emotional frustration. Soulcraft is a radical departure
from the way the world looks at life, because it encourages us to
place all of our grief and all of our sorrow in the context of God's

purpose and provision. Before we dwell on our brokenness, before we feel the depth of our emptiness, before we measure the weight of our burdens, some very important truths deserve to be considered. We may not be in the mood for it, but the importance of this consideration is both greater than our feelings and crucial for our feelings. We may not even hear—truly hear—what is said, but it should be said anyway. The truth is too great not to be told in the midst of our boredom and brokenness.

In order to "Carry each other's burdens," and "fulfill the law of Christ" (Gal 6:2) we need to begin with God. An in-depth understanding of human need requires an in-depth understanding of divine purpose. It is like the piano student listening to Brahms or a medical student studying human anatomy. They thus begin to learn appreciation for how things should be. Budding musicians have to hear how an instrument really sounds before they are inspired to practice. Medical students learn how a healthy body functions before they diagnosis and treat diseases. Soulcraft works the same way. That which is good is set in contrast to that which is evil. We let the rhythms of grace inspire our souls and give us a song to sing. If all we know is a mournful tune of despair and brokenness we haven't yet discovered the real reason for relationships.

Without God we have no beginning; everything is formless, empty, dark and silent. This is how the Bible describes the nothingness that preceded God's creation of the heavens and the earth, and this is how it is in the world of our own making. When you insist on a self-made world—one that exists by your own engineering, your own ingenuity, your own arrangement and your own rules—you then have a world—your own little world—that looks like the nothingness that there was before God created. It has no real beginning, and has no real end, and in between it lacks significance, meaning, purpose—it lacks life itself! It is a strange paradox, perhaps the strangest paradox of all, that one can exist in God's creation without God; without his Word, his order, his life and light. Soulcraft chooses the world of God's creating over the world of our making. God is not our invention, designed to please our whims. We are

God's creation designed to fulfill his will. "Creator creates creation" is affirmed; "creation creates Creator" is rejected. The deceptive and utterly disastrous inversion is denied.

So for the time being we put aside that which is "formless and empty." We refuse to be intimidated by the "darkness . . . over the surface of the deep." We begin with faith, not fear. As God began with nothing, we begin with nothing but God. As God overruled the chaos, we overrule everything but the rule of God. This is a wonderful place to begin, "in the beginning God . . ." (Gen 1:1-2).

God's Relational Gifts

Everything has a beginning, and our beginning could not have been better. God's creation has so much to say about us that we must not only begin at the beginning but remain there long enough to appreciate what we have been given. When a couple stands at the altar on their wedding day, are they aware of whom they stand before? If only marriages would begin the way Genesis begins with the clear, uncontested, simply presented, sovereignly powerful reality of God. This would make for a true beginning. Isn't it ironic that a beautiful couple, well-educated, physically fit, worldly-wise and in their prime, can come to the altar oblivious to God? How can this be? Unlike the pastor who says, "Dearly beloved we are gathered here to join this couple in holy matrimony," the prophet would say,

> Do you not know?
>   Have you not heard?
> Has it not been told you from the beginning?
>   Have you not understood since the earth was founded? . . .
> The LORD is the everlasting God,
>   the Creator of the ends of the earth.
> He will not grow tired or weary,
>   and his understanding no one can fathom. (Is 40:21, 28).

How could the Alpha and Omega, the beginning and the end, be unknown in the middle of life? How could we turn heaven's symphony: "Holy, holy, holy is the Lord God Almighty, who was, and is, and is to come" (Rev 4:8), into a solo jingle: "Me, Me, Me"?

"In the beginning God . . ." and there is truly no other reality from which to begin. Everything else is pointless and purposeless. Where we begin makes all the difference; it determines what world we live in—a world of our own making or the world of God's creating. The world of our making is filled with idols, chaos and darkness. But the world of God's creating is filled with wisdom, order and light. Apart from God our personal world remains in chaos, darkness and nothingness.

"And God said, 'Let there be' . . . And God saw that it was good" (Gen 1:3, 9). The first thing said is that which *God said*. Creation speaks volumes.

> The heavens declare the glory of God;
> the skies proclaim the work of his hands.
> Day after day they pour forth speech;
> night after night they display knowledge. (Ps 19:1-2)

But it doesn't stop there! God's word not only creates but guides, directs and commands.

> The law of the LORD is perfect,
> reviving the soul.
> The statutes of the LORD are trustworthy,
> making wise the simple.
> The precepts of the LORD are right,
> giving joy to the heart.
> The commands of the LORD are radiant,
> giving light to the eyes.
> The ordinances of the LORD are sure
> and altogether righteous. (Ps 19:7-9)

The first thing said is that God said, "Let there be . . ." Silence is broken, darkness dispelled. Nature does not have a life of its own. Nothing can be deified, from the stars to the trees, because it is all created, commanded into existence. Creation is subservient to the subject of the first sentence of the Bible, God. God created. God spoke, not in an authoritarian tone, for there was no resistance to his will.

This was not the bark of a drill sergeant but the voice of the Author, Artist and Composer. "Let there be . . ." gives permission for creation to exist freely and gracefully, reflecting the glory of the Creator. God called the light "day" and the darkness "night." God made. God blessed. And over all, God gave his all-encompassing, comprehensive verdict on creation: It is good, very good; all of it is good. It is good morally and materially, spiritually and physically, aesthetically and ethically. Goodness ranges over this vast cosmos shot through with rationality. The void is filled by the voice of God. Herein lie meaning, purpose and love. Gifts given by God. Rhythms of grace. God is the Composer and Conductor, inspiring the song, setting the beat, filling life with unity and coherence.

Boredom
Internalizing this sweet truth, regardless of how sour life has been, is basic to being healthy and whole in our life in Christ. God's voice, which we so desperately need to hear, is meant to create out of our formless and empty worlds the fullness of life that God intended. God's desire is to bring us into his large world of order, beauty and rhythm. The problem is that in God's good creation we tend to create our own void. The practical implications are many. Consider, for example, the bane of modern life: the fear of boredom. As a culture we seem to feel compelled to create a self-sustaining, self-stimulating momentum of activities and experiences in order to feel alive. Self-importance appears directly proportionate to the pace of life, as if going faster and faster increases a sense of self-worth. By sustaining the physical and material momentum of life we do not have to think deeply about the meaning and purpose of life.

The repetitive performances of daily life are not tuned to the rhythms of grace. Maxed-out schedules make meaningful friendships and worship nearly impossible. Nobody has time for anything. Everybody is booked. Marriages often begin with both husband and wife working at jobs that demand their undivided attention. Parenting becomes a function of daycare, preschool, videos and television. In some households the CD player, radio and television are never turned off.

The measure of our age is enthusiasm, zealotry, hype and stress. We are a driven people, filling our "free" time with expensive pleasures and self-indulgent diversions. Ronald Dahl, a professor of psychiatry and pediatrics at the University of Pittsburgh Medical Center writes,

> I'm concerned about the cumulative effect of years at these levels of feverish activity. It is no mystery to me why many teenagers appear apathetic and burned out, with a 'been there, done that' air of indifference toward much of life. As an increasing number of friends' children are prescribed medications—stimulants to deal with inattentiveness at school or antidepressants to help with the loss of interest and joy in their lives—I question the role of kids' boredom in some of the diagnoses. . . . The pace of life and the intensity of stimulation may be contributing to the rising rates of psychiatric problems among children and adolescents in our society.[1]

The Danish Christian thinker Søren Kierkegaard, writing in the mid-1800s, warned that boredom would be considered the root of all evil and that overcoming it would be the passion of the age. He was right. "There is a restless activity which excludes a person from the world of the spirit, setting him in a class with the brutes, whose instincts impel them always to be on the move."[2] The substitution of momentum for meaning and a busy life for a full life robs the soul of its own music.

Kierkegaard foresaw the impact boredom and its resulting restlessness would have on relationships. He sarcastically reasoned that it would be preferable for people to remain uncommitted so they could be free to do what they wanted when they wanted to. Friendship, marriage and children are the enemies of freedom, because they require commitment, fidelity and roots. When people are committed to one another they cannot afford to "move aimlessly around the world."[3]

Kierkegaard forecasted that, because of the effort to escape boredom, the goal of modern life would be to amuse oneself with trivial things. "One should, in spite of mature years, be able to prove the truth of the proverb that children are pleased with a rattle and tickled with a straw."[4] What one does or doesn't do no longer matters as long as one is doing something. "The whole secret lies in arbitrariness," wrote Kierkegaard satirically. "People usually think it easy to be arbitrary, but it requires much study to succeed in being arbitrary so as not to lose oneself in it, but so as to derive satisfaction from it."[5] When boredom is considered the root of all evil, the goal of life is to make everything arbitrary. People determine in a serious way that nothing is all that serious.

Wiley Miller's *Non Sequitur* comic strip captures the theme in a picture: A college student stands at a chalk board working out a complicated math problem that takes up the length of the board, only to follow the equal sign with the word "Whatever."[6] No commitment or responsibility is considered more important than the freedom to seek present-moment happiness. The absolute importance of being arbitrary guarantees relief from boredom and assures a constant flow of distractions and diversions. What Kierkegaard sarcastically anticipated as an emerging possibility has become a way of life for many today.

> It is extremely wholesome thus to let the realities of life split upon an arbitrary interest. You transform something accidental into the absolute, and as such, into the object of your admiration. This has an excellent effect, especially when one is excited. This method is an excellent stimulus for many persons. You look at everything in life from the standpoint of a wager, and so forth. The more rigidly consistent you are in holding fast to your arbitrariness, the more amusing the ensuing combinations will be.[7]

Soulcraft restores the rhythm to life by calling us back to God's "Let there be . . ." His voice separates the light from the darkness and establishes meaning and purpose. Creation week concludes with a satisfying rest. Each day begins not with the morning but with the evening, so that when we rise at dawn, we know that the Lord God, who never sleeps, has gone before us. Each week ends with a sabbath rest, a memorial to God's promise and a reminder that life does not depend upon our effort. "The observance of Sabbath rest is a break with every effort to achieve, to secure ourselves, and to make the world into our image according to our purposes."[8] The measure of a person is not in what is achieved but in what is received. As John Greenleaf Whittier wrote in his hymn,

> Take from our lives the strain and stress,
> And let our ordered lives confess
> The beauty of Thy peace.[9]

We are not rootless, landless highwaymen, seeking easy prey for personal gain. Over and against the arbitrariness of modern life stand the absolutes of God. Life is not like modern art that begs the interpreter rather than the artist to be original. God writes the score, setting the beat and determining the rhythm.

"The heavens declare the glory of God; the skies proclaim the work of his hands. . . . The precepts of the LORD are right, giving joy to the heart" (Ps 19:1, 8). David delights in expounding on the impact of God's special revelation. He does not want us to miss the clarity of the Word of God. Through the Lord's law, statutes, precepts and commands nothing is left out that we need for guidance. The words chosen to convey the meaning of God's Word "indicate the precision and authority with which God addresses us, while fear, or reverence, emphasizes the human response fostered by His word."[10] The powerful purpose of God's word is to "evoke intelligent reverence, well-founded trust, detailed obedience."[11]

It is up to us whether we choose God's rhythms of grace, but God has done his part in making his will known. There is only one Composer, only one Conductor, and without him there is no soul music.

Incarnation

In the middle of Psalm 19, David draws a picture that is meant to inspire wonder and gratitude. It is a metaphor for joy.

> In the heavens he has pitched a tent for the sun,
>   which is like a bridegroom coming forth from his pavilion,
>   like a champion rejoicing to run his course.

> It rises at one end of the heavens
>> and makes its circuit to the other;
>> nothing is hidden from its heat. (Ps 19:4-6)

The journey of the sun as it appears in the sky moving from east to west is like a bridegroom on his wedding day traveling to the house of his bride to join her. The visual impact of this picture evokes joy and celebration. The long-awaited wedding day has arrived, and bride and bridegroom are to be united. The metaphor also causes us to think of Jesus, the incarnate One, the Bridegroom, coming forth to claim his bride. More than a beautiful picture, it is an awesome reality.

There is an inseparable relational link between creation and the incarnation. In the coming of Christ we are blessed with what we need to restore God's creation purposes. On the last day of Jesus' first full week of ministry he went to a wedding (Jn 2). It is not by accident that the second Adam began his earthly ministry by blessing a marriage. History began with a marriage (Gen 2) and will climax with the marriage supper of the Lamb.

> Let us rejoice and be glad
>> and give him glory!
> For the wedding of the Lamb has come
>> and his bride has made herself ready. (Rev 19:7)

Like his mother and his disciples, Jesus was at the wedding to bless the couple and celebrate their marriage. The wedding was neither incidental to nor a pretext for a prearranged display of power, but it was an occasion to manifest God's glory. All weddings should be.

Weddings begin with a call to worship. "This is the day the LORD has made; let us rejoice and be glad in it" (Ps 118:24). The bride is radiant; the groom is beaming. We may even feel the weight of glory. Light and life are alive! Everything is positive: music is celebrative, the mood is festive, and the future is bright. The wedding day pulses with the wonder of creation, God's creation, and whether it is acknowledged or not, the pulse is palpable.

God's blessing runs through it.

Jesus was at the wedding like everyone else. He was a single man who was part of a larger family of relationships, an extended family of concern, comfort and community. Jesus' home culture had an advantage over ours because the community was put ahead of the individual, thus assuring the importance of both. Hebrew culture affirmed the significance of the person in the larger context of family and nation. Instead of the lone individual trying to make community, as is often the case in our culture, the individual belonged in a community and drew identity, strength and comfort from enduring relationships.

What distinguished Jesus and set him apart from the rest of the wedding guests was a crisis. Not what we would call a major crisis, but in the culture of his day more than an embarrassing moment. The wedding feast ran dry. There was no more wine. And since wine was a symbol of celebration and a sign of God's blessing and provision, its absence was duly noted. One senses a hint of panic in Mary's voice as she came to Jesus and said, "They have no more wine," as if to say, "Do something!" Implied in her response was an understanding of Jesus and a confidence in his ability, even in a matter as practical as the need for wine.

More than the wine was symbolic at this wedding feast in Cana of Galilee. It appears that John meant for us to draw a parallel between Jesus' first week of public ministry and creation week. Both weeks began with proclamation: "God said, 'Let there be . . .'" (Gen 1:3) and the prophet said, "I am the voice of one calling in the desert, 'Make straight the way for the Lord'" (Jn 1:23; see Is 40:3). The two voices are linked. The Lord God, maker of heaven and earth, called the prophet to speak. On the second day of Jesus' ministry John prepared the way for redemption, "Look, the Lamb of God, who takes away the sin of the world!" (Jn 1:29). As God made the world, God will redeem the world. The Creator creates out of nothing—nothing but chaos, emptiness and darkness. The Redeemer redeems us out of the darkness of sin and death.

During that first week of public ministry Andrew and another disciple stayed with Jesus. Their fellowship brings to mind the experience of Adam and Eve with God in the Garden of Eden. The incarnate One came to restore us to the fellowship first experienced by Adam and Eve in God's creation. The fruit of Andrew's evangelism is reminiscent of God's command "be fruitful and increase in number" (Gen 1:28). The physical and spiritual dimensions of God's blessing were woven together. As the week progressed the circle of disciples expanded. Both weeks ended with a memorial to God's glory.

Creation week ended with sabbath rest, not because the Lord God was exhausted and needed to take a break—God did not need to recuperate on the seventh day. God celebrated. Jesus' first week of public ministry finished on a similar note. This "beginning" of miracles, performed by Jesus in Cana of Galilee, reminds us of the miracle of creation, "In the beginning God created the heavens and the earth" (Gen 1:1), and Jesus' ministry helps us begin to understand what creation is all about. C. S. Lewis described the miracle of changing water to wine as a miracle of the old creation. "Every year as part of the Natural order, God makes wine. . . . Once, and in one year only, God, now incarnate, short circuits the process: makes wine in a moment: uses earthenware jars instead of vegetable fibers to hold the water."[12]

Through the incarnation, the Lord of creation displays the first fruits of a whole new order. The wedding in Cana causes us to anticipate the marriage supper of the Lamb. The message of both weeks is that God reveals his glory in creation and through the incarnation. "The Word became flesh and made his dwelling among us. We have seen his glory, the glory of the One and Only, who came from the Father, full of grace and truth" (Jn 1:14).

We cannot possibly dance to the rhythms of grace apart from the soul music of our Creator and Redeemer. If Jesus is not Lord of our lives we'll end up doing everything in reverse, taking pride in turning wine into water.

Until we hear the heavens declaring the glory of God and experience the joy that comes from obeying the precepts of the Lord, we will have trouble understanding who we really are. We'll never catch on to what life and relationships are all about. We'll always feel like something important is missing. But when we get hold of the rhythms of grace and Jesus comes into our lives, we will know the joy of dancing on foundations that no one can ever destroy.

We need to be joyfully receptive of the gifts of God and be truly grateful. Humility graciously responds to God's rhythms of grace, finding in his creation the order, beauty, meaning and purpose essential for life. Receiving these gifts is what it means to live in Christ and to receive him as our Lord and Savior. The humble believer worships the holy God in gratitude for the gift of salvation through his Son, and then for life itself with all its joys and blessings.

In God's creation and redemption there is an expansiveness and freedom that exceeds our imagination. We are recipients of so much more than we could ever realize. Daily life was meant to be shaped by the rhythms of grace. Our being is shaped in his likeness, and by the Holy Spirit we reflect God's glory. We are invited out of that which is formless, empty and dark into God's deeply interpersonal creation, where friendship and family, communion and community are blessed by our Lord and Savior.

> Don't be deceived, my dear brothers. Every good and perfect gift is from above, coming down from the Father of the heavenly lights, who does not change like shifting shadows. He chose to give us birth through the word of truth, that we might be a kind of firstfruits of all he created. (Jas 1:16-18)

3

THE SOULFUL
SELF

"What can a man give in exchange for his soul?"

MATTHEW 16:26

SELF-WORTH IS NOT A HUMAN ACHIEVEMENT BUT A DIVINE ENDOW-
ment. We are made in the image of God, which means we are made
for communion and community, for rational reflection and righteous obedience, for worship and work. We are called into a personal, face-to-face relationship with God and with one another.

The essence of who I am comes from God and is received by me as a
gift. "So God created man in his own image, in the image of God he created him; male and female he created them" (Gen 1:27). We have a soul
because God created us with a soul. This means that I am not my own,
that which is most dearly "Me" is not mine. The genesis of soulmaking
lies not in ourselves but in our Creator and Lord. Jesus made this clear:
the value of our soul is beyond our means. It always has been and
always will be. Who we are and to whom we belong is a critical issue,
especially when it comes to relationships. How we see ourselves has a
great impact on our friendships and commitments. Our self-understanding shapes our expectations of self-fulfillment. When all is said
and done are we me-centered or God-centered? That is the question!

My wife, Ginny, recently took a graduate course here in San Diego. The first day of class began in a typical enough fashion. The students were asked to introduce themselves. Most of them gave their names and briefly explained why they were taking the course. But the normal routine was upset by one student who strutted to the front of the classroom, drew a big circle on the chalkboard and in the middle of the circle wrote the word "ME" in large capital letters. "I am going to talk about ME!" he declared and then carried out his threat. Before returning to his seat, he informed the class that he was brilliant, had made more money than anyone else present and stood on the verge of achieving fame. Only in California!

Most people could not conceive of putting on such a serious display of egotism in public. They would shudder at the thought. But what we would never do in public we do in our hearts—in our souls. We are pathologically self-centered. It is as if we had gone to the chalk board, drawn a large circle, filled the circle with a capital *M* and a capital *E*, and turned around to face the world in proud admiration.

Of all the obsessions and hang-ups we struggle with, self-centeredness heads the list. It is at the root of both our insecurity and our pride. When our primary goal is to please ourselves, or even to please others for our own sake, we invariably end up hurting the people around us as well as ourselves. In a soulless world, self-centeredness is the only rational recourse, but in a world of God's making, self-denial is the way to self-fulfillment. Christians should understand this. Theoretically, there ought to be little ambiguity regarding the difference between a me-centered world and a God-centered world, but it's not that easy. We struggle daily with the challenge of being God-centered in a world that is self-centered. The soulful self lives in a soulless culture.

Soulless

Brilliant people tell us that the soul does not exist. They believe that the essence of life is explained by nature alone. Everything is a product of biochemical reactions, a function of material substance and brain synapse. To them the essence of human life is simply a matter of physics and chemistry. We don't have a soul, we have a microchip. Reducing humankind to bargain basement prices is not new; people have been doing that for a long time. If people believe that millions of years of evolution have transformed us from tiny sacs of nucleic acids to the human beings we are today, they usually are not too interested in the soul. One who claims that the human brain— three pounds of wet, gray porridge—defines who and what we are, both as individuals and as a species, eliminates many deep questions with the swipe of an eraser and proves the old Puritan adage, "When you ungod God, you unman man."

The impact of secularism through the physical and human sciences has been to reduce the human being from a person to a product. The cause may be a seven-hundred-million-year process or biological drives, environmental conditioning or societal forces, but the bottom line is the same. If a human being is a complex machine, a technologically sophisticated animal or a biologically driven sexual creature, there is no room for talking about the soul. People would prefer to speculate on extraterrestrial life and interplanetary space travel.

The late Carl Sagan envisioned that thousands of years from now our descendants would be scattered throughout the cosmos, peopling other worlds. In *A Pale Blue Dot* Sagan predicts that the human race will achieve significance through pioneering planetary space travel and settlement. Future generations "will gaze up and strain to find the blue dot in their skies." They will "marvel at how vulnerable the repository of all our potential once was, how perilous our infancy, how humble our beginnings, how many rivers we had to cross before we found our way."[1]

The distinguished scientist Loren Eiseley describes humankind as the zenith of the evolutionary process. In his *Encyclopaedia Britannica* article entitled "The Cosmic Orphan" he writes:

> The thing that is you bears the still-aching wounds of evolution in body and brain. Your hands are made-over fins, your lungs come from a swamp, your femur has been twisted upright. Your feet are a

reworked climbing pad. You are a rag doll resewn from the skins of
extinct animals. Long ago, two million years perhaps, you were
smaller; your brain was not so large. We are not confident that you
could speak. Seventy million years before that you were an even
smaller climbing creature. . . . You were the size of a rat. You ate
insects. Now you fly to the moon.[2]

Others have been less optimistic. Nietzsche puts it bluntly: "Man is
a disease on the skin of the earth." Samuel Beckett says it graphi-
cally. His thirty-five-second play entitled "Breath" opens with a pile
of rubbish on the stage. The lights brighten and then fade. The audience hears a recorded cry, an inhaled breath and then a final cry.

Novelist and social commentator Tom Wolfe captures the soul-
defying reductionism of modern culture in a *Forbes* article entitled
"Sorry, but Your Soul Just Died": "The notion of a self—a self who
exercises self-discipline, postpones gratification, curbs the sexual
appetite, stops short of aggression and criminal behavior . . . is
already slipping away . . . slipping away . . . slipping away." In its
place evolutionary psychologists propose a genetic determinism
that explains, if not excuses, deviant behavior. Wolfe observes,

> The male of the human species is genetically hardwired to be polyga-
> mous, i.e., unfaithful to his legal mate. Any magazine-reading male
> gets the picture soon enough. (Three million years of evolution made
> me do it!) Women lust after male celebrities, because they are geneti-
> cally hardwired to sense that alpha males will take better care of their
> offspring. (I'm just a lifeguard in the gene pool, honey.) Teenage girls
> are genetically hardwired to be promiscuous and are as helpless to
> stop themselves as dogs in the park. (The school provides the con-
> doms.) Most murders are the result of genetically-hardwired compul-
> sions.[3]

Psychology has played its part in the loss of the person. "It is fair
to say," writes philosopher Stephen Evans, "that the rise of the
human sciences in the twentieth century has been marked by the
demise of the person."[4] Freud reasoned that the whole mind, particularly the unconscious, is biological in origin. People are largely the
product of amoral and irrational instinctual forces. B. F. Skinner, the

famous behaviorist, saw humankind simply as biological organisms conditioned by the environment to respond in a complex variety of ways. Sociologists in the tradition of Émile Durkheim made their contribution to the demise of the person by seeing people as the product of impersonal societal forces.

Movements in philosophy have further depersonalized the person. For example, the radical claims of naturalism which conclude that the human animal is the product of time and chance and is devoid of meaning and purpose, have been embraced schizophrenically. On the one hand is the objective world, which is impersonal, irrational and meaningless, and on the other hand is the subjective world which is of our own making. The essence of humanity is self-generated. Thus there are absurdity, nothingness and purposelessness in the objective real world, but in the subjective world of our own making there is authenticity, meaning and self-actualization. This way of reasoning has profoundly affected the way many think.

The only thing left to believe in is oneself. Individuals create their own belief systems. As Sheila Larson explains in *Habits of the Heart,* "My faith has carried me a long way. It's Sheilaism. Just my own little voice." Defining "Sheilaism," she says, "It's just try to love yourself and be gentle with yourself. You know, I guess take care of each other."[5]

Modern life is a reaction to these reductionistic perspectives of the person. People try to create meaning through a customized lifestyle, by means of sports, music, politics, sex, family or relationships, hoping to resist the perceived meaninglessness of the larger world. This has led to a fixation with image and it helps to explain why people go to extremes to re-invent themselves. There is little to believe in that is larger than the self.

It is drilled into children to believe in themselves. Second graders in our neighborhood elementary school recite the following pledge:

I pledge allegiance to myself, and to who I want to be.
I can make my dreams come true if I believe in me.
I pledge to stay in school and learn the things I need to know,
to make a world a better place for kids like me to grow.
I promise to keep my dreams alive, and be all that I can be.

I know I can, and that's because
I pledge to stay alcohol-, tobacco- and drug-free!

Each successive generation raised with a materialistic, naturalistic worldview is becoming tougher, more self-indulgent and more self-centered. The we-expect-more-of-everything outlook imposes a long list of expectations on the search for self-fulfillment. These intangibles include "creativity, leisure, autonomy, pleasure, participation, community, adventure, vitality, stimulation, and tender loving care."[6] The only moral duty many people acknowledge appears to be the moral duty to themselves. Basing his conclusion on national surveys, social analyst Daniel Yankelovich writes, "Instead of a concern with moral obligations to others pursued at the cost of a personal desire, we have the concept of duty to self pursued at the cost of moral obligations to others. Personal desire achieves the status of an ethical norm."[7]

When Frank Sinatra stood center stage and belted out, "I Did It My Way," he unabashedly sang our national anthem. But he was not singing soul music—he was boasting. The song says, "I am me, and what are you going to do about it."

Ironically, even our culture's interest in spirituality and religion seems to reinforce self-centeredness. The *New York Times Magazine* ran a special series entitled "God Decentralized" that concluded that Americans are reshaping religion for themselves. "More and more, Americans appear to be turning to religion (in some form, however unorthodox) even though they are unsure if they believe in God."[8] Observers say that the real issue in this quest for the sacred is personal existence, not the existence of God.

Spirituality is experienced as a private, usually weekend-only option. The emphasis is on self-realization and self-discovery, and shares values with eastern mysticism, pagan idolatry and gnostic spirituality. Moral absolutes are deemphasized in a "live and let live" duty-to-self ethic. Felt needs and personal opinions transcend orthodox convictions. Realities of sorrow, pain, aging, disease and death are glossed over. Coping with stress, realizing one's dreams and finding happiness are the modern equivalent to salvation. In our soulless culture spirituality is not God-centered but me-centered.

Please don't write this discussion off as too abstract for personal impact. The questions "Who am I, and to whom do I belong?" are basic to our self-understanding. They are surely critical to our personal sense of self-worth and to our attitudes toward friendship. How can meaningful premarital counseling proceed without reference to these questions? Could the disregard for God and the soul be linked to the high number of unwed mothers, unknown fathers and unwanted children? How can a wedding be performed in the name of Jesus without considering the soul? If we boast of being captains of our souls and masters of the universe, perhaps we should expect broken homes and painful divorces.

We cannot live as if we are the center of the universe without experiencing consequences. Daniel Yankelovich wisely observes,

> By concentrating day and night on your feelings, potentials, needs, wants and desires, and by learning to assert them more freely, you do not become a freer, more spontaneous, more creative self; you become a narrower, more self-centered, more isolated one. You do not grow you shrink.[9]

Many people have told us that we don't have a soul, but only one person has said that we can't afford one. Only Jesus has said that my soul is so expensive that even if I gained the whole world I couldn't afford my very own soul: "What good will it be for a man if he gains the whole world, yet forfeits his soul? Or what can a man give in exchange for his soul?" (Mt 16:26). The reality of the soul changes everything. The me-centered world of our own making is nothing but myth. Reality is the God-centered world of creation and eternity.

No matter how vocal and pervasive the experts may be in arguing for the absence of soul, the Word of God and the human heart confirm otherwise. We have been created for the challenge to love the Lord with all our heart, soul and mind, and our neighbor as ourselves (see Deut 6:5; Mt 22:37-39). All the rhetoric in the world cannot touch the enduring reality of the God-given soul. As Jesus said, "Do not be afraid of those who kill the body but cannot kill the soul. Rather, be afraid of the

One who can destroy both soul and body in hell" (Mt 10:28).

"You Know Me"

Self-understanding, Jesus insisted, is not based on a set of beliefs as much as on an act of self-surrender. The soulful self finds its rest in God. Every truly self-aware person can identify with C. S. Lewis's discovery. At the age of thirty-one, while a student at Oxford, Lewis painfully realized that the secret to self-fulfillment was not to be found in himself. "I gave in, and admitted that God was God, and knelt and prayed," he recalls. "I had tried everything in my own mind and body; as it were, asking myself, 'Is it this you want? Is it this?'" Even Lewis's noble pursuit of joy proved unfulfilling.

> I thus understood that in the deepest solitude there is a road out of self, a commerce with something which by refusing to identify itself with any object of the senses, or anything whereof we have biological or social need, or anything imagined, or any state of our own minds, proclaims itself sheerly objective.[10]

To know yourself is to know in the depth of your being that you are fully known. As the apostle Paul says, "Now I know in part; then I shall know fully, even as I am fully known" (1 Cor 13:12).

What is important, then, is being able to say with David in the depth of our being, "O LORD, you have searched me and you know me" (Ps 139:1). Psalm 139 is a powerful portrayal of God's parental love for us. I remember first being impressed with this psalm when our youngest child, Kennerly, was born. She was born on Wednesday, February 20, 1985, and on the following Sunday I preached on Psalm 139. More than most fathers I was humbled by her birth, even as I was humbled by God's previous provision in the adoption of our two sons. I had been told that due to surgery for cancer it was highly unlikely that I would be able to have children. In time, we pursued adoption and God wonderfully provided Jeremy and Andrew for us. And then after ten years of marriage Ginny became pregnant with Kennerly. Each of our children has been a reminder of God's parental love and that we are his children.

There is nothing like the birth of a child to make a mockery of the belief in nature alone. I stood in the delivery room and held our seven-pound newborn, and I was overwhelmed by the sheer glory of her. David asks, "What is man that you are mindful of him, the son of man that you care for him?" He then answers his own question, "You made him a little lower than the heavenly beings and crowned him with glory and honor" (Ps 8:4-5). The birth of a child causes us to re-examine the meaning of life, to contemplate God's sovereignty and to feel our dependence upon God. A child's dependence on human parents is so obvious; our dependence upon God is so real.

The Lord God's knowledge of me is complete. It is intimate, immediate, comprehensive, persistent and sovereign.

> O LORD . . . you know when I sit and when I rise;
> you perceive my thoughts from afar.
> You discern my going out and my lying down;
> you are familiar with all my ways.
> Before a word is on my tongue
> you know it completely, O LORD. (Ps 139:1-4)

It is very freeing to be truly known and understood, accepted and loved. In spite of my sin and because of God's great mercy, I am invited into his fellowship which sustains and supports me. I am not a cosmic orphan or a master of the universe but a child of God.

> You hem me in—behind and before;
> you have laid your hand upon me.
>
> Such knowledge is too wonderful for me,
> too lofty for me to attain. (Ps 139:5-6)

I cannot escape this relationship, nor do I want to. It is this relationship that defines me, secures me and understands me. Within it I'm free to "rise on the wings of the dawn" or "settle on the far side of the sea" (Ps 139:9), but I am never independent from God's guidance or protection. God is the answer to my inherent fears of anonymity and loneliness. From fear of the dark to the fear of death,

I will fear no evil,
　　for you are with me;
your rod and your staff,
　　they comfort me. (Ps 23:4)

I know what it means to call my daughter mine, not in a possessive, domineering sense but in a way that I pray secures her identity,
strengthens her confidence and frees her to become a mature
adult—a God-centered woman. How much more effective is God's
parental love because his love is untainted by selfish motives, foolish fears and ignorance. The Lord God knows us from the inside-
out, from top to bottom and from beginning to end.

For you created my inmost being;
　　you knit me together in my mother's womb.
I praise you because I am fearfully and wonderfully made;
　　your works are wonderful,
　　I know that full well.
My frame was not hidden from you
　　when I was made in the secret place.
When I was woven together in the depths of the earth,
　　your eyes saw my unformed body.
All the days ordained for me
　　were written in your book
　　before one of them came to be. (Ps 139:13-16)

In spite of my many weaknesses, Kennerly is happy to have me
as her father—at least most of the time! She does not resent that her
father is older and wiser than she is (I may not always be wiser, but
I will always be older). Convinced of my love, she seeks my wisdom, considers my counsel and listens to my advice. How much
more then should I be impressed by the wisdom and counsel of
God, my Maker and Redeemer. "How precious to me are your
thoughts, O God!" (Ps 139:17).

Kennerly looks to her father to protect and defend her. I enjoy
being my daughter's advocate, guardian and defender. And just as
my daughter turns to me, I turn to my heavenly Father. "If only you
would slay the wicked, O God!" (Ps 139:19). If I am a true dad, my

daughter will learn that she can also come to me and vent her feelings and frustrations, her anger and her pain. As David turned to God and vented his hatred of evil, we need to learn how to pour out our anger and despair to God. "Do I not hate those who hate you, O LORD, and abhor those who rise up against you?" (Ps 139:21).

David ends the psalm by inviting the Lord to examine his heart and expose his sin. More than anything else he is glad to be fully known by his God. He is well aware that nothing escapes God's notice. His thoughts and feelings are an open book before him. In fact, everything about him, past, present and future, is completely comprehended by God. Finally, the psalmist personally invites God's scrutiny and testing. "Search me, O God, and know my heart; test me and know my anxious thoughts" (Ps 139:23).

As my teenage son would say, David is "keeping it real, holding it tight" with God. Whatever defensiveness or self-serving bias David might have been tempted to hold has evaporated in the soul-penetrating heat of communion with God. He is fully aware that the only way to truly know himself is to know God deeply. It is one thing for a father to try to understand, protect and provide for his daughter, but it is another thing when she longs for spiritual discernment in her life. Our prayer as parents should be that our children will go beyond us and seek the wisdom of God for themselves. Augustine said that the key to spiritual growth could be summarized in three words: "Humility! Humility! Humility!" and surely David illustrated that humility.

Freud explains away the deep-seated emotion poured out in Psalm 139 and dismisses the reality of the all-knowing, all-loving, holy God. He claims in *The Future of an Illusion* (1928) that a parent-child relationship is responsible for the illusion of God.

> When the growing individual finds that he is destined to remain a child forever, that he can never do without protection against strange superior powers, he lends those powers the features belonging to the figure of his father; he creates for himself the gods whom he dreads, whom he seeks to propitiate, and whom he nevertheless entrusts with his own protection. Thus, his longing for a father is identical with his

need for protection against the consequences of human weakness.[11]

I have claimed just the opposite—that a parent-child relationship is at best but a faint, albeit tender, reflection of God's abiding parental love. The choice is ours between a world of our making and the world of God's creating. Either the Creator creates creation or creation creates the creator. In a multitude of practical ways we choose between being me-centered or God-centered.

Many people have a familiarity with the tenets of the Christian faith. They believe in God and espouse an orthodox understanding of humankind, but they still don't know who they are and to whom they belong. J. I. Packer, in his own inimitable way, puts his finger on the issue:

> Though we negate secular humanist doctrine, we live by its value system and suffer its symptoms: Man-centeredness as a way of life, with God there to care for me; preoccupation with wealth, luxury, success, and lots of happy sex as a means to my fulfillment; unconcern about self-denial, self-control, truthfulness, and modesty; high tolerance of moral lapses, with readiness to makes excuses for ourselves and others in the name of charity; indifference to demands for personal and church discipline; prizing ability above character, and ducking out of personal responsibilities—is any of that Christian? The truth is that we have met the secular humanist enemy, and ethically, it is us.[12]

This helps to explain why so many professing Christians suffer from spiritual schizophrenia. Theoretically they know about the soul, but in practice they live soulless lives. Jesus said to his disciples, "If anyone would come after me, he must deny himself and take up his cross and follow me. For whoever wants to save his life will lose it, but whoever loses his life for me will find it" (Mt 16:24-25). This involves relinquishing control, surrendering ourselves to God and dying to the sinful self. Soulcraft involves the daily work of distancing ourselves from past practices that work against the soul and embracing those practices that honor God and enrich the soul. We are off that old list, that way of life that took advantage of others, abused our bodies and bowed before idols. We have been "cleaned up and given a fresh start by Jesus, our Master, our Messiah, and by

our God present in us, the Spirit" (1 Cor 6:11 The Message).
Self-worth is not a human achievement but a divine endowment.
It is God who invests us with value and meaning. Human significance is God-given, by virtue of the fact that we are made in God's
image. The value of the person is not optional; the measure of the
person is not in what is achieved but in what is received from God.
We are more than exquisite chemical equations or angst-filled emotions; we resonate with the Spirit of God. We are called into a personal, face-to-face relationship with our God and one another.
What John Calvin wrote in 1536 is still true:

> Our wisdom, in so far as it ought to be deemed true and solid wis-
> dom, consists almost entirely of two parts: the knowledge of God and
> of ourselves. . . . No person can survey himself without immediately
> turning his thoughts toward God in whom he lives and moves;
> because it is perfectly obvious, that the endowments which we pos-
> sess cannot possibly be from ourselves. . . . It is evident that a person
> never attains to a true self-knowledge until he has previously contem-
> plated the face of God, and come down after such contemplation to
> look into himself. . . . The knowledge of God and the knowledge of
> ourselves are bound together by a mutual tie.[13]

Holy! Holy! Holy!

Psalm 139 is filled with references to the first-person personal pro-
nouns: *I, me* and *my.* The emphasis, however, is not on the self but
on the Lord. The best way to avoid self-centeredness, as David
knew so well, is not by pretending that the self does not exist or by
self-consciously trying to eliminate all references to the personal. To
be truly God-centered is a deeply personal experience. Instead of
living according to the constant refrain "Me! Me! Me!" we enter into
a hymn of praise and adoration: "Holy, holy, holy is the Lord God
Almighty, who was, and is, and is to come" (Rev 4:8). Everything
about me becomes centered in the Lord Jesus Christ, my abilities
and disabilities, my hopes and fears, my friends and enemies, my
past and future, my daily tasks and long-range goals.

4
WHOLENESS

*"No one who puts his hand to the plow and looks back
is fit for service in the kingdom of God."*

L U K E   9 : 6 2

W*E HAVE EXPLORED THE VALUE OF THE PERSON CREATED IN THE*
image of God. How we see ourselves in relationship to God is foundational to how we relate to others. It effects how we make friends and how we feel whole. Being single presents a unique challenge to soulcraft, one that is faced by each and every follower of Christ. Some people remain single for their entire lives, but we all start single and many of us will end up single because of death or divorce. Whether we are fit for Christian service, make good friends and become happily single or happily married depends on how complete we are as single adults. The message of the gospel is that a single person in Christ can be truly complete and joyfully whole. Singleness expressed in Christ-centered wholeness is a powerful testimony to the grace and peace of Christ.

The very word *single* is double-edged. It ironically implies both freedom and isolation, autonomy and separation. We both envy and pity the caricature of the single person: on the one hand the single person has the freedom to be the self-actualized autonomous self that we fantasize about so much, but on the other hand the single person faces the dreaded loneliness of the seemingly-unfulfilled relational self.

Being sexually active does not make a person more a man or a woman than does celebacy. Sexuality should not be confused with having sexual intercourse. Sexual fulfillment is a much greater issue than genital sex and has far more to do with self-control, self-discipline and self-sacrifice. Our over-sexed culture has gone a long way in proving the biblical point that sex makes a poor object of devotion. The real quest in our culture is not to have sex but to experience intimacy. The longing of the soul is not for sex but for meaningful companionship.

Marriage for many comes in the middle of a relationship, between a beautiful beginning and a painful ending. It is often preceded by an affair in which a couple explores the fleeting emotion of present-moment happiness and contemplates future commitment. Popular culture has arrived at the point of sexual distrust by exhausting itself on sex. The Christian culture was meant to arrive at the point of sexual fulfillment by reserving sex for the holy commitment of marriage. The world has known for some time what many Christians are finding out the hard way, that the pleasure principle is more of an addiction than a prescription for happiness. Jesus knew what he was talking about when he said, "whoever loses his life for me will find it" (Mt 16:25).

A Seinfeld Single

I expect that television's top-rated sitcom *Seinfeld* will linger in the popular imagination for some time to come. It offers a laughable, if not tragic, caricature of thirty-something single life. As a modern version of *The Abbott and Costello Show*, it's funny; but as commentary on who we are, it's sobering. Jerry, Kramer, George and Elaine are amazingly self-absorbed and self-centered, and their shared narcissism seems to be the tie that holds their friendship together.

Through these four singles we see ourselves and our friends, but underlying the comedy of George's super-thick wallet, Kramer's wild entrances and Elaine's choice of boyfriends is the message that life is boldly superficial. Life is the sum of daily trivialities, pet peeves and personal idiosyncrasies. The show portrays sex as just another overrated thing people do for themselves whenever and with whomever they can. It is part of life, like washing your hair or buying groceries. Sex happens.

In *Seinfeld*, commitment, fidelity and virtue are avoided at all cost. Whatever romance there is between a man and a woman is short-lived and reduced to a joke. In one of the show's more controversial episodes, George's fiancée dies, having poisoned herself by licking cheap wedding-invitation envelopes. George, relieved of the prospect of marriage, can hardly contain his joy. It was inconceivable to these Seinfeld singles that people could live for anyone other than themselves. The show is about four people who take the most insignificant details of their lives more seriously than they take life itself. In almost a decade of episodes God never gets a straight line. What is not so funny is that the caricature fits our culture like a pair of Spandex shorts. The search for meaning is only a quest for present-moment happiness; growing up is unnecessary.

Jesus Was Single

Being single and a disciple of Jesus may be one of the toughest kingdom callings today. In Christian circles a single person is often made to feel like only half a person, and a divorced or widowed person like a second-class Christian. After the age of thirty, single people's lives can become strained and awkward, especially in the church. Their singleness types them, placing them in a category that seems to define them as less than whole. The never-married or the long-since unmarried are treated like relational wannabes. It is the rare single person who is not negatively impacted by the Christian community's practice of socializing as couples and focusing on the family. Many singles are the people most committed to Christ and yet most vulnerable in the culture and in the church.

For the most part, we do not take Jesus' singleness seriously. We

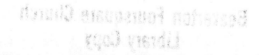

do to Jesus what we can't stand others doing to us. We place him in a category and then say that the category does not relate to us. By virtue of his incarnation we distance ourselves from the power of his example, even though the incarnation was for the purpose of his identification with us in our humanity. Remember that the apostle Paul says that our attitude "should be the same as that of Christ Jesus" (Phil 2:5). His full humanity and his complete humility invite our participation in his life. Our Lord and Savior has gone lower than we have, to show us how to live the upward call of God. Jesus meets us in our weaknesses, and because he shared our vulnerabilities and temptations we can share in his life. Far from being an excuse, the incarnation is the reason that we can take the example of Jesus seriously.

When Jesus assumed "the very nature of a servant" (Phil 2:7) he showed us how to live fully for God as a single young adult. However, because of the sexual preoccupation of our age, many have trouble relating to Jesus because he seems to them asexual. It is ironic that by virtue of his singleness and celibacy, Jesus is rarely considered as an example of authentic singleness. It is true, Jesus does not offer an over-the-counter practical guide to dating or a how-to manual on finding a wife. But Jesus does show us how to live fully and freely with or without a spouse, and he does it as a single person!

Contrary to the opinion of some, the Bible presents Jesus as a sexual being. His sexuality was a real factor in his relationships with both sexes. Far from using his masculinity to distance himself from women, Jesus related to women in a very meaningful and profound way. When Jesus spoke to the Samaritan woman at Jacob's well, he met a woman whose sordid sexual past would have offended most law-abiding Jewish males. But Jesus encountered her as a real person. His questions quickly went to the core of her being and provoked a discussion as deeply theological and personal as any we find in the Gospels. The disciples' surprise at finding Jesus in dialogue with this woman implies not only the culture's awareness of gender but also Jesus' intention to respect this woman as a real person in need (Jn 4).

Jesus' evident sensitivity to those in need, his resistance to being bullied by the cultural elite, and his ability to cultivate loyal friendships among both women and men implies a self-assured masculinity. He was comfortable with his sexual identity and with who he was as a person. His strength and sensitivity appealed to both women and men. Luke tells us that Jesus was supported by a number of women, including several who, like Mary Magdalene, had been healed of evil spirits or diseases, as well as others who appear to have been financially well-off, such as Joanna, who was married to the manager of Herod's household (Lk 8:2-3).

Jesus' sexuality was also implied by the criticism he received from the religious leaders. Far from being a standoffish, holier-than-thou moralist, Jesus befriended "tax collectors and sinners" (Mt 11:19). Some of these so-called sinners were prostitutes who appreciated the message of Jesus far more than some members of the religious establishment. On one occasion, when Jesus was invited to dinner by a Pharisee named Simon, a woman with a reputation for promiscuity was overwhelmed by Jesus. She stood behind him sobbing so hard that her tears wet his feet. She wiped his feet with her hair, kissed them and poured perfume on them. She had given her body to many men, but now she was giving her heart to Jesus. All the while, Simon thought to himself, "If this man were a prophet, he would know who is touching him and what kind of woman she is—that she is a sinner" (Lk 7:39).

The woman had touched Jesus and was not rebuked; this stirred Simon's criticism. How could this sexy woman with an erotic reputation get away with touching Jesus, who had a prophetic reputation. It didn't fit. It was wrong. Simon was offended by what he judged to be a tainted touch. What other touching could there be between a woman and a man but a lustful touch?

Simon saw only a fornicator, but Jesus saw a woman seeking forgiveness. She represented the people Simon pretended not to see, but she was the kind of woman Jesus made eye contact with when he said, "Blessed are you who weep now, for you will laugh" (Lk 6:21).

Jesus addressed the Pharisee: "Simon, do you see this woman?"

What an understatement! Simon hadn't missed a thing. Her appearance, her sound, her scent dominated the room. "I came into your house," Jesus continued:

> You did not give me any water for my feet, but she wet my feet with her tears and wiped them with her hair. You did not give me a kiss, but this woman, from the time I entered, has not stopped kissing my feet. You did not put oil on my head, but she has poured perfume on my feet. Therefore, I tell you, her many sins have been forgiven—for she loved much. But he who has been forgiven little loves little. (Lk 7:44-47)

For once, this woman had met a man who treated her like a woman, not as a sex object or as someone to be scorned but as a person who deeply wanted to be a woman of God. Jesus told her, "Your sins are forgiven." Ignoring the stir this caused to the rest of the dinner party, Jesus said to the woman, "Your faith has saved you; go in peace" (Lk 7:48, 50). It dehumanizes Jesus to speak of him as asexual, especially when the male-female dynamic was a real part of his life.

Jesus manifested fearlessness without being arrogant and a sensitive spirit without being sentimental. The disciples saw his courage when he faced angry crowds or the raging seas. They experienced his compassion when he healed the sick and blessed the children. In Jesus there was a composure and a confidence that both genders could appreciate and learn from. He provoked deep passions among his followers that found expression in ways unique to each gender. When Martha hosted a dinner in honor of Jesus, Mary used the occasion to express her love for Jesus in the most extravagant way she could think of. She took "a pint of pure nard, an expensive perfume," and "she poured it on Jesus' feet and wiped his feet with her hair. And the house was filled with the fragrance of the perfume" (Jn 12).

Paul Barnes, a musician friend of mine, called my attention to the important difference between being sensual and being sensuous. If this were a *sensual*, carnal act, Mary would be coming on to Jesus. Her thoughts for Jesus would be lustful, not loving; her actions, erotic, not endearing. Instead, this wonderful scene was *sensuous*, like a bouquet of roses, filling the air with a delicious fragrance. Her thoughtful display of devotion was appealing, not enticing; her actions delightful, not deviant. Mary's lavish outpouring of perfume was not intended to be sexy but sensory, filling the room with the fragrance of her love. What Mary did was holy, not hedonistic, and it was done as only a woman would do it. Peter, James and John, left their fishing nets; Mary poured out her expensive perfume.

Jesus says enough about purity and lust, fidelity and adultery, marriage and divorce to silence any criticism that he was out of touch with the real issues facing men and women. He did, however, see much larger issues than marriage and sex. Our culture may be consumed by the topic of sex, but Jesus was not and his message to us places sexuality in the larger context of soulmaking and discipleship. In the mind and actions of Jesus, personal devotion to God and obedience to God's will takes precedence over any other considerations. This does not render him asexual but instead frames sexual issues in the light of true spirituality and personal wholeness.

Jesus makes it clear that marriage is not the overriding duty that Judaism makes it out to be. Nor does Jesus see the single person as an autonomous individual self. Jesus did nothing less than redefine the meaning of family, and unlike today's evangelical rhetoric, he did not focus on the nuclear family. "Who is my mother, and who are my brothers?" Jesus asks, and then pointing to his disciples, he says, "Here are my mother and my brothers. For whoever does the will of my Father in heaven is my brother and sister and mother" (Mt 12:48-50). Jesus saw the salvation-shaped world of the single person as a large, grace-filled world.

> I tell you the truth, . . . no one who has left home or brothers or sisters or mother or father or children or fields for me and the gospel will fail to receive a hundred times as much in this present age (homes, brothers, sisters, mothers, children and fields—and with them, persecutions) and in the age to come, eternal life. But many who are first will be last, and the last first. (Mk 10:29-31)

We turn now to see the impact of Jesus' teaching on singleness.

Knowing God

Whether we are single or married, Jesus teaches that we are ruled by an overarching commitment. In many ways he gives us a single message: "No one can serve two masters. . . . You cannot serve both God and Money" (Mt 6:24). "Come to me, all you who are weary and burdened, and I will give you rest. Take my yoke upon you and learn from me, for I am gentle and humble in heart, and you will find rest for your souls. For my yoke is easy and my burden is light" (Mt 11:28-30). "If anyone would come after me, he must deny himself and take up his cross and follow me" (Mt 16:24).

Jesus calls for single-minded devotion, total life commitment and whole-hearted passion for God. Anything less is not the gospel according to Jesus. He makes it clear: "Seek first his kingdom and his righteousness" (Mt 6:33). This was a hard message in Jesus' day and it is a hard message today. We simply must reject any notion of Christianity "lite" or weekend spirituality. People can't possibly follow Jesus only in their spare time as if soulcraft were a neat hobby or interesting pastime. If a person has really heard the call of Jesus there is no turning back. Jesus had a way of driving this point home even though it cost him followers. Instead of lowering the cost and making it more appealing, Jesus seems intent on stressing the cost of discipleship.

Luke writes about Jesus' impatience with excuses, delays and competing priorities. One day Jesus was approached by a man who said, "I will follow you wherever you go." But instead of gladly receiving him, Jesus discouraged him, "Foxes have holes and birds of the air have nests, but the Son of Man has no place to lay his head." To another man Jesus said, "Follow me." But the man replied, "Lord, first let me go and bury my father." Surely fulfilling his family obligations until his father passed away sounded reasonable to Jewish ears but not to Jesus'. "Let the dead bury their own dead, but you go and proclaim the kingdom of God." First things first was Jesus' unyielding priority. Still another man said, "I will follow you, Lord; but first let me go back and say good-by to my family." Jesus replied, "No one who puts his hand to the plow and looks back is fit for service in the kingdom of God" (Luke 9:57-62).

There appears to be an ascending order of legitimacy in the requests made by these eager would-be disciples. Luke implies that the first person turned away from Jesus for personal comfort, the second for family obligations and the third for the common courtesy of saying good-by to his family. How could Jesus be so unreasonable? How could he be so radical?

Every believer ought to feel the intensity of Jesus' absolute call to discipleship, but for a moment consider the implications for the single Christian specifically. Is a single person faced with Jesus' lordship inclined to say, "I will follow the Lord, but . . . first let me find a husband or wife"? Is there not a temptation to make sexual intimacy and marriage a priority, even rivaling salvation itself?

Singles experience temptations similar to Jesus' experience in the wilderness. As Jesus went head-to-head with the devil, so does the single believer. The tempter comes to the single person and says, "If God really loved you, you would be happily married by now." Or, "If God wanted you to remain a virgin you wouldn't feel such a strong sex drive." Or, "You're a biological human being, what does God expect?" Sometimes the voice of the tempter can be heard in the well-meaning but misguided Christian friends or parents who claim that single people are only half the persons they could be. "We're just praying that your life will someday be complete." "When will you grow up, find a mate and settle down?"

The temptation may be to scout the bar scene or go from church to church searching for a potential partner. The situation may feel as hopeless as turning stone into bread or as desperate as casting oneself down from the pinnacle of the temple. Single people may be tempted to do virtually anything and may even toy with the idea of living like a *Seinfeld* single just long enough to know what it feels like. It is helpful to remember that Jesus our Lord faced powerful temptations as a single adult. Single people can follow his lead by responding to Satan with biblical conviction: "Away from me, Satan! For it is written: 'Worship the Lord your God, and serve him only'" (Mt 4:10).

The most important truth for us to realize is that personal wholeness flows from our commitment to Christ and not from sexual
experience. His call to discipleship is a higher calling than marriage
and defines us far more completely than a spouse ever could. Anyone can choose to have sex or to get married; for a single believer to
remain unmarried, no matter how painful, is a radical commitment
to God's will and God's timing. Michael Cavanaugh writes,

> Singleness is neither a stigma nor a social disease. It's a matter of
> choice. . . . You may not have become single in the first place because
> you chose to be. Someone else may have gotten the divorce. Someone
> else may have broken the engagement. Someone else may have died.
> But, right now, you are single by choice. If you wanted to be married
> today, you could be. . . . If you had no criteria, no real guidelines, or
> no moral standards to speak of, [you] could find someone who'd be
> willing to marry you. Anybody who doesn't have any standards can
> get married.[1]

A single believer who chooses to be faithful to Christ is responding to the will of God with the same attitude that Mary expressed, "I
am the Lord's servant. . . . May it be to me as you have said" (Lk
1:38). Singleness for the right reasons is not a matter of fate but of
faithfulness, and we need to see it through the eyes of the Lord, who
honors those who honor him with their whole being.

If truly knowing God is the overriding consideration in life, his
call to single-minded discipleship will never be rationalized away.
Our completeness in Christ will mean more to us than getting into a
relationship or experiencing sex. One of the dangers of living in an
oversexed culture such as ours is that faithfulness to God regarding
sexual distractions and relational temptations is thought to be old-
fashioned. We would do well to restore the intensity with which
Christians in the past guarded their sexual purity and their passion
for single-hearted devotion.

Hudson Taylor, destined to become one of the great nineteenth-
century missionaries to China, was deeply in love with a gifted young
woman, Miss V., who had won his affection almost from the moment
they met. If he had had a salaried position he would have proposed

marriage, but he didn't feel the freedom to do so until he had sufficient financial support for going to China. He wrote to his sister,

> I have not, as you know, the slightest idea how I shall go [to China]. But this I know, I shall go either alone or married. I know God has called me to the work, and He will provide the means. . . . It is not reasonable to suppose that Miss V. would be willing to go and starve in a foreign land. I am sure I love her too well to wish her to do so. You well know I have nothing, and nothing to hope for. Consequently I can enter into no engagement under present circumstances. I cannot deny that these things make me very sad. But my Father knows what is best. "No good thing will he withhold." I must live by faith, hang on by faith, simple faith, and He will do all things well.[2]

A year and a half later, the nineteen-year-old Taylor was still deeply in love and hoping to find a way to marry Miss V. But as time went on it became evident that she did not share his passion for serving the Lord in China. Finally in December of 1851 she told him that she was unprepared to go to China. Taylor was crushed. His dream of two years was over. Writing to his sister, he said:

> Satan seemed to come in as a flood, and I was forced to cry, "Lord, save me!" Still Satan suggested, "You never used to have trials like this. You cannot be on the right path, or God would help and bless you more," and so on, until I felt inclined to give it all up. . . .
>
> Yes, [God] has humbled me and shown me what I was, revealing Himself as a present, a very present help in time of trouble. And though He does not deprive me of feeling in my trial, He enables me to sing, "Yet I will rejoice in the Lord, I will joy in the God of my salvation." I can thank Him for *all*, even the most painful experiences of the past, and trust Him without fear for all that is to come. [3]

Five long years passed, and Hudson Taylor had concluded that it was probably God's will for him to remain single in order to carry out his calling, and then he met Maria Dyer in China. She was impressed with him from the beginning. In spite of the fact that many of the missionaries disliked Taylor's adoption of Chinese dress and ways, Maria found him authentic. "He seemed to live in such a real world, and to have such a real, great God."[4] Taylor's biographer describes Hudson's feelings about her: "In everything she satisfied his mind and heart; not only embodying his ideal of womanliness but being herself devoted to the work to which his life was given. As one who having put his hand to the plough dared not look back, he could rest in the assurance that she would help and not hinder him in his special service."[5] Six weeks after the wedding on January 20, 1858, Hudson Taylor wrote,

> Oh, to be married to the one you *do* love, and love most tenderly and devotedly, that is bliss beyond the power of words to express or imagination conceive. There is no disappointment there. And every day as it shows more of the mind of your beloved, when you have such a treasure as mine, makes you only more proud, more happy, more humbly thankful to the Giver of all good for this best of earthly gifts.[6]

In *The Hiding Place* Corrie ten Boom tells the dramatic story of her life as a determined saint in the anti-Nazi underground. The woman of God she became was forged in her willingness to accept her singleness as from God. When she met a man named Karel through her brother Willem, she was only fourteen, but she knew immediately that she had fallen "irretrievably in love." "I was going to love Karel forever," she writes.[7]

Seven years later Corrie and Karel began to see each other on a regular basis. She was twenty-one and he was twenty-six. For Corrie it was a dream come true. They took long walks each day and began to dream of a future together. And then one day her brother asked, "has Karel led you to believe that he is serious?" Corrie blushed. "I . . . no . . . we . . . why?"

"Because, Corrie," Willem continued, "this is something that can never be. You don't know Karel's family. They've wanted one thing since he was a small child. They've sacrificed for it, planned for it, built their whole lives around it. Karel is to . . . 'marry well' is the way I think they put it." Corrie was confident that she knew Karel's heart, and even though he became an assistant minister in a town some distance way, their letters back and forth kept her love for him as intense as ever.

And then one day, completely unexpectedly, Karel came to visit. Corrie answered the doorbell to find Karel standing there with a young woman beside him. "Corrie, I want you to meet my fiancée." Somehow Corrie, with the help of her father and sister, got through the thirty minute visit, but before the front door closed behind Karel and his fiancée, she had fled to her room. She writes:

How long I lay on my bed sobbing for the one love of my life I do not know. Later, I heard Father's footsteps coming up the stairs. For a moment I was a little girl again waiting for him to tuck the blankets tight. But this was a hurt that no blanket could shut out, and suddenly I was afraid of what Father would say. Afraid he would say, "There'll be someone else soon," and that forever afterward this untruth would lie between us. For in some deep part of me I knew already that there would not—soon or ever—be anyone else.

The sweet cigar-smell came into the room with Father. And of course he did not say the false, idle words.

"Corrie," he began instead, "do you know what hurts so very much? It's love. Love is the strongest force in the world, and when it is blocked that means pain.

"There are two things we can do when this happens. We can kill the love so that it stops hurting. But then of course part of us dies, too. Or, Corrie, we can ask God to open up another route for that love to travel.

"God loves Karel—even more than you do—and if you ask Him, He will give you His love for this man, a love nothing can prevent, nothing destroy. Whenever we cannot love in the old, human way, Corrie, God can give us the perfect way."

I did not know, as I listened to Father's footsteps winding back down the stairs, that he had given me more than the key to this hard moment. I did not know that he had put into my hands the secret that would open far darker rooms than this—places where there was not, on a human level, anything to love at all.

I was still in kindergarten in these matters of love. My task just then was to give up my feeling for Karel without giving up the joy and wonder that had grown with it. And so, that very hour, lying there on my bed, I whispered the enormous prayer:

"Lord, I give to You the way I feel about Karel, my thoughts about our future—oh, You know! Everything! Give me Your way of seeing Karel instead. Help me to love him that way. That much." And even as I said the words I fell asleep.[8]

The timely wisdom of Corrie's father recalls Paul's prayer for the believers at Philippi, "And this is my prayer: that your love may abound more and more in knowledge and depth of insight, so that you may be able to discern what is best and may be pure and blameless until the day of Christ" (Phil 1:9-10). My prayer is that when I need loving spiritual direction I would be guided by the Spirit of God, not the spirit of the age. Christ's radical love made all the difference in the world for Corrie. May we allow God to work in our lives the way she allowed God to work in her life. As Jesus said, "Peace I leave with you; my peace I give you. I do not give to you as the world gives. Do not let your hearts be troubled and do not be afraid" (Jn 14:27).

Humility or Humiliation
If there is any stigma attached to singleness it certainly doesn't come from the New Testament. "It is good for a man not to marry," declares the apostle Paul in the very context in which he upholds the value of marriage. He points to his own singleness as a sign that the Jewish law of the family had been transcended in Christ. "I wish that all men were as I am. But each man has his own gift from God; one has this gift, another has that" (1 Cor 7:1, 7). The capacities for celibacy or marriage are abilities God graciously bestows on us for the edification of his church, just as much as teaching, giving or speaking in tongues (see Mt 19:10-12). Like other gifts, the gift of singleness may last only for a time. On the other hand, we may seek after the gift of marriage but not obtain it. Paul was not reticent about advocating singleness for the sake of the gospel. He commended singleness as one viable, even commendable, response to the problems confronting the church at Corinth.

Instead of seeing marriage as a prerequisite for service, Paul saw singleness as a preference for service. His counsel to us would be to make God's purpose for our lives our number one priority.

Does today's evangelical emphasis on the ideal Christian life match with the biblical picture of costly discipleship? Or have we created a false recipe for Christian happiness, which includes falling in love, sexual intimacy in marriage, a successful career and healthy, well-adjusted children? "Jesus loves you and has a wonderful plan for your life" looks suspiciously like the American dream. Often it is hard for us to accept that God has in mind a greater agenda than our personal peace and happiness.

Joni Eareckson Tada's diving accident left her paralyzed from the neck down, but it certainly did not cripple her soul. Ten years after her near fatal accident in the waters of Chesapeake Bay, and while she was still single, she quoted Oscar Wilde: "In this world there are two tragedies. One is not getting what one wants, and the other is getting it." Joni makes this observation:

> I suggest there are likewise only two joys. One is having God answer all your prayers; the other is not receiving the answer to all your prayers. I believe this because I have found that God knows my needs infinitely better than I know them. And He is utterly dependable, no matter which direction our circumstances take us.[9]

Remember the Word of the Lord spoken through the prophet Jeremiah, whom God had commanded to remain single (Jer 16:1-2): "For I know the plans I have for you . . . plans to prosper you and not to harm you, plans to give you hope and a future. Then you will call upon me and come and pray to me, and I will listen to you. You will seek me and find me when you seek me with all your heart" (Jer 29:11-13).

The message of the gospel is that a single person in Christ can be fully complete and truly whole—a powerful testimony to the grace and peace of Christ. Humility before God overcomes whatever humiliation is imposed by the world and the church. Humility frees the single person to enjoy life to the full. Singleness as a sign of wholeness points to the completeness of life in Christ.

5
FRIENDSHIP

"I no longer call you servants. . . . Instead, I have called you friends."

J O H N   1 5 : 1 5

G OD DESIGNED US IN SUCH A WAY THAT THE MEASURE OF OUR communion with him is reflected in the depth of our relationships with others. The natural corollary to abiding in Christ is enduring friendships. Soulcraft insists that true spirituality is worked out in true relationships. Just as we cannot find ourselves apart from relating to God, we cannot be ourselves apart from relating to others. The wholeness we find in Christ empowers us to make true friends. There is a remarkable symmetry between our communion with God and our community with one another. Soulcraft reminds us that our friendship with God and our faithfulness to one another are two sides of the God-centered sacramental reality we call life.

The term *friends* is unusually elastic. It stretches from non-enemies and acquaintances to those we love deeply and trust completely. It is apparent that we automatically realize that there are many different types of friends, from casual "Hi, how are you?"

friends to earnest, soul-confiding friends. Our days go better with a multitude of friends.

There is the checkout clerk at the grocery story who knows us because we shop there all the time. We'll even choose her line when other lines are shorter, just to banter about prices and the weather and to hear how her kids are doing. We keep going back to the same car mechanic, even though he may charge a little more for his service, because we can trust him. He tells us the truth about our car and doesn't treat us like we are ignorant fools because we know little about fixing cars. Besides, after years of working on our car, he is familiar with both the car and the driver. We consider him a friend. We're often not really close to our neighbors, but we're friendly. If a neighbor needs to borrow a tool or one of the kids across the street is locked out, we're eager to help.

We all relate to the kind of friendship that makes daily life go just a little bit smoother. Even a modicum of decency, respect and regard for others usually assures us of this level of friendship. We give a little and receive a little.

Sometimes when I am walking down a crowded street or getting on an elevator I remind myself that I am surrounded by people who are made in the image of God, people for whom Christ died. When I keep that simple yet overwhelming fact in mind, it helps me to make eye contact, smile more and not be so quick to shut out the people around me. "There are no ordinary people," writes C. S. Lewis. "You have never talked to a mere mortal."[1] I believe that, and I want to relate to people behind the counter and on the highway with that in mind.

But we know we need to experience friendship in a deeper, more internal way. Convenience-oriented friendships are useful, companion-level friendships are encouraging, but soul-nurturing friendships are invaluable. We seek friendships that go beyond giving and getting and the commerce of the working world. Some people are especially good at networking. They seem to have friends everywhere, but these connections are often not the friendships that strengthen the soul and remove the pain of loneliness. A crowded appointment schedule and a Rolodex crammed with telephone numbers offer no assurance that a person has true friends.

Nor does the fun factor necessarily indicate a friendship that helps define the self and shape the soul. We can hang out with people and go surfing or golfing or whatever and have a great time but never really confide in them or truly know them. Every age group experiences this kind of entertaining friendship. It is as if an invisible line has been drawn through the relationship that says that conversations and experiences can only go so far and no further. The moment that unwritten rule is violated the atmosphere changes. This helps to explain how good friends who have traveled together, played together and laughed together may not really know one another. Their relationship is based on shared activities rather than a shared spirituality. They have a lot of fun together, but they are not soul mates. When the conversation switches from football to faithfulness or from fashion to prayer, a wall goes up. If the activities were to cease, so would the friendship.

What a Friend
It is reasonable to conclude that when God says it is good for a man or a woman not to be alone, he intends something more than a pragmatic relationship to make life easier or a pleasure-based friendship to make life fun. It is the friendship with worth beyond utilitarian and entertainment value that our souls long for and need if we are to become emotional and spiritually mature.

The old gospel hymn "What a Friend We Have in Jesus" reminds us where we should begin. As you would expect, soulcraft defines friendship on the basis of Christ's friendship with us. Our freedom and capacity to be true friends rests on the fact that we have been befriended by Christ Jesus. *Everything* about our friendships flows from our enduring relationship with Christ. This fact should not be overlooked or minimized, as if it were a pious truth isolated from our human relationships. Our friendship with Jesus needs to be honored and remembered in a way that is at least as special as, if not far beyond, our relationship with our "best friend."

We tend to forget this primary relationship with Christ when we lament that we are friendless and unloved. Even when everyone else lets us down, Jesus promises, "I am with you always" (Mt 28:20). King David understood this truth when he wrote, "Though my father and mother forsake me, the LORD will receive me" (Ps 27:10). Before we listen to the experts and motivational speakers on "how to win friends and influence people," we should hear what Jesus has to say about friendship. Before we memorize the seven easy steps toward making "friendships that work for you" we need the wisdom of Christ to shape our thoughts and feelings about friendship.

"Abide in Me"
Soulcraft takes its cue from Jesus, who explored with his disciples the meaning of friendship on the night he was betrayed. The very context in which Jesus spoke underscored the radical contrast between his self-sacrifice on the one hand and the disciples' self-centeredness. There was Judas, the "in it for what he could get out of it" friend, who was about to betray Jesus with a kiss and sold him out for a measly thirty pieces of silver. And there were the rest of the disciples who, in that night of confusion and chaos, would surprise even themselves by becoming fair-weather friends. When their own lives were at risk they fled the scene to save themselves. It was in this tense, threatening context that Jesus calmly presented the truth about soul-shaping friendship.

According to Jesus, the first principle of friendship is simply: "Abide in me" (Jn 15:4 KJV). We should not be surprised by this truth, nor dismissive of it on grounds that it sounds too spiritual or pious. Isn't this what soulcraft is all about? We need the spiritual maturity to understand the direct relationship between our devotional life with God and our relational life with others. Practically speaking, this means that we have an abiding relationship with God that deserves to be nurtured, cultivated and acknowledged with gratitude. Instead of lamenting our lack of friends, we begin with the one Friend who has given his life for us and promised to never leave us nor forsake us. It is this abiding relationship with Christ that gives us our personal identity and emotional security, as well as the freedom to risk relating to others.

One of the most beautiful pictures of friendship in the Bible is that of the relationship between Ruth and Naomi. At a point in her life when Naomi had nothing left to give, not even a faint promise on the horizon, Naomi insisted that her two daughters-in-law, Orpah and Ruth, return to their native country and start life over. Naomi's husband and her two sons, Orpah's and Ruth's husbands, had died. Naomi's life had hit rock bottom. Homeless and poor, she had no place else to go but to return to Bethlehem and hope that her distant relatives would help her get back on her feet.

Orpah accepted Naomi's advice. We read that she "kissed her mother-in-law good-by, but Ruth clung to her. 'Look,' said Naomi, 'your sister-in-law is going back to her people and her gods. Go back with her'" (Ruth 1:14-14). But the bond between Naomi and Ruth was not situational or circumstantial. We are told that Ruth "clung" to Naomi. It is the same word used in Genesis to describe the relationship between husband and wife, "a man will leave his father and mother and be united to his wife," or as an older version says, he will "cleave to his wife" (Gen 2:24). Ruth was not going to let go of her relationship with Naomi. Her response to her mother-in-law was filled with affection and resolve. "Don't urge me to leave you or to turn back from you. Where you go I will go, and where you stay I will stay. Your people will be my people and your God my God. Where you die I will die, and there I will be buried. May the LORD deal with me, be it ever so severely, if anything but death separates you and me" (Ruth 1:16-17).

This is a remarkable statement. It reveals the depth of Ruth's character and the power of her friendship with Naomi. Far from being sentimental, it evidences forethought and sober consideration. Ruth freed Naomi from feeling responsible for her. Their bond did not rest on what Naomi could provide for Ruth but on what they shared together. Ruth's commitment was for life and the pledge she made to Naomi was founded on her relationship to Naomi's God.

Ruth invoked the name of Yahweh, "May the LORD deal with me, be it ever so severely, if anything but death separates you and me."

Another powerful picture of friendship in the Bible is that of the relationship between David (Ruth's great grandson) and Jonathan. Their vowed commitment to one another reflects the wisdom of the first principle of friendship. Jonathan said to David, "Go in peace, for we have sworn friendship with each other in the name of the LORD, saying, 'The LORD is witness between you and me, and between your descendants and my descendants forever'" (1 Sam 20:42). At the center of their enduring friendship was the Lord who affirmed and authenticated their relationship. To intentionally place the Lord between them was to pledge themselves to both integrity and sacrifice. Their word to one another could always be trusted and they would sacrifice their lives for the sake of each other. It is significant that Jonathan, rather than David, initiated the covenant. The son of David's archenemy, Saul, was used by God to affirm David's life and calling. It would be hard to measure the value of this friendship for salvation history.

Both of these examples of friendship underscore the centrality of one's relationship to God as a foundation for being a true friend. I believe that for the Christian this is true even when the friendship is with a person who does not know Christ. Through the years I have had close friends who were not professing Christians. Even though they did not share my passion for Christ I think they would say I was a better friend to them because of Christ than if I had related to them apart from my Christian identity and convictions. In other words, they attributed at least some of the qualities of our friendship to the fact that I follow Christ.

I don't think Christians can be true friends to nonbelievers and conceal their God-centered identity. Friendships with nonbelievers must neither compromise our relationship with Christ (Jas 4:4) nor impose our convictions on the non-Christian. It is important to realize that by its very nature such a friendship is limited, because the bond between the friends is not Christ. The friendship may be self-defining (Prov 27:17), but such friends do not become soulmates. "As iron sharpens iron, so one person sharpens another" (Prov 27:17) may describe a friendship without the bond of Christ. But Jonathan's description of his friendship with David, "The LORD is witness between you and me" (1 Sam 20:42), highlights a deeper bond. The apostle Paul warns us not to become invested in relationships that may lead us astray (2 Cor 6:14), but he also encourages us to befriend those who are in the world both for their sake and for the gospel's (1 Cor 5:9-11).

When we look at inspiring pictures of friendship founded on a mutual relationship to the Lord, as in the lives of Ruth and Naomi, and David and Jonathan, it is important to be sensitive to the sort of emphasis we bring to these biblical examples. We can use these examples to inspire and instruct us to befriend others as Ruth befriended Naomi, and Jonathan befriended David; or we can use them to make ourselves feel badly that we have no close friends like a Ruth or a Jonathan. I remember listening to a preacher eloquently expound on David and Jonathan's relationship only to ask the congregation with great emotional feeling, "Do you have a friend like Jonathan? Who strengthens your hand in God? Who cares enough about you to pray for you? Do you have a friend like Jonathan?" By asking the question in this way he caused many people in the congregation to lament their lack of close friends. But if he had asked, "Are you a friend like Jonathan?" he would have encouraged us to examine our responsibility to be a friend like Jonathan. Depending on our emphasis when we consider this already emotionally charged issue, we can either bemoan our relational losses or be challenged to make relational gains by strengthening the character of our friendship. Instead of feeling the absence of Jonathan-like friends, we can, with the help of God, be Jonathan-like friends.

Jesus didn't wait for us to befriend him. He proved his friendship in the most extreme way possible: "Greater love has no one than this, that he lay down his life for his friends" (Jn 15:13). The challenge to love one another is based squarely on the power of Christ's love for us. His love and friendship allows us the freedom from guilt, the security of acceptance and the identity of belonging that make being a true friend not only a possibility but our calling. God, in Christ, has taken the friendship initiative on our behalf. Whenever we are tempted to lament taking what seems to be all the initiative in developing friendships, we can remember that Christ took all the initiative with us. This truth renews our courage to befriend others. As the apostle John writes, "Dear friends, since God so loved us, we also ought to love one another. . . . We love because he first loved us" (1 Jn 4:11,19).

Real Friends
Soulcraft insists on looking at friendship from the unique perspective of God's love for us and Christ's love in us. This is our first principle. No matter whom we are befriending, we should let the attitude of Jonathan be our conscious thought: "The LORD shall be between me and you" (1 Sam 20:42 NRSV). For it should be our desire to evidence in all of our relationships that we have been befriended by Christ. It is his love that empowers our love and friendship.

The second principle of soul-nurturing friendship emerges from the distinction Jesus made between being a servant and being a friend. "I no longer call you servants," Jesus said to his disciples, "because a servant does not know his master's business. Instead, I have called you friends, for everything that I learned from my Father I have made known to you" (John 15:15). Christians know that being a servant is a high calling. We are called to serve. Our obligation and responsibility to be our brother's keeper and sister's helper is emphasized throughout the Word of God. Jesus insisted on it by systematically removing all cultural, racial and ideological barriers and obstacles that would get in the way of our service. Jesus' parable of the Good Samaritan is a classic portrait of our moral obligation to meet our neighbor's need—even when our neighbor is a never-before-seen stranger in the ditch (Lk 10:25-37).

Of course, Jesus also teaches that there is a difference between serving others and spoiling them. Service, as defined by Jesus, never means catering to people's every whim or propping up their egos. We are not meant to cast pearls before pigs or get so wrapped up in serving that we forget Christ's priorities (Mt 7:7; Lk 10:38-42). The high calling of Christian service is never meant to degenerate into self-depreciating labor that spoils the recipient with false notions of self-importance. Jesus warns us against both a distorted version of service and an inflated notion of service. Christian service requires neither the humiliation of enslavement nor the intimacy of friendship. It is certainly positive and providential if being a servant develops into becoming a friend, but for that to happen the relationship will change from unilateral service to interdependence.

There is considerable confusion on this point. Often when people are wishing for friends they are actually looking for servants who will meet their emotional and relational needs. We don't always see this dynamic for what it is; seeking servants instead of friends reaps relationships full of burdens, obligations, even impositions. We do it to others and they do it to us. Under the guise of seeking friendship we seek donors who will give to our projects, volunteers who will work for our cause counselors who will listen to our problems, companions who keep us company, motivators who will boost our morale and pastors who will affirm us. Seeking help is not wrong, but we should call it for what it is: service, not friendship. The word *friend* is elastic, but it can be stretched too far.

Jesus makes a distinction that underscores a crucial relational truth. When our particular needs motivate our relational initiative we are looking for a servant, not a friend. We should be honest with ourselves. Too often we start into a so-called friendship with a need-meeting agenda that imposes on our would-be friend an unexpected burden. By refusing to acknowledge, even to ourselves, that we are looking for help, we set the relationship up for failure. Instead of simply enjoying a friend we require the work of a servant. And when our needs are not met we feel empty and disappointed.

Over time Dan Lam became a very close friend of mine, but our relationship started out with a straightforward request for help. The pastoral staff affectionately called Dan "the Asian Invasion." His reputation preceded our first encounter. I had been told told that Dan was a visionary with a passion for Christ. I was prepped to anticipate his intensity and his true zeal for missions. When we first met by appointment in my office, Dan laid out the call to service as directly as anybody I had ever met.

"I want you to disciple me," he said. "Can you do it?"

Knowing what I knew about Dan, I said, "I think it would be better the other way around."

"No, can you disciple me?"

"Okay, how about we disciple one another?" I proposed.

"No, I don't have time for you. Can you disciple me? I need somebody to pray for me and discuss God's work. I need someone to hold me accountable."

I found Dan's honesty refreshing. And his approach to ministry made me want to serve with him. His appeal for help was on the basis of our shared commitment to Christ and our call to service. He didn't ask me to be his friend, he asked me to serve him. Out of our weekly times of prayer and discussion emerged a ministry to Mongolia, and thanks to the Lord, a friendship that never would have happened if Dan had insisted first on being my friend. When Dan died in a plane crash in Siberia, I lost a dear friend whom I look forward to seeing in eternity.

Service can be requested, organized and implemented, but friendship develops naturally in the providence of God. The surest way to kill a friendship is to insist on it. In our first-name culture, where everyone knows your name but nobody knows where you live, friendliness can be easily orchestrated. But real friendship is a gift. The kind of friendship that is a true inner good and that nurtures the soul is far removed from the giving-getting contract of business associates.

We might think of friendship as a good tennis match—not the competitive version we watch on TV but the recreational pastime we participate in. In order to really enjoy tennis we need to have some level of competency with the basics. It helps to be able to get the ball over the net with some consistency, and, as we all know, this takes practice. We also need a partner who can return our serve and volley. It is often difficult to find players that are evenly matched, but having a good game depends on it. If the person on the other side of the net can hardly return the ball, the game isn't much fun (except to someone who likes feeling superior). The same is true when the other player is so advanced that whenever she swings she hits an ace (that's only fun for someone who likes picking up tennis balls all the time). The relational give and take of friendship is like tennis. It needs to be evenly matched. Friendship is not a one-way street. If all the emotion and care is only going in one direction the friendship will not last long.

The give and take of true friendship is innocent and uncalculated, uncoerced and spontaneous. That is not to say that genuine friendship lacks commitment and structure, but like love itself it is not engineered or programmed. Friendship is born of *mutual* respect, *shared* concern and *common* cause. It involves a meeting of the minds, an enjoyment of each other's company, and the freedom to feel at home with one another. C. S. Lewis pictures friends standing side by side with their eyes looking ahead, unlike lovers who look at one another face to face. Friendship "must be about something," Lewis observes. "That is why those pathetic people who simply 'want friends' can never make any. The very condition of having friends is that we should want something else besides friends. . . . Those who have nothing can share nothing; those who are going nowhere can have no fellow-travelers."[2]

The reason Jesus gives for calling his disciples *friends* instead of *servants* is that he has confided in them. Servants don't know the master's business; they simply do the master's bidding. But Jesus affirms that friends know what's going on. There is an implicit trust between friends as they experience life together and share their souls. The matrix of friendship is companionship and conversation. In a nonhierarchical, open, informal, spontaneous way, friends confide in one another, trust and depend on each other.

There is a natural, organic development to friendship that leads to deep feelings of responsibility and intimacy. There is no formula for achieving this, but faithfulness to the commands of Jesus makes friendship possible. Eugene Peterson is right when he says, "Characteristically, we do not make pronouncements to one another or look up texts by which to challenge one another; we simply talk out whatever feelings or thoughts are in our hearts as Jesus' friends."[3]

However, this does not mean that people will become friends or remain friends in spite of what they do. It is an odd, idealistic notion that claims that friendship is without conditions or responsibilities. Our ability to confide in friends is related to our confidence in the character of our friends, and their confidence in us is reflected in their willingness to listen to us. Jesus gives us a very important truth in his description of friendship, which deserves to be carefully understood. Jesus said, "You are my friends if you do what I command" (Jn 15:14). Our first reaction to this condition of friendship may be to narrow its focus to the relationship between Jesus and his followers. But what is said here applies to all soul-nurturing friendships. We don't lay down commandments that our friends must follow, but Christ does; we depend on this wisdom not only in our relationship to the Lord but in our relationships with one another. Obedience to the commands of Christ—whether conscious or unconscious—is implicit in any true friendship. For the sake of friendship we are called into the large world of God's making, where relationships are defined by forgiveness, integrity, righteousness, self-sacrifice and goodness. In other words, we agree with God on what makes intimate, trusting relationships work.

Soulcraft wisdom excludes a worldly form of friendship that is willing to sacrifice integrity and righteousness for the sake of the relationship, knowing that these immoral concessions and breaches of integrity eventually destroy friendship, as well as character. A true friend will never ask you to lie for him or her, because it violates the foundation of true friendship. The best way to be a loving friend is to be obedient to the commands of Christ.

Jesus kept nothing back from his friends. He shared everything with them. "For everything that I learned from my Father I have made known to you," is the bottom line of costly friendship (Jn 15:15). There is no better expression of true friendship than to share with your friend everything God has given to you.

Master of Ceremonies

The story behind our relational life is similar to the truth behind our salvation. In a very real sense we do not make friends, we receive friends. Friendship is a gift. Divine providence is the blessing of God's great faithfulness going before us, conducting the symphony, weaving the tapestry, supervising the project, writing the poetry that we call life. We can rest secure in our friendship with God and in the wisdom that he has shared with us. We're not one decision away from blowing it. The success of our lives does not rest on chance or blind fate. Building friendships is not a performance-driven, human achievement but a slow work of God's grace. C. S. Lewis writes:

> A secret Master of the Ceremonies has been at work. Christ, who said to the disciples "You have not chosen me, but I have chosen you," can truly say to every group of Christian friends, "You have not chosen one another but I have chosen you for one another." The Friendship is not a reward for our discrimination and good taste in finding one another out. It is the instrument by which God reveals to each the beauties of all the others.[4]

Finally, it should be said that the exclusive, well-defined character of soul-nurturing friendship does not mean in any way that friendship is exclusionary. This is one of the beautiful truths of Christ-centered friendship. It has a solid identity, but it is always open. There is no friendship quota or imaginary limit that says enough is enough. There is room at the table for one more. There is always the potential and the promise of new friends becoming dear friends. When friends must have you all to themselves and are offended at the thought of sharing your friendship with others, then you know there are artificial restrictions imposed on your relationships. When it comes to friendship Jesus gives a simple command: "Love each other" (Jn 15:17). That command alone is enough to let us know that there is always more to receive of the grace-filled blessing of friendship.

6
TWO LOVES

"For this reason a man will leave his father and mother and be united to his wife, and they will become one flesh."

GENESIS 2:24

ONE OF THE DRAMATIC WAYS GOD CHOOSES TO BLESS THE RELAtionship between two friends is through marriage. The relationship between a husband and wife is meant to take friendship to a unique and challenging level. Both intimacy and responsibility are heightened and intensified in marriage. By divine design, marriage was created to point beyond itself to our union with God in Christ. The relationship between our devotional life with God and the potential for human intimacy and commitment through marriage is to be received with gratitude. These are inseparable relational dynamics that nurture the soul and give glory to God.

True soulcraft discerns the high calling of both singleness and marriage. The single person's experience of wholeness in Christ and the married person's experience of oneness in Christ may do more for the cause of Christ and his kingdom than does any other feature of the household of faith. Who we are in our life together, whether we are single or married, testifies to the power of the gospel of Jesus Christ. Insightful love discerns what only God can provide for us. Whether we are single or married, we discover the fruit of righteousness nurtured in a relational life centered in Jesus Christ. Whenever the church favors either singleness or marriage it loses the fullness of what the Lord intended. The person who knows how to be single is ready for marriage, and the person who knows how to be married understands and respects the single person. Jesus says, "This is how everyone will recognize that you are my disciples—when they see the love you have for each other" (Jn 13:35 The Message). Soulcraft is learning how to love one another the way Jesus loves us and to manifest the love of Christ whether we are single or married.

Greater Love

God's illustrations are always the best, and when describing God's love for us the Lord chooses an analogy that is bound to get our attention. In a biblical theology of marriage, logic moves from the greater to the lesser truth: God's love is the source for all human love. But often our hearts can better grasp the meaning of God's love through the power of a metaphor. A picture is worth a thousand words, and one of the most effective pictures illustrating the love of God is that of the love between a husband and wife.

Human love helps us to grasp the meaning of God's love for us. Parental love is an example of God's love, "As a father has compassion on his children, so the LORD has compassion on those who fear him" (Ps 103:13). Marital love is also a picture of God's love for us, "As a bridegroom rejoices over his bride, so will your God rejoice over you" (Is 62:5).

Divine love transcends all human love and is the source for marital love. The love between a man and a woman points to the even greater reality of God's love for us. Both marital love and divine love are real, but redemptive love—"God so loved the world that he gave his one and only Son" (Jn 3:16)—takes precedence over romantic love. Soulcraft distinguishes between these two loves and cherishes the bond between them.

There is a negative and a positive side to this analogy between
human love and divine love. The prophets cast God in the role of
the jilted lover. The very people whom God had vowed to love and
cherish spurned his love and looked for lust: " 'You have lived as a
prostitute with many lovers—would you now return to me? . . . Like
a woman unfaithful to her husband, so you have been unfaithful to
me, O house of Israel,' declares the LORD" (Jer 3:1, 20).

The Word of the Lord through Ezekiel is graphic: "When I looked
at you and saw that you were old enough for love, I spread the cor-
ner of my garment over you and covered your nakedness. I gave
you my solemn oath and entered into a covenant with you, declares
the Sovereign LORD, and you became mine" (Ezek 16:8). Using the
language of the day, Ezekiel tells us that the Lord is married to his
people, pouring out his affection and grace upon them. But they
brazenly rebel and degrade their beauty, offering themselves "with
increasing promiscuity to anyone who passed by" (16:25). Adultery
is the prophet's metaphor for idolatry—sexual infidelity stands for
spiritual faithlessness. "You adulterous wife!" cries the Lord. "You
prefer strangers to your own husband! Every prostitute receives a
fee, but you give gifts to all your lovers, bribing them to come to you
from everywhere for your illicit favors" (Ezek 16:32-33).

John the Baptist felt like the best man at a wedding, overjoyed to
see the bride and groom united in marriage. The coming of Jesus
made him think of the Old Testament analogy between marital love
and God's love. "The bride belongs to the bridegroom. The friend
who attends the bridegroom waits and listens for him, and is full of
joy when he hears the bridegroom's voice. That joy is mine, and it is
now complete" (Jn 3:29).

Jesus likens the coming of the Messiah to a wedding banquet.
"The kingdom of heaven is like a king who prepared a wedding
banquet for his son." But instead of greeting this joyous news with
glad participation, the invited guests refuse to come. In a shocking
twist that recalls the prophets' angle on this analogy, the servants
are killed for delivering the good-news invitation, "Come to the

wedding banquet." The outraged king sends out his army and wipes out those on the original guest list and tells his servants, "Go to the street corners and invite to the banquet anyone you find." But even then a guest shows up who has no business being at the party. By refusing to change his clothes, he insults the king and mocks the celebration. Drastic measures are taken. The king orders, "Tie him hand and foot, and throw him outside, into the darkness, where there will be weeping and gnashing of teeth." The reality-stretching extremes of Jesus' allegory stress the eternal consequences of refusing to participate, or even to participate fully, in the marriage supper of the Son. "For many are invited, but few are chosen" (Mt 22:1-14).

Jesus tells another wedding story using irony and a touch of humor to make a serious point. Whoever heard of planning a wedding for midnight? But in the parable of the ten bridesmaids that is exactly what happens. The groom is more than a little late. He is so late the wedding party falls asleep. Five of the bridesmaids are prepared for a delay and five are not.

When the call finally arrives that the bridegroom is coming, the five bridesmaids who have brought an extra supply of oil for the lamps are prepared, and the five who haven't are not. The foolish bridesmaids are reduced to begging, "Give us some of your oil; our lamps are going out." The wise bridesmaids reply, "No, there may not be enough for both us and you. Instead, go to those who sell oil and buy some for yourselves." I imagine that buying oil at that time of night would be like trying to buy a Big Mac after McDonald's closes. By the time they return, they find the door to the wedding banquet locked and an uncooperative servant dismisses them curtly, saying, "I tell you the truth, I don't know you" (Mt 25:1-13).

The finality of being shut out doesn't fit the context of a village wedding, but it certainly fits the message of Jesus. His parable harkens backward to the Old Testament and forward to John's Revelation: Be prepared. The coming of Christ is like the coming of the bridegroom for his bride. "Blessed are those who are invited to the wedding supper of the Lamb!" (Rev 19:9).

Marriage as a metaphor for our relationship with God was on the mind of the apostle Paul too: "Husbands, love your wives, just as Christ loved the church and gave himself up for her to make her holy, cleansing her by the washing with water through the word, and to present her to himself as a radiant church, without stain or wrinkle or any other blemish, but holy and blameless." Paul goes on to quote from Genesis: " 'For this reason a man will leave his father and mother and be united to his wife, and the two will become one flesh.' This is a profound mystery—but I am talking about Christ and the church" (Eph 5:25-27, 31-32).

These two loves, marital love and divine love, romantic love and redemptive love, are meant to support and illuminate each other. The lesser love, the love between husband and wife, is meant to help us grasp more completely the personal intimacy and earnestness of God's love for us. The greater love, God's sacrificial, saving love, is meant to be the source, strength and standard for human love. The power and intensity of the oneness experienced between a man and a woman points to the greater mystery of our oneness with God in Christ.

Lesser Love
An appreciation for these two loves and how they relate to one another is especially important for a couple entering into marriage. Christians and non-Christians alike tend to impose on marriage a burden that marriage was never meant to bear. Many books on love and marriage are filled with practical relational advice on how to make a marriage work, but they are silent when it comes to the love of God that preserves and protects marital love. When the pursuit of sexual intimacy in a loving marriage becomes the ultimate quest for love, marriage becomes an idol and each partner a god. Salvation is sought within this intimacy and the power of eros feels like a sacred power.

A scenario in Garrison Keillor's novel *Wobegon Boy* is typical of how many view love and marriage. John Tollefson's mid-life crisis climaxes in a relationship with Alida after his pilgrimage through

numerous sexual relationships and a career in talk radio. If there is
any such thing as ultimate love, it is the weekend romance that goes
well. Present-moment happiness is all that is essential in life.

Together John and Alida agree to forget the past. She doesn't
want to hear about his many lovers. Salvation is the immediate feeling of well-being stirred by good sex, cuddling and relaxed conversation over freshly brewed coffee. "A person could live his whole
life exactly this way and be content," John muses to himself. "You
wouldn't need to see the world, or be a raging success; it would be
enough to be well loved."[1] Tollefson can't stop himself from thinking about marriage. He wrestles within himself over a deep desire to
protect and honor their special intimacy by committing himself to
Alida in marriage. She is his antidote to emptiness, his ticket to
"magnificence." In his mind he proposes:

> My darling Alida, you are the love of my life, and now all I need is a
> life to go with you. What I have, my darling, is a lifestyle, the life of
> people in commercials. I have a nice house and nice things and every
> couple of weeks I have you, the goddess Aphrodite, but I have no
> coherent story of my life. I am part of no struggle, have nothing at
> stake. I'm a fussy man in a blue suit who consumes fine wines. . . . I
> need passion, blood, magnificence. You are the only magnificence I
> know. Marry me.[2]

For Alida, marriage is the antithesis to the bond of intimacy they
share. "There is nothing so mean as the doldrums of marriage," she
says. "I saw my parents go through it. Those sour arguments about
money and in-laws and the stuff about 'If you loved me, you'd want
to spend more time with me.' Why would we ever wish that on us?"
She loves her freedom too much to give up her independence, and
then she explains, "after a couple of weeks I get ravenous for you,
and I can't wait for us to get back together and take our clothes off
and make love like a couple of cougars. I love our weekends. We
fasten onto each other for two complete days, no distractions, no
anything other than us. We each have lots to talk about, we're each
starved for each other's company. It couldn't be better."[3]

Alida knows intuitively that marriage ultimately exposes the emptiness of the lesser love's "magnificence." Sexual intimacy cannot make a life out of a lifestyle. Weekend ecstasy cannot support transcendence. Aphrodite is the goddess of present moments not the God of eternal truths. To put sexual or marital intimacy at the center of one's life, with the hope that meaning and purpose can be based upon this relationship is to guarantee failure. Unless the lesser love is empowered and protected by the greater love, marriage bears an impossible burden. That is one reason why so many marriages are unhappy and sexual intimacy so fleeting. To make the other the object of our idolatrous devotion is self-centered and ultimately ruinous. Only when God's love for us and our love for God is truly our first love can marriage become what it was designed to be, an experience of the grace and peace of Christ our Lord.

The Bible's consistent use of human love as a metaphor for divine love helps to dispel the notion that they are rival loves. Far from being in competition with God's love, marital love was given as a gracious expression of God's love. These two loves enhance one another in beautiful harmony. But if the greater love is forgotten for the sake of the lesser love, the two become rival loves locked in competition.

The issue is one of priority, not intensity of feelings. The feeling a husband has toward his wife is on a different plane than his feeling for God. If a husband truly loves his wife, loving God will always mean more in his life. Jesus spells it out in the most radical terms. The difference between the greater love and the lesser love is as great as the difference between love and hate. "If anyone comes to me and does not hate his father and mother, his wife and children, his brothers and sisters—yes, even his own life—he cannot be my disciple" (Lk 14:26). The best way for natural love to be strong and tender is to bow before divine love.

Soulcraft takes precautions against placing these two loves in competition. How can a woman's love for God remain strong if she chooses to unite her life in marriage to a man who does not share her love for God? How can a man honor God by marrying a woman who does not know Christ? The relationship of the two loves is painfully practical at this point and should not catch us off guard. There should be no surprise here for believers intent on following Jesus. How can we obey Jesus' command to deny ourselves, take up our cross and follow him (Luke 9:23), and marry someone who has no interest in following Jesus. I am not speaking here to a person who has come to Christ after being married but to a believer who chooses to ignore the meaning and power of God's greater love for the sake of the lesser love.

Today's ready acceptance of mixed marriages, with one spouse a believer and the other not, is a sad reflection of the church's false humility. "Who are we to say that this man or this woman should not be married?" At a critical time we bow before the pressure of the world and validate the lesser love at the expense of the greater love. But what is thought to be humility is in fact our humiliation. We retreat from the radical Word of Christ and in the end the married couple suffers.

C. S. Lewis writes:

> It is too late, when the crisis comes, to begin telling a wife or husband or mother or friend, that your love all along had a secret reservation—"under God" or "so far as a higher Love permits." They ought to have been warned; not, to be sure, explicitly, but by the implication of a thousand talks, by the principle revealed in a hundred decisions upon small matters. Indeed, a real disagreement on this issue should make itself felt early enough to prevent a marriage or a Friendship from existing at all.[4]

If we ever hope to achieve the oneness God intends for husband and wife we shall have to be honest about the two loves and let the greater love rule the lesser love.

Created Other

The word *sex* implies a split, a division—the parting of the human race in two.

> So God created man in his own image,
>   in the image of God he created him;
>   male and female he created them. (Gen 1:27)

The poetic emphasis of this life-shaping truth is creation. Male and female are not the yin and yang of an evolutionary synthesis but the created reflection of the image of God. Is there more to this sexual division than estrogen and testosterone? Is our masculinity or femininity the primary truth about us or is it secondary to the real meaning and significance of our identity?

What I find surprising is the degree to which moderns accept reductionism, a dehumanized, animalistic understanding of the human person, as the rational explanation for relationships. The "nature alone" argument makes reproduction the key reason for sexual division and the force behind life itself. Sex is the defining factor, the primary truth, of what it means to be human. Made in the image of animals, humans are biologically programmed to reproduce themselves and protect their young. Anthropologist Helen Fisher offers this explanation for the existence of two sexes: "No one knows how two separate sexes evolved in the primordial goo, . . . but somehow, billions of years ago, individuals of two complementary strains developed. Then two separate sexes emerged. And their continually varying offspring lived and multiplied the eons of our restless, changing past."[5]

Fisher contends that males are by nature more interested in sexual variety in order "to spread their genes." Females, on the other hand, are biologically driven "to acquire resources . . . and to secure better or more varied DNA."[6] For Fisher, "Profound reproductive forces that evolved across eons of daily mating throughout our shadowed past," explain everything from falling in love to serial monogamy.[7] "Year upon decade upon century we replay these ancient scripts—strutting, preening, flirting, courting, dazzling, then capturing one another. Then nesting. Then breeding. Then philandering. Then abandoning the fold. Soon drunk on hope, we court anew. Eternal optimist, the human animal seems restless during reproductive years, then settles in as he or she matures."[8]

According to Fisher, human sexuality takes its cues from "jungle love." She traces the story of human love and the "sexual imperative" back to apes in an effort to explain human patterns of sexual adventure and promiscuity. Locked in human genes is a built-in, primitive "reproductive strategy" that makes men and women breed and breed again. Fisher believes that today's modern "gorilla tactics"—loving and leaving—are truer than the sexual morality of the Puritans to the primal sexual patterns deeply ingrained in us.

The question follows: Do we better understand the mystery of marriage by exploring the mating habits of chimps or by reflecting on the revelation of God? Are we best understood according to our biological drives or according to the biblical testimony that we are made in the image of God? The Bible affirms that we are soul beings first and sexual beings second. Male and female sexuality goes to the core of our personhood, but it is not the most comprehensive truth about us. By virtue of the fact that we are made in the likeness of God, the person is a spiritual being first and a sexual being second. Furthermore, human sexuality is not rooted in primal mating rituals and reproductive strategies but in the image of God.

In Genesis, three important truths are highlighted about the human person and sexual division.

First, there is a qualitative difference between humans and other living creatures. Humans are endowed by God with the capacity to love, to worship and to communicate. These attributes find no true parallel in the animal world. That is why we speak of the person as having a soul. Only humankind bears the designation of having been made in God's image. This distinction is also seen in the creation of Eve, for among the animals no suitable helper could be found for Adam. That which was inferior to Adam was not suitable for Adam.

Second, the cohumanity of men and women is stressed in several specific ways. The language of Genesis 1:27 makes it plain. Henri Blocher explains that being made male and female

> will never be anything more than a second truth about man and woman. By underlining the likeness, Genesis provides protection against the coarse machismo of the Mediterranean male, but also against the suspect cult of an Eternal Feminine, and against Romantic speculations which make the masculine and the feminine, like yin and yang, the ultimate principles, the two poles of being.[9]

The equal humanity of the two sexes is also seen in Adam's relationship and response to Eve. Adam is passive in the creation of Eve; only God is active. Eve is made not to Adam's specifications but according to God's plan. "So the LORD God caused the man to fall into a deep sleep; and while he was sleeping, he took one of the man's ribs and closed up the place with flesh. Then the LORD God made a woman from the rib he had taken out of the man, and he brought her to the man" (Gen 2:21-22). The imagery used to describe the creation of woman stresses her equality with man. Adam has no control over Eve. To name her "woman" is for the sake of joy, not power. He receives her as a gift from God. Both the woman and the man belong to God and owe their being to God before they belong to each other. Adam exclaims,

> This is now bone of my bones
>   and flesh of my flesh;
> she shall be called "woman,"
>   for she was taken out of man. (Gen 2:23)

His powerful, poetic language is as beautiful as it is stark. He is no longer alone. He has met his match in the fullest and most beautiful way. They are equal but not the same.

Third, the Bible teaches that the reason for two separate sexes is for the sake of relationship, not reproduction. The primary truth is that the *other* is created for companionship, not copulation. There is profound purpose for the differences between the sexes that advances the fulfillment and enjoyment of each sex. The human experience of oneness depends upon a dramatic otherness, not sameness, and works in us deeply from the inside out. In relating to the other we meet the truly fulfilling self—not a narcissistic self but a loving, caring and sharing self. The journey of self-denial in relationship to the other is the path to self-fulfillment.

It is not contradictory to say that our gender is a secondary truth about us, and at the same time to affirm that our sex is at the core of our being. Sexuality is more than body parts, hormones and cultural roles. By virtue of being made in the image of God, we are ushered into a drama far, far greater than the "survival of the fittest" or the "culture wars." Femininity and masculinity permeate the entire person, assuring a fundamental complement in being, intelligence, feeling and will.[10] The other is not just another but a truly distinct, wholly unique being through whom we are reminded of our need for each other.

One of the most impressive qualities of a loving marriage is its complementary character. Humble spouses appreciate this, as do their children. It is no joke when we introduce our spouse as our "better half." I grew up benefitting from this impressive duality of personality, ability and creativity within the shared work of my parents' marriage. Now I experience this unity-in-duality firsthand in ways that continue to surprise me even after twenty-three years of marriage. My wife is just so different from me, and those who know us know how very much I need her. We have distinct intensities and personalities, diverse capabilities and capacities, and different strengths and weaknesses.

Take, for example, our response to criticism. I am in a vocation in which I tend to get a lot of criticism, and my personality is such that if left to myself I would dwell on it. Thankfully, I am married to a woman who takes criticism of her husband lightly and helps me move on positively. If Ginny absorbed criticism about me as a reflection on her or was overly empathic with me, we would both become oversensitive and unfit for ministry. Her ability to frame criticism in a larger picture, her understanding of people and her sense of humor help to restore a right perspective in me.

Otherness was created for the holy purpose of reminding us that we are incomplete in and of ourselves. Whether single or married, we were made for community. The Lord intended for all of us, from children to seniors, to benefit from the oneness of the marriage relationship in the bond of family life and in the body-life of the saints.

One Flesh
We cannot miss noticing the only negative assessment God made of creation, "It is not good that man should be alone" (Gen 2:18). "The remark amazes us," writes Henri Blocher. "Scripture could not

underline better the degree to which solitude contradicts the calling of humanity."[11] God's selfless love ordained human sexuality as a provision for our own good. Walter Brueggemann wisely observes:

> Sexual identity is part of creation, but it is not part of the creator. The text provides no warrant for any notion of the masculinity and femininity or androgyny of God. Sexuality, sexual identity, and sexual function belong not to *God's person* but to *God's will* for creation. . . . Sexuality is ordained by God, but it does not characterize God. It belongs to the goodness God intends for creation.[12]

Although the gift of sex in a lustful world may be twisted into a serious liability, God intends sex as a blessing, both for our fulfillment and for our growth in faithfulness. The "one flesh" imagery of Genesis requires discernment if we are to understand the fullness of God's provision. The term *flesh* is loaded with different connotations. At first glance it may seem pejorative, recalling the contrast between living in the flesh and living in the spirit (Gal 5:17). The New Testament speaks of "corrupted flesh" (Jude 23) and the sins of the flesh. In the New International Version of the Bible, *flesh* is often equated with a "sinful nature" (Rom 8:3-5). The apostle Paul writes of crucifying the flesh "with its passions and desires" (Gal 5:24) and warns against living for the flesh (Gal 6:8). Christians remain "in" the flesh but are not "of" the flesh (see Gal 2:20); they agree with Paul when he writes that "nothing good dwells in me, that is, in my flesh" (Rom 7:18 NASB).

Paul's worst fears about the flesh are confirmed by a quick word search on the Internet. Type in *flesh,* hit a key, and cyberspace puts out the welcome mat to hardcore pornography. There are invitations to every form of sexual perversion, leaving little doubt what *flesh* stands for in the world.

The positive meaning of the term *flesh* is also emphasized in the Bible. When we think of the "one flesh" metaphor in Genesis we are reminded of the apostle John's description of our Lord's incarnation: "The Word became flesh and made his dwelling among us" (Jn 1:14). *Flesh* is used here in reference to the incarnation to underscore the full humanity of Jesus. At the feeding of the five thousand Jesus said, "I am the living bread that came down from heaven. If anyone eats of this bread, he will live forever. This bread is my flesh, which I will give for the life of the world" (Jn 6:51).

In its pure form the Genesis description of "one flesh" refers to the whole of human nature. Therefore the union of husband and wife in a "one flesh" relationship embraces every dimension of their humanity. Within the extended family a new microcommunity is formed through this oneness. That is why we find the cryptic line, "For this reason a man will leave his father and mother and be united to his wife" (Gen 2:24). Dietrich Bonhoeffer is quick to reject the rationalization that some might adopt in light of this verse in favor of its more meaningful message:

> This passage does not justify running away from the worldly order of connection with our father and mother. It is the profoundest way possible of describing the depth and seriousness of belonging to one another. This ultimate belonging to one another is undoubtedly seen here in connection with man's sexuality.[13]

The physical union of husband and wife in sexual intercourse is the "sacrament" of an all-encompassing union. God intended a marriage of minds as well as of bodies, of emotions as well as of finances. When the groom is asked "Do you take this woman to be your wedded wife?" is there a part of her that he refuses to take? Her career? Her family? Her past? When the bride is asked, "Do you take this man to be your wedded husband?" is there a part of him that she subtracts from the relationship? His health? His manners? His ambition? Marriage is not like buying a car, when you choose your option package. When you marry, you marry into everything about that person. That doesn't mean that everything about your spouse is perfect and should remain fixed, but it does mean that there is nothing about the other that is left outside of the relationship.

A contractual arrangement may state otherwise, but a covenant relationship is grandly inclusive of all that you are and will be. The biblical expression "to know" is more than a euphemism for having sex. It is a telling reference to the totality of marriage and a reminder that God's primary purpose for marriage is not reproduction but relationship.

Mike Mason writes,

> To put it simply, marriage is a relationship far more engrossing than we want it to be. It always turns out to be more than we bargained for. It is disturbingly intense, disruptively involving, and that is exactly the way it was designed to be. It is supposed to be more, almost, than we can handle. It was meant to be a lifelong encounter that would be much more rigorous and demanding than anything human beings ever could have chosen, dreamed of, desired, or invented on their own.[14]

We should be careful to understand this because it is easy to get swept along by the rhetoric of romantic adventure and begin to make the goal of marriage "the dangerous and unpredictable depths of a real interpersonal encounter."[15] When we speak of marriage as being more than we bargained for we can express this in terms of romance or in terms of commitment. We can let our imagination run in the direction of our romantic dreams, or we can turn our attention to marriages that endure with love the harsh edge of ordinary life. "More than we bargained for" may mean dealing with forgiveness, cancer or financial setbacks. We don't want to be fooled into thinking that the intriguing part of marriage is discovering ourselves more fully. Of course personal insights will come and we will discover feelings that we never thought we had, but they tend to come more often in the middle of the night when we're pacing the floor with a colicky baby than they do over romantic dinners in expensive restaurants.

The oneness of marriage is a beautiful, powerful experience, but it has some hard edges, definite limits and immense commitments. "More than we bargained for" has to do with sexual purity before marriage, fidelity in marriage, and mutual submission throughout marriage. It has to do with the soul's "Amen" to God's revealed will more than it has to do with the inner recesses of the secret self.

The questions are so straightforward; the promises so simple. The pastor asks the groom:

Do you take this woman to be your wife, and to live together after God's command in holy marriage? Do you promise to be her considerate, faithful, and loving husband and to submit your life to the authority of God's Word? Do you covenant to love her, support and serve her, guide and cherish her in prosperity and in adversity; in sorrow and in happiness; in sickness and in health; and forsaking all others, be united to her so long as you both shall live?"

The same questions are then addressed to the bride, "Do you take this man to be your husband, and to live together after God's command in holy marriage? . . ."

The decisive "Yes" response to these life-embracing, all-encompassing questions is reminiscent of creation. "And God said, 'Let there be . . .'" Empowered and entrusted by God, the word of the groom and the corresponding word of the bride create marriage. Once they were two strangers, now they are "one flesh." Marriage speaks of the power of God's "Amen" and the love of a bride and groom's timeless, unqualified "Yes" to each other.

One Lord

To insist on finding the ultimate, soul-saving love in one's spouse is to drain the energy and joy right out of marriage. No matter how real and beautiful the oneness of the marriage relationship may be, we are reminded of our need for the greater love. Augustine's prayer says it so well, "Our hearts are restless until they find their rest in Thee."[16] The final lesson that marriage teaches us on "otherness" and "oneness" is that the primary Other before whom we bow is our Creator and Redeemer. The ultimate oneness that satisfies the soul is that of loving and obeying the Lord God. Marriage is a powerful analogy of Christ's love for us and our love for Christ. Soulcraft distinguishes between the lesser love and the greater love and rejoices in the truth. "We know and rely on the love God has for us. God is love. Whoever lives in love lives in God, and God in him" (1 Jn 4:16).

7

BODY & SOUL

"The man and his wife were both naked, and they felt no shame."

GENESIS 2:25

I N THE PREVIOUS CHAPTER WE EXPLORED SOME OF THE PROFOUND theological and relational dimensions of what God intends for marriage. The next three chapters focus on religious and secular reactions to the biblical ideal of sexual intimacy in marriage. It would be nice if we could move immediately from the biblical ideal of marriage to biblical insights on how to develop a marriage, but there is some rough terrain to negotiate first. The work of soulcraft is carried out in less than ideal conditions. There are frustrations and tensions and obstacles to spiritual maturity that require insight and discernment.

In the broad sweep of church history Christians have run the gamut from sexual aversion to sexual immersion. If we are serious about doing soulcraft we need to examine these two extremes and seek God's perspective. Biblical wisdom is often disregarded in a tug of war between asceticism and hedonism. Like a skilled bobsled team shooting down a straightaway, soulcraft steers right down the biblical fast track, rightly dividing the Word of truth. Love must "abound more and more in knowledge and depth of insight" (Phil 1:9), so as to guard the soul from sin and free the soul for life.

Early believers and contemporary saints have both had difficulty distinguishing between love and lust. Many of the early church fathers were convinced that the body and soul were engaged in a constant war, but today many believers feel they owe it to themselves to indulge their bodies. The pendulum swings from suppressing the body to dwelling on the body. One believer is taught that love is lust and another believer is taught that lust is love. In ancient times many Christians equated beauty with shame and in modern times many equate shame with beauty.

Augustine instructed husbands and wives to engage in passionless sex, but today church-sponsored seminars promote passionfilled sex. I have attended church services in other cultures where men and women sit on separate sides of the aisle for fear that mixing the sexes distracts from worship. And I've gone to church-youthgroup pool parties where, while most of the teenagers are dressed sensibly, several are wearing next to nothing. Yet to imply that a skimpy bikini or a mini-brief swimsuit is inappropriate invites the criticism that one is being prudish. On the relationship between body and soul the church is often like a bobsled hitting a curve either too high or too low, ricocheting off the walls, and bouncing down the runway. Learning how to hit the straightaway just right is the work of soulcraft. The challenge is to know how to embrace sexuality and spirituality in a way that fulfills God's will for body and soul.

Early Church Fathers

It was difficult for Christians living in Roman culture not to be adversely affected by mainstream thinking, just as it is difficult for us not to be unduly shaped by the spirit of the age. Ancient medical science reasoned that women were inferior to men. They believed that a lack of sufficient energy at conception inhibited women from becoming men. "Women . . . were failed males," writes Peter Brown in his monumental work *The Body and Society: Men, Women, and Sexual Renunciation in Early Christianity.* "The precious vital heat had not come to them in sufficient quantities in the womb. Their lack of heat made them more soft, more liquid, more clammy-cold, altogether more formless than were men."[1]

Christians labored under the false but common notion that frequent sexual activity not only decreased the fertility of the male seed but robbed the soul of spiritual energy. In making his case for the soul's presence at conception, Tertullian (c. 155-220), one of the leading church fathers, reflected on the spiritual implications of the science of the day:

> In a single impact of both parts, the whole human frame is shaken and foams with semen, as the damp humor of the body is joined to the hot substance of the spirit. And then, (I speak of this at the risk of seeming improper, but I do not wish to forego my chance of proving my case) in that last breaking wave of delight, do we not feel something of our soul go out from us?[2]

Early Christians developed convictions that led them to conclude that total sexual self-renunciation was desirable if one was fully committed to Christ. Sex and marriage were identified with the "present age." Theologians quoted the words of Jesus:

> The people of this age marry and are given in marriage. But those who are considered worthy of taking part in that age and in the resurrection from the dead will neither marry nor be given in marriage, and they can no longer die; for they are like the angels. They are God's children, since they are children of the resurrection. (Lk 20:34-36)

To walk in singleness of heart and to overcome doubleness of soul required a divorce from the common passions and pursuits of ordinary people.

It was wrongly thought that the concept of the new creation requires a dualism of spirit and flesh. Paul's words to the Corinthians in A.D. 54 became for many their whole theology of sexuality and marriage: "It is good for a man not to marry. But since there is so much immorality, each man should have his own wife, and each woman her own husband" (1 Cor 7:1-2). The words were pulled out of context, misapplied and misconstrued to mean that marriage itself was no more than a defense against desire. For large segments of the church, marriage was for the weak, not the strong. Brown observes, "The married person, whose heart was inevitably divided, was almost of necessity a *half-Christian.*"[3]

Serious Christian discipleship entailed a denial of one's sexuality. Tertullian made it clear what was the better way. "By continence you will buy up a great stock of sanctity, by making savings on the flesh, you will be able to invest in the Spirit."[4] Tertullian believed that abstinence from sex was the most effective technique with which to achieve clarity of soul.

> Let us look at our own inner world. Think of how a man feels in him-self when he abstains from a woman. He thinks spiritual thoughts. If he prays to the Lord, he is next door to heaven; if he turns to the Scriptures, he is all of him present to them; if he sings a psalm, it fills his whole being with enjoyment; if he exorcises a demon, he does so confident in his own strength.[5]

Tertullian's emphasis had an impact on other theologians including Cyprian, Ambrose, Jerome and Augustine in the Latin West.

Sexual renunciation was perceived in the Eastern Church as an act of personal spiritual freedom. To renounce sexual intercourse was to cut all ties with "the present age," reestablish the human freedom lost in the fall, regain the Spirit of God and undo the power of death. Brown observes:

> Many Christians already took for granted habits of rigorous sexual abstinence and had long practiced rites of baptismal initiation that linked the beginning of the true life of Christians with the perpetual renunciation of sexual activity.[6]

> Baptism was presented as a rite of effective desexualization. The ini-tiates stepped naked into the baptismal pool. They were thought to have put off the sexualized 'garments' of their old body. They stood beside the pool like little children.[7]

With a few notable exceptions, such as Clement of Alexandria

(c. 150-215), church leaders exalted the spiritual life above ordinary life and relationships. Sexual renunciation and virginity, it was believed, helped to preserve the original, unadulterated state of the union of body and soul. The tragedy of this history of Christian sexual renunciation is that the church for centuries labored under a false and twisted interpretation of the Bible. Who can say how many Christian young people grew up believing that if they were to follow Christ wholeheartedly they had to disavow any desire for marriage and family? The church taught that marriage degraded the body, dulled the spirit and divided the heart. Lifelong virginity symbolized the purity of a past when the human race was not yet polluted with sexual sin, and the hope of a future when there would be no sexual desire.

Spiritual perfection was measured in degrees of sexual withdrawal. The body, especially in its sexuality, was considered the soul's archenemy. As pressure increased for priests to remain celibate even in marriage, virgin young women were encouraged to think of themselves as the "brides of Christ," their "untouched flesh" serving as a symbol of the "purity of soul" realized by those engaged to Christ and Christ alone.[8]

Augustine

There is no early church father greater than Augustine, bishop of Hippo (354-430). His powerful grasp of theological truth and his impact on Christian thought through the centuries is difficult to exaggerate, but his legacy is marred by his distorted understanding of the body and soul. Instead of challenging the prevailing religious perspective as he had done in other areas, he used his powerful intellect to erect a wall between the soul and sex. It was impossible for Augustine to think of sex untainted with lust. This "greatest of all bodily pleasures" endangered the soul. "So possessing indeed is this pleasure," wrote Augustine, "that at the moment of time in which it is consummated, all mental activity is suspended."

Augustine insisted that a married couple intent on following the apostle's admonition that "each of you should learn to control his own body in a way that is holy and honorable, not in passionate lust like the heathen, who do not know God" (1 Thess 4:4-5), would prefer to beget children without "the heat of lust."[9] For Augustine the impact of the Fall was that sexual intercourse was forever steeped in shame. That is why, according to Augustine, married couples engage in sex in private, under the cover of darkness. If their action were righteous they would seek the light.[10]

Augustine's insights into sexual lust's power to rule the soul are worthwhile, but it was impossible for him to imagine that sex between husband and wife could be beautiful and righteous. Before the Fall Adam and Eve were devoid of the "wild heat of passion" arousing their bodies. Augustine takes pains to describe their intercourse as pure obedience: "Without the seductive stimulus of passion, with calmness of mind and with no corrupting of the integrity of the body, the husband would lie upon the bosom of his wife." They fulfilled God's mandate to "be fruitful and multiply" (Gen 1:28 NASB) through "placid obedience" apart from the "disease of lust" and the "violent acting of lust."[11]

It is likely that Augustine's own sexual past haunted him and reinforced his negative conclusions about sex. Augustine lived with the same woman from the time when he was eighteen until he was thirty-one. In order to advance his career he left open the possibility of marrying into a higher social class. When the time came for him to move from Carthage to Milan he decided he would look for a wife who was a member of an upscale, well-positioned Milanese Catholic family. His concubine returned to Africa bound by a vow to have no further sexual relationships.

The spiritual intensity with which Augustine and his mother sought a wife appears inconsistent with their spiritual indifference toward the woman with whom he had lived for thirteen years. Augustine's conversion took place during the crisis of his soul-wrenching struggle with sexual desire. He seems to have truly loved his first mistress. One wonders: if he had married her and they had raised their son, Augustine might have been free of the sexual trauma that possessed him.

The frustration and sinfulness of his own sexual passion was undoubtedly intensified when he rejected the woman he loved, became engaged to a young girl twenty years his junior, and then had an affair with a third woman. Augustine's apparent inability to distinguish love from lust caused him to equate the feelings he had for his "old mistresses" as only so much evil desire. He came to the conclusion that the only way out of his sexual nightmare was "continence," abstaining from sexual activity. What was "sex" but a toy that any adult should be able to live without. Besides, there were so many virgin young men and women and chaste older widows, that Augustine felt he, too, should be able to remain celibate. He understood his spiritual struggle as a choice between the allure of sex and the vow of chastity.

On the one hand, "The very toys of toys, and vanities of vanities, my old mistresses, still enthralled me; they shook my fleshly garment, and whispered softly, 'Dost thou part with us?'" And on the other hand,

> The chaste dignity of Continence . . . smiled on me with an encouraging mockery, as if to say, "Can't you do what these youths and maidens can?" . . . I blushed beyond measure, for I still heard the muttering of these toys, and hung in suspense. And she again seemed to say, "Shut up thine ears against those unclean members of thine upon the earth, that they may be mortified (Col 3:5). They tell thee of delights, but not as doth the law of the Lord thy God.[12]

It was in the midst of his struggle with this sexual tension that Augustine's famous conversion took place. He was convinced that he could not come to Christ without renouncing marriage: "For You did so convert me unto Yourself, that I sought neither a wife, nor any other of this world's hopes."[13]

Because of his own sexual history, the history of the church and the spirit of the times, Augustine saw all sexual desire as a compulsive enemy of the spirit that required vigilant resistance. On the positive side, Augustine could never be found guilty of underestimating the power of sex. He certainly never belittled the force of sexual temptation, nor could he be accused of ignoring this sensitive subject.

On the negative side, however, he denied the gift of love and sex in the bond of marriage. Sexual desire could only be the enemy and never a blessing from God. When he was nearly seventy he wrote:

"Against this drive, which is in tension with the law of the mind, all chastity must fight: that of the married couple, so that the urge of the flesh may be rightly used, and that of continent men and virgins, so that, even better and with a struggle of greater glory, it should not be used at all."[14] As far as Augustine was concerned "the Christian married couple must 'descend with a certain sadness' to that particular task: for in the act of married intercourse itself, their very bodies spoke to them of Adam's fall."[15]

New Testament Church

The apostles were ahead of Augustine in dealing with these issues, and their answers were decisive. The threat of an otherworldly, spiritualized asceticism plagued the early church. From the beginning there were Gnostic dualists who despised the body and promoted a spiritual elitism which aspired to live above the ordinary activities of life, such as marriage, family and physical labor. False teachers were laying down rules: "Do not handle! Do not taste! Do not touch!" (Col 2:21). They were, in Paul's words, "hypocritical liars, whose consciences have been seared as with a hot iron. They forbid people to marry and order them to abstain from certain foods, which God created to be received with thanksgiving by those who believe and who know the truth" (1 Tim 4:2-3).

Paul's view on celibacy was quite different from that of the Gnostics, as we have seen. He gave permission for people to remain single for the sake of the gospel. One did not have to marry to be whole. Singleness or marriage depended upon God's leading in a person's life. "But each man has his own gift from God; one has this gift, another has that" (1 Cor 7:7).

The apostles deftly refute life-denying asceticism by emphasizing God's creation and God's incarnation. Physical life is not to be despised but enjoyed, for it is sanctified by God. Divine acts of creation and redemption infuse life with meaning and purpose and manifest the glory of God. "For everything God created is good, and nothing is to be rejected if it is received with thanksgiving, because it is consecrated by the word of God and prayer" (1 Tim 4:4-5). That is why the apostle Paul was compelled to write, "See to it that no one takes you captive through hollow and deceptive philosophy, which depends on human tradition and the basic principles of this world rather than on Christ. For in Christ all the fullness of the Deity lives in bodily form" (Col 2:8-9).

Robert Farrar Capon writes:

> The goal of all Christian self-denial is the restoration, not the destruction, of nature; the removal, not of matter, but of perversion. . . . The Christian religion is not about the soul; it is about man, body and all, and about the world of things *with* which he was created, and *in* which he is redeemed. Don't knock materiality. God invented it.[16]

Paul's counsel is so clear and straightforward on the divine value of ordinary life that in hindsight it is difficult to understand the church's fourth century position on sexuality. The early church fathers misunderstood Paul. They interpreted the apostle's admonition to practice self-control (1 Thess 4:4; 5:6, 8; 1 Tim 3:2; 2 Tim 3:3; Tit 1:8; 2:2, 5-6, 12) as the requirement of sexual abstinence in marriage and a celibate priesthood. Undoubtedly this misunderstanding would have been condemned by Paul, who writes, "To the pure, all things are pure, but to those who are corrupted and do not believe, nothing is pure. In fact, both their minds and consciences are corrupted. They claim to know God, but by their actions they deny him" (Tit 1:15-16).

It is difficult to imagine the extent of the suffering caused by the church's insistence on tearing apart body and soul. The false guilt, the frustrated marriages, the celebration of celibacy, and the disparagement of marriage and family—all because the church did not have a biblical theology of sexuality, marriage and family. Moralistic sexual repression, as Paul well knew, does not solve but rather exacerbates the sinful, sexual nature. "Such regulations indeed have an appearance of wisdom, with their self-imposed worship, their false humility and their harsh treatment of the body, but they lack any value in restraining sensual indulgence" (Col 2:23).

A Love Song

In spite of the fact that the name of God is never mentioned in the Song of Songs, it is a deeply theological book—but not in the sense in which the early church fathers thought it was. In light of the preceding discussion, it may surprise you to learn that the Song of Songs was the most popular biblical book in the Middle Ages, but it was not popular because it celebrated romantic love and sexual intimacy. The Song was fashionable because it was interpreted as an allegory illustrating the love of Christ for his bride, the church. One of the first proponents of this interpretation was Origen (185-254), who wrote a ten-volume commentary and a series of homilies on the Song. With painstaking analysis, every description, every metaphor was turned into a statement about God's love for us and our love for God.

Commentary by Bernard of Clairvaux (1090-1153) was typical of the age: " 'Let Him kiss me with the kisses of His mouth' (1:2). Who is it who speaks these words?" Bernard asks. "It is the bride. Who is the bride? It is the soul thirsting for God."[17] The beloved's search for her lover is the believer's search for God (1:7). The beloved's dependence upon her lover (1:15-16) is the believer's dependence upon God. The beloved's longing for her lover is the church's longing for Christ. The bridegroom's embrace of his bride is God's embrace of us.[18] Human love is but a booster rocket to be jettisoned after men and women grasp the true meaning of spiritual love. "For having left behind in the body all earthly cares and bodily obstacles, the soul will forget everything except God and attend to nothing else but God. 'My beloved is mine, and I am his'" (2:16).[19]

Ironically, the spiritualized version of the Song of Songs drove out the spiritual meaning of God's Word. This well-crafted collection of love songs describing the relationship between two lovers celebrates the beauty and energy of love between a man and a woman. The Song is an inspired canonical commentary on Genesis 1:27: "So God created man in his own image, in the image of God he created him; male and female he created them." To meditate on the

Song of Songs is to follow the admonition of the apostle Paul: "Whatever is true, whatever is noble, whatever is right, whatever is pure, whatever is lovely, whatever is admirable—if anything is excellent or praiseworthy—think about such things" (Phil 4:8).

The Song does not express the ancient hang-ups about the body, which disparaged the physical and material qualities of God's good creation. There is no Platonic dualism anticipated in this Hebrew celebration of human love. Neither is there an exaltation or deification of physical passion. The Song is the antithesis both of ancient fertility cults and of modern hedonism. Pleasure is not divorced from commitment, and love is not synonymous with lust.

The Song begins with deep yearnings of love, longing for intimacy, feelings of insecurity, pressures from family, and uncertainty as to the whereabouts of the lover. Human emotions are worthy of deep thought, careful exploration of meaning, and loving expression. Feelings and emotions merit reflection and contemplation. Of all the biblical books, perhaps this is one of the strongest in commending the importance of psychology.

Tom Gledhill offers this splendid description of the love song that tops all love songs:

> The capacity to delight in physical beauty, to be attracted by members of the opposite sex, the desire to form secure and intimate relationships, and to express love and affection in demonstrably physical ways—these are all a very fundamental part of our common humanity. The Song of Songs is an unabashed celebration of these deeply rooted urges. In beautiful poetic language, the Song explores the whole range of emotions experienced by the two lovers. . . . So we have a strong biblical affirmation of love, loyalty, beauty and sexuality in all their variety.[20]

Couples in love have much to learn from the Song of Songs about how to express their affection for each other. They would do well to reflect on the Song as an example of how to praise each other: "How beautiful you are, my darling! Oh, how beautiful! . . . All beautiful you are, my darling; there is no flaw in you. . . . Who is this that appears like the dawn, fair as the moon, bright as the sun, majestic as the stars in procession?" (Song 4:1, 7; 6:10).

The Song of Songs proves that the heart is worthy of exegesis! Soulcraft enjoys the labor of love that goes into describing the feelings we have for our beloved. I remember the time I hastily penned a few lines on a birthday card for my wife, Ginny. She read the card, smiled and moved on to her next card. My daughter, who was ten at the time, picked up my card, read it and then turned to me and said, only half jokingly, "You call yourself a writer." That little incident has stayed with me, and I recall it whenever I write a card to Ginny. Now I think of writing cards as an opportunity to express my love to her.

The language of love is neither explicitly vulgar nor technically clinical. Affection creatively uses the power of metaphor to impact all five senses. The love of the beloved is more delightful than wine, a more pleasing fragrance than the choicest perfume, more pictur-esque than the most beautiful garden, sweeter than honey, better than anything money could possibly buy. The beloved likens her lover to a beautiful apple tree in the forest and he likens her to a wild flower among the thorns. She is a beautiful well-protected gar-den, an orchard of fruit trees, filled with all kinds of flowers and spices, resplendent with color, covered with fragrance, watered by a flowing stream. Her lover has taken her to the banquet hall and "his banner over me is love" (Song 2:4).

Highly literal or very analytical people may struggle with the poetic medium, and modern readers may need help interpreting the metaphors. After all, a literal interpretation of "hair like a flock of goats" or "teeth like a flock of sheep just shorn" (Song 4:1-2) is hardly attractive and actually quite comical, but a poetic reading captures the essence of the metaphor: her hair reminds her lover of the grace-ful motion of a flock of mountain goats descending the distant peak; her teeth are white and sparkling, perfectly matched and symmetri-cal, like sheep sheared to their smooth skins, glistening white.

The Song of Songs revels in the physical and emotional side of love. It is a canonical warning to all those who would disparage the body and be unduly embarrassed with the physical side of love. John Chrysostom, the great preacher of Antioch in the fourth century, wrote to a man named Theodore, attempting to dissuade him from leaving the ascetic brotherhood to marry the woman with whom he had fallen in love:

> I know that you are now admiring the grace of Hermione, and that you judge that there is nothing in the world to be compared to her beauty; but if you choose, O friend, you shall yourself exceed her in beauty and grace, as much as golden statutes surpass those which are made of clay. . . . For the groundwork of this physical beauty is nothing else but phlegm, and blood, and liquid, and bile, and digestive juices. . . . So that if you consider what is stored up inside those beautiful eyes, and that straight nose, and the mouth and the cheeks, you will affirm the well-shaped body to be nothing else than a whitened sepulcher; the parts within are full of so much uncleanness.[21]

Chrysostom would have us look at a beautiful woman and see a dead corpse. Author Mike Mason offers a decidedly different perspective when he writes of his wife:

> I still haven't gotten used to seeing my wife naked. It's almost as if her body is shining with a bright light, too bright to look at for very long. I cannot take my eyes off her—and yet I must. To gaze too long or too curiously is, even with her, a breach of propriety, almost a crime. It is not like watching a flower or creeping up to spy on an animal in the wild. No, my wife's body is brighter and more fascinating than a flower, shier than any animal, and more breathtaking than a thousand sunsets. To me her body is the most awesome thing in creation. Trying to look at her, just trying to take in her wild, glorious beauty, so free and primal, so utterly unchanged since the beginning of time, I catch a small glimpse of what it means that men and women have been made in the image of God. If even the image is this dazzling, what must the Original be like?[22]

The basic assumption that sexual intimacy is a gift from God is nowhere stated in the Song, but it is everywhere implied. The Song challenges conventional wisdom on romantic love and sexuality. Love is compatible, not competitive. There is a uniting of the whole person: body, soul and spirit. While masculinity and femininity are celebrated, it is the couple's mutuality that is foundational to their love. They are eye to eye, face to face, life to life.

Throughout the Song restraint is emphasized: "Do not arouse or awaken love until it so desires" (2:7; 3:5; 8:4). Love should be allowed to take its natural course and not be rushed. The Song wisely depicts love's development as a challenge. It is hard to wait, but the waiting is essential for love to grow. Waiting involves yearning and longing, allowing anticipation and expectation to grow. Insecurities must be faced. Understanding between the lovers needs to grow. Satisfaction with each other must mature. Love needs time to make up its mind. As Tom Gledhill writes, "Do not force love-making or a love relationship; let it blossom naturally in due season, for the process cannot be hurried artificially."[23] Love moves toward realization not piecemeal but holistically.

Heresy and Humiliation

Through the years I have focused much more on what the early church fathers said about Christ than on what they said about sex. Their insistence on refuting heresies against the nature of the incarnate One impressed me. The Nicaean and Chalcedonian Confessions are powerful statements defending the humanity and deity of Christ. These early theologians tenaciously taught that Jesus did not just appear to be human; he was human. It is ironic that those who fought so hard to preserve the biblical testimony about the real humanity of Jesus shied away from our own full humanity. The physical side of being spiritual is precisely what the incarnate One accomplished through his life, death and resurrection. All that we are, including our sexuality, is redeemed in Christ.

It is a sad fact that through the ages many sincere followers of the Lord have been humiliated by the very God-given gifts intended for their blessing. What was condemned allegedly for spiritual reasons hurt not only the body but the soul. By equating love with lust these believers sought to make sexual intimacy between husband and wife impossible. By denying the physical and romantic dimensions of human love they turned the "spiritual life" against God's very own creation. And to this day their glory is their shame.

8

EAST OF EDEN

*"And Cain went away from the LORD's presence and lived in
a land called 'Wandering,' which is east of Eden."*

GENESIS 4:16 TEV

T HERE IS NOTHING NEW ABOUT LIVING IN A SEX-CRAZED CULTURE.
When it comes to sex, the people of God have always been resident
aliens living in the wilderness. Now is not the time for panic or
excuses—the apostle John offers this encouragement, "You, dear
children, are from God and have overcome them, because the one
who is in you is greater than the one who is in the world" (1 Jn
4:4)—but if there ever was a time to be "as wise as a serpent and as
harmless as a dove" it is now. Unlike Lot, who was challenged to
flee Sodom, we have no place to run to. Unlike Noah, who was res-
cued by a flood as well as from a flood, we are immersed in a lust-
filled culture with no rescue in sight. Sex saturation is the order of
the day. Lust, fornication and adultery permeate the modern way of
life. We live in the "burbs" of Babylon and stroll the streets of
Corinth. We all live east of Eden in the company of Cain.

Soulcraft distinguishes between sexual desire and sexual lust: the
former is rooted in God's original design, the latter in human

depravity. Sexual desire is healthy; sexual lust is unhealthy. The Greek word for lust combines sexual desire and possession. There is a difference between looking and lusting, between appreciating and devouring, and the line between them is located in the soul. Lust is not simply a matter of treating someone of the opposite sex as a sex object. That is too narrow a definition. It is using the other person to feed one's sexual appetite. Lust is divorced from love; it spurns care, denies communion and disregards commitment. The Bible underscores the goodness of sexual desire and the badness of sexual lust. Sexual intimacy is meant to be encouraged and protected in the personal, public, sacred commitment of marriage. Lust is a dehumanizing, depersonalizing drive to indulge the sexual appetite.

When I was on a mission trip to Mongolia several years ago, I spent a few days in Beijing. It was springtime, and each evening I saw scores of couples walking slowly, hand-in-hand, enjoying each other's company. Romance was in the air. The tenderness of touch, whispered conversations and time alone in public impressed me as something that I had not seen for a while. I shared this experience with a friend, who had recently returned from Bosnia. He said that he had experienced the same thing walking the streets of Sarajevo. We agreed that there is something beautiful missing in a culture in which young people waste no time jumping into bed. Halfway around the world romance is alive and well among people who have experienced harsh economic and political circumstances. The West's sexual self-indulgence interferes with the very intimacy our culture longs for.

No Shame

We are told in Genesis that Adam and Eve "were both naked, and they felt no shame" (Gen 2:25). This absence of shame was a result of their oneness. Their union was complete in body and soul. Nothing came between them. No insecurity. No dehumanizing thoughts. No compulsion that turned one person into a sex object or consumed the other for the sake of sexual gratification. Neither one of them felt on display or worried about not measuring up to the other's expectations. Their satisfaction was mutual and their intimacy complete.

Shame entered the human drama as a result of sin. Broken fellowship with God meant broken fellowship with each other. Separation from God caused an internal separation and a relational separation. Adam and Eve were no longer true to their soulful selves, nor were they true to one another. "Shame is the expression of the fact that we no longer accept the other person as the gift of God," writes Dietrich Bonhoeffer. "In the unity of unbroken obedience man is naked in the presence of man, uncovered, revealing both body and soul, and yet he is not ashamed. Shame only comes into existence in the world of division."[1] The root cause of shame is the unnatural, disobedient and dysfunctional violation of body and soul. Sin makes us terribly vulnerable, insecure and fundamentally dissatisfied with ourselves and others.

As a result of Adam and Eve's sin, "the eyes of both of them were opened, and they realized they were naked; so they sewed fig leaves together and made coverings for themselves" (Gen 3:7). In their pathetic attempt to cover up we see their helplessness—their utter embarrassment. Sin had opened their eyes to a world independent of the Creator"—the world of the autonomous self and selfish desire. John captures this world when he writes, "For everything in the world—the cravings of sinful man, the lust of his eyes and the boasting of what he has and does—comes not from the Father but from the world. The world and its desires pass away, but the man who does the will of God lives forever" (1 Jn 2:16-17).

The first couple's sensitivity to shame appears in marked contrast to modern culture's insensitivity to shame. There is a bold, in-your-face, deal-with-it shamelessness which is difficult to explain apart from the fact that hearts have become extremely hard. Deep down, people know what is right. "They show that God's law is not something alien, imposed on us from without, but woven into the very fabric of our creation. There is something deep within them that echoes God's yes and no, right and wrong" (Rom 2:15 The Message). But they work against their very own conscience to conceal their shame (Jn 3:19).

Shame is sensitivity to the painful and unnatural separation of the body and soul; shamelessness is the absence of pain due to the dulling, if not deadening, of spiritual sensitivity. The lust of the flesh rules in spite of the muffled cry of the soul. The body becomes an idol, an object of veneration, the sole center of being and the only hope for glory. The soul is treated as expendable. The popular language of love has become a euphemism for lust. The work of soulcraft requires distinguishing God-given sexual desire from God-denying sexual lust. Author Paul Mickey offers a helpful definition:

> Lust is any excessive desire, any uncontrollable urge for immediate gratification. . . . Lust may involve a craving for food, alcohol, sports, new fashions, success, sex. . . . Lust of any type is dangerous because it is self-centered, mechanistic, inflexible, and insensitive to the needs of others. . . . Lust is selfish, insensitive self-gratification. Lust is a powerful force that is rooted deeply in our selfish, rebellious nature.[2]

Soul-scarring cultural conditions require soulcraft discernment. Factors that sear the conscience and deaden the soul should be discussed, not ignored. To begin with, there is a coarsening quality to daily life that fouls the air for romance and love. Youth are exposed to crude, dehumanizing sexual explicitness. People who are otherwise dignified and cultured think nothing of using vulgar sexual expressions and jokes. Speaking crudely about sex appears to be a compulsory habit necessary for social acceptance. Explicit sexual vulgarity has seemingly competed against love poetry and won. These days, talk radio "experts" consider having sex and being in a relationship to be two different things. They encourage teenagers to "test their equipment," to "get out there and have fun." "It doesn't hurt to score once in a while," they say. Popular FM stations schedule early evening programs that discuss the optimum size of the penis or the experience of group sex.

The apostle Paul writes, "For it is shameful even to mention what the disobedient do in secret" (Eph 5:12), but now it is shameful to repeat what is openly discussed on afternoon television talk shows. Mardi gras-style debauchery pervades college campuses, and sexual innuendo relentlessly invades the work place. "We live in a constant bath of depersonalized, imaginary, highly provocative sexuality," writes Tim Stafford. "To the modern person, this seems normal; he is barely aware of it."[3]

What's Love Got to Do with It?

In *The Bonfire of the Vanities* Tom Wolfe tells what his lead character, Sherman McCoy, was thinking to himself as he walked down Fifth Avenue:

> It was in the air! It was a wave! Everywhere! Inescapable! . . . Sex! . . . There for the taking! . . . It walked down the street, as bold as you please! . . . It was splashed all over the shops! If you are young and halfway alive, what chance did you have? . . . Who could remain monogamous with this, this, this tidal wave of sexual desire rolling across the world? . . . You can't dodge snowflakes, and this was a blizzard! He had merely been caught in it. . . . It meant nothing. It had no moral dimension. It was nothing more than getting soaking wet.[4]

Mainstream culture has severed the link between sex and morality while shifting the moral focus to sexual harassment. There is widespread passive approval of premarital sex, adulterous affairs, homosexual practice and pornography, but a growing sensitivity to sexual harassment and date rape. Ironically, our culture is callously indifferent toward the sin of consensual extramarital sex but sensitive to sexual innuendo in the work place. This comes at a time when women and men discuss and joke about sex in ways that previous generations would have found disgustingly vulgar and crude.

The selective nature of today's sexual sensitivity is peculiarly narrow. A man may be unfaithful to his wife with cultural approval, but talking about such infidelities at work could result in his being fired. Sexual activity among minors is accepted as a fact of life, but consensual sex with a minor is a felony. Homosexual practice is celebrated. Pedophilia is condemned. Abortion is a popular form of birth control amidst growing sensitivity about child abuse. Pornography and violence are big box office draws, but rape is a serious crime. As a culture, we have the good sense to know that some things are wrong, but it is a fragmented, selective sense of right and wrong.

Professor Allan Bloom writes in *The Closing of the American Mind:*

> I once asked a class how it could be that not too long ago parents
> would have said, "Never darken our door again," to wayward
> daughters, whereas now they rarely protest when boyfriends sleep
> over in their homes. A very nice, very normal, young woman
> responded, "Because it's no big deal." That says it all. This passion-
> lessness is the most striking effect, or revelation, of the sexual revolu-
> tion, and it makes the younger generation more or less
> incomprehensible to older folks.[5]

Bloom finds modern students "flat-souled." They feel no guilt or
shame about illicit sex. Sex is a thing in itself, to be studied, ana-
lyzed, performed and experienced.

> Many live together, almost without expectation of marriage. It is just
> a convenient arrangement. They are not couples. . . . They are room-
> mates, which is what they call themselves, with sex and utilities
> included in the rent. Every single obstacle to sexual relationships
> between young unmarried persons has disappeared, and these rela-
> tionships are routine.[6]

Sex is everywhere, but love is hard to find. Students are giving up
their bodies but holding back their hearts. A self-protective loveless-
ness may maximize erotic freedom, but it retards the soul. Shamelessness may be due in part to sexual overexposure, but the greater
reason may be the lack of love; the cynical, hard heart is not willing
to show love. Men and women have had so many "lovers" that they
don't have any idea of what love is. As C. S. Lewis observes,

> There is no safe investment. To love at all is to be vulnerable. Love
> anything, and your heart will certainly be wrung and possibly bro-
> ken. If you want to make sure of keeping it intact, you must give your
> heart to no one, not even to an animal. . . . Wrap it carefully round
> with hobbies and little luxuries [sexual pleasure and personal desire].
> . . . Avoid all entanglements; lock it up safe in the casket or coffin of
> your selfishness. But in that casket—safe, dark, motionless, airless—it
> will change. It will not be broken; it will become unbreakable, impen-
> etrable, irredeemable.[7]

The work of soulcraft is to break open that casket, smash that coffin, and release the heart from its cultural bondage and self-imposed imprisonment. Soulcraft teaches the heart the difference between love and lust and seeks to reunite body and soul.

Samson

The writers of the Word of God are not shocked or stymied by lust. They are well aware of what we are up against. The ancient character of Samson vividly illustrates the pleasure-seeking strategy of the modern person. Samson was calculated in his pretense of not knowing. He acted stupid by design, seemingly oblivious to the obvious nature of his self-destructive behavior. His ancient story is a strangely modern tale. Read the story of Samson in the book of Judges (chaps. 13—16) and you will be forgiven for wondering why he is included among the heroes of faith whose names are recorded in Hebrews (11:32).

Samson's life reads like a Hollywood script for an R-rated movie. It is difficult to find very much, if anything, in Samson's life that is commendable. In some respects he is a pathetic character, driven by selfish passions and powerful lusts. His one redeeming quality is that he reminded the Israelites of who the enemy was. We are told that the Lord "was seeking an occasion to confront the Philistines," and Samson, in spite of himself, was the man to provoke this confrontation. It is hard to imagine that salvation history had come to this: God preserving the distinctive character of his people through a judge who is consumed by lust.

Imagine Samson seducing and being seduced; first he was involved with the Philistine woman whom he begged his parents to get for him as a wife, then with the prostitute in Gaza, and finally with Delilah. The testimony of God's people surely was at an all time low. One wonders if Samson had any practical idea of the Ten Commandments or the celebration of the Passover. Did he have a clue about the faithfulness of Abraham or the meekness of Moses or the courage of Joshua? When I read of Samson—his unbridled lust, his recreational violence, his flirtation with the world, his apathy to the things of God—I find a biblical "hero" that I definitely do not want to be like. I am inclined to say, "Lord, help me not to become like Samson!"

At nearly every point Samson is a disappointment, a spiritual disaster waiting to happen. Samson was called to live apart from mainstream culture and to evidence his dedication and devotion to God through his Nazirite vows: "No razor may be used on his head, because the boy is to be a Nazirite, set apart to God from birth, and he will begin the deliverance of Israel from the hands of the Philistines." "The Nazirite would say a definite no to certain perfectly natural things in order to show how definite was the yes he was saying to something more important, his dedication of himself to God."[8] Yet Samson's life was characterized not by devotion but by defiance. His life exemplifies not understanding and insight but ignorance and foolishness. He just didn't get it. He was clueless, frustratingly slow and inexcusably blind to the will and ways of God.

The final chapter of Samson's life unfolded after nearly twenty years of willful promiscuity. He was still running down to Philistine country, driven by sexual lust. He was no closer to understanding the work of God than he was when he began his tenure as Israel's judge. He still acted more like a Philistine than an Israelite. How could he be so resistant to the will of God? He didn't give the Israelites or Philistines the slightest impression that faithfulness to God mattered to him.

His experience with Delilah was déjà vu—history repeating itself. In nearly twenty years of leadership Samson hadn't grown up a bit, but the Philistines had become even more determined to remove this Israelite Goliath. They promised Delilah 140 pounds of silver (eleven hundred shekels) if she could lure him into showing her the secret of his great strength so that they could tie him up and subdue him.

So Delilah, using all of her charm and seduction, cleverly and subtly asked Samson, "Tell me the secret of your great strength and how you can be tied up and subdued." At this point you can be forgiven for being exasperated with Samson. Samson played along and gave her an answer: "If anyone ties me with seven fresh bowstrings (made from animal intestines), I'll become as weak as any other man." So he presumably fell asleep and the Philistines, with Delilah's help, wrapped Samson in these strings made of gut. But when Delilah shouted, "Samson, the Philistines are upon you!" he snapped the chords like frayed strings. A coy game of seduction and flirtation went back and forth between Delilah and Samson three times. She tied him down with new ropes and even tried weaving his lengthy hair into the fabric on a loom, but each time Samson broke free.

Finally, after changing her tactics from seducing to nagging, Delilah succeeded. "How can you say, 'I love you,' when you won't confide in me? This is the third time you have made a fool of me and haven't told me the secret of your great strength." We are told that "with such nagging she prodded him day after day until he was tired to death" (Judg 16:16).

Weary with this harangue Samson told her everything: "No razor has ever been used on my head, because I have been a Nazirite set apart to God since my birth. If my head were shaved, my strength would leave me, and I would become as weak as any other man." So when Samson fell asleep with his head on her lap the Philistines shaved his head and when he awoke he was powerless. There was nothing magical about Samson's long hair. It was a symbol that he was set apart to God. The real tragedy, of course, was not that he lost his hair but that the Lord had left him.

The Philistines seized Samson and gouged out his lust-filled eyes and marched him through the gates of Gaza that he had previously single-handedly removed to defy the Philistines. He became a trophy to be paraded and displayed, a symbol of the virility of the Philistine god Dagon. Samson's capture and humiliation was cause for great excitement and celebration. Thousands of Philistines assembled at the temple of Dagon to gloat over their victory and see Samson perform for them. "Bring out Samson to entertain us!" they shouted.

They stood him among the pillars and they laughed and jeered and mocked this one-time single-man army, now reduced to a blind and beaten spectacle who needed to be led by the hand. And Samson prayed, like he had done many years before when he feared he would fall into the hands of the Philistines (Judg 15:18). And once again God answered his prayer. But even this final prayer is a reflection of the selfish motives that characterized Samson from beginning to end: "O Sovereign LORD, remember me. O God, please strengthen me just once more, and let me with one blow get revenge on the Philistines for my two eyes" (Judg 16:28).

God's powerful act of judgment against the Philistines was reduced in the mind of Samson to revenge for his two eyes. He thought nothing of the reputation of Yahweh. Samson was still only thinking of himself and of getting even with his enemies. He died never having seen the larger purpose and the true calling of his life. He was a tragic paradox: clever but not wise; strong but weak; lustful but not loving; blessed by God but addicted to himself.

The life of Samson is a powerful illustration of the relevance of the Bible when it comes to the subject of lust. His example is unnerving. Samson's life vividly pictures the downward pull of evil versus the upward call of God. "I press on toward the goal to win the prize for which God has called me heavenward in Christ Jesus" (Phil 3:14). Instead of pursuing spiritual maturity, Samson was always going after the Philistines to fulfill his own desires and impulses. He is a particularly appropriate character for us to learn from in our sex-crazed world. Dealing with lust is not only a physical and psychological issue but a spiritual issue. Freud thought that people had pursued God as a substitute for sex, but it is the other way around: sex has become a substitute for God. The passionate gravity of Samson's soul belonged to God, but he kept giving his soul away to Philistine women.

Samson needed a "self-conscious distant early warning line" guarding the soul.[9] Job made a covenant with his eyes "not to look lustfully at a girl" (Job 31:1). Joseph was determined not to be seduced by Potiphar's wife. The latter two were aware of the potential power of seduction and they intentionally dealt with it. Sexual immorality "is never a sudden, spontaneous, and totally unexpected act. It is always preceded by a longer drama, at the beginning of which you are not helpless."[10] Samson learned about women and sex in the Philistine culture and he let sex become the overriding, dominant, obsessive fixation of his life. He refused to overcome lust with love. The basic acts of obedience, such as fidelity, honesty, love and purity were foreign to Samson's life.

God's decision to work through us to accomplish his will is hardly convenient and certainly not neat. It is almost unthinkable that the living God who spoke creation into existence would use people like us to work and minister in his name. Surely it must be a burden to God to accomplish his kingdom work through us. Like the hero whom nobody should be like, we are often known more for our hypocrisy and inconsistency than for our authenticity and consistency. We, like Samson, have a propensity toward sin. We easily lose heart, drift away and give in to the pressures around us.

We have a love-hate relationship with today's "Philistine" culture, and we find it easier to look like Philistines than to act like the followers of Jesus. How frustrating it must be for God to put up with us. We are at times very crude instruments. Samson shows us that enormous potential can be squandered in trivial, lustful pursuits. But Samson's life also reminds us that in the mess of hypocrisy, deception, manipulation and lust, God prevails. God's grace wins the day.

The Blame Game

Samson's refusal to "get it," to understand what God really wants in a leader, makes us more aware of how we excuse and rationalize lust. A modern version of a Samson-style struggle with lust is depicted in *Leadership*, a journal for pastors. In *The War Within: An Anatomy of Lust* one Christian leader vividly describes his personal battle with lust.[11] Exposing the evil power of lust, the author traces his story from witnessing "exotic dancers" and feeding his lust with pornography to his full-blown sexual addiction. He ably describes his "downward spiral of temptation," his elaborate rationalizations and his spiritual schizophrenia. He also recounts his commitment to healing. What impresses me about the article, however, is something that more than likely was unintended by the anonymous author. He implies perspectives that remind me of Samson and his inability to "get it" when it came to the war within. The author describes degrees of lustful intensity that he feels range from normal, innocent lust to abnormal, obsessive lust. He begins the article by making a significant distinction: "I remember vividly the night I first experienced lust. Real lust—not the high school and college variety. Of course as an adolescent I had drooled through *Playboy,* sneaked off to my uncle's room for a heart-thumping first look at hard-core pornography." This distinction may sound discerning, but it is deceptive. What the author dismisses as adolescent lust may be instrumental in what he calls "the adult onslaught of mature, willful commitment to lust."[12] The pressure is on from early adolescence to separate body and soul. As Jesus reminds us, there is no innocent lust that we can afford to treat lightly (Mt 5:29).

In his description of his battle with lust, the author of the article sees himself as a passive victim of cultural forces, biological drives and relational pressures. He writes of socio-historians in the future offering explanations "of why men who grew up in church homes are oversexed and vulnerable to attacks of lust and obsession, and why women who grew up in those same environments emerged uptight and somewhat disinterested in sex."[13] He laments that we have "sex drives that virtually impel us to break rules God laid down."[14] Samson would have undoubtedly found some comfort in this perspective.

Sometimes the strategies of self-deception become very complex, especially when it comes to lust. Translating volitional choices into passive acts of fate is a technique that separates body and soul and negates the responsibility of the individual. The author observes himself as if forces beyond his control had taken over. He says things like, "I found myself stalking the streets of the seedy areas looking for lust."[15] And, "So far, none of the scary, negative argu-

ments against lust had succeeded in keeping me from it."[16] I can
hear Samson making similar appeals to explain his actions.

In subtle ways the author seems to blame his wife for his failure
to be open and honest. "I have wondered why God let me struggle
for a decade before deliverance: maybe I will one day find out my
wife required just that much time to mature and prepare for the one
talk we had that night. Far smaller things had fractured our marriage for months."[17] And in the end he implies that his lust was
related to his wife's inadequacies. When after ten years of deception
he confessed, it came out as an indictment against his wife. "I hurt
her—only she could tell how much I hurt her. It was not adultery—
there was no other woman for her to beam her resentment toward,
but perhaps that made it even harder for her. . . . Now she heard
what she had often suspected, and to her it must have sounded like
rejection: You were not enough for me sexually, I had to go elsewhere." But could any wife prove adequate to fulfill and quench his
ungodly lusts? In the end the impression one receives is that the
unseen forces—his sexually repressed childhood, his male sex drive
and the sexual inadequacies of his wife—conspired against him,
leading to his obsessive lust.

We confront the same temptations to divorce body and soul that
Samson and this Christian leader faced. The pressure is on to
blame everything from today's sexual mores, early-childhood
parenting, internal biological drives and one's spouse. The strategies of self-deception that justify and fortify disobedient sexual
behavior are powerful forces that are not easily tamed. However,
Samson didn't have to live in his self-made, lust-filled, ven-
geance-seeking world. At any time he could have done the most
obvious things to reverse his descent into Philistine culture. He had a
heritage to draw on and vows to embrace. As it did for Samson,
sometimes ignorance requires hard work. We have to insist on spiritual apathy, psychological games and moral excuses. But the power
is there, God's grace is sufficient, the pattern of worldly conformity
can be broken! Samson is the hero nobody should emulate but everyone can learn from.

Jesus on Sex

Soulcraft works to reunite body and soul by avoiding the pitfalls of sexual aversion and sexual immersion, neither of which (an ideology of asceticism nor the indulgence of hedonism) being what our Creator and Redeemer had in mind. To accomplish this reunification soulcrafters follow Jesus, who dethrones and demystifies the power of sexual lust (Mt 19:1-12), reaffirms the purity of sexual desire within the sanctity of marriage (Mt 5:27-32), and prioritizes sexuality in relationship to time and eternity (Mt 22:29-32). As I said earlier, Jesus bases personal wholeness on knowing God, not on sexual intimacy.

Jesus states the truth about sex, and all the reason and power of the Creator's will and word back up his every thought. Jesus' brevity on the subject of sex may be explained in part by the context. Jesus spoke to people who were shaped by the Old Testament commandments. As the gospel moved out and confronted cultures in which there was a lack a biblical moral vision, more was said about sexual obedience. The One "in whom are hidden all the treasures of wisdom and knowledge" (Col 2:3) delivered his spiritual direction with such clarity and conciseness that only the stubborn and hard-hearted can fail to grasp his meaning.

Jesus dethroned sex from deserving any absolute loyalty by establishing the powerful priorities of the kingdom of God and the gospel of reconciliation. Jesus neither denies nor discourages sexual desire. He simply and naturally places it under his Lordship. "But seek first his kingdom and his righteousness, and all these things will be given to you as well" (Mt 6:33). Sexual desire is subsumed under the call of discipleship. As Jesus says, "If anyone would come after me, he must deny himself and take up his cross and follow me" (Mt 16:24).

Jesus assumes the goodness of sex within the bounds of marriage. It requires no defense or emphasis. The incarnation and its impact on Mary and Joseph and on Elizabeth and Zechariah point powerfully to the importance of marriage and family. If Jesus' silence on this subject is disturbing, it is only because of the preoccupation and controversy we bring to the subject. We must be careful to read Jesus in light of the whole counsel of God rather than using his silence as an invitation to revise and re-imagine truth in our own image.

When Jesus addresses the subject of sexual lust, he reaffirms the union of body and soul in the most graphic way possible. He is not interested in technical, legal definitions of what constitutes adultery. He was interested in a person's soul and body. No one can really separate them. The sins of the heart impact us just as if we have committed them in the flesh. "You have heard that it was said, 'Do not commit adultery.' But I tell you that anyone who looks at a woman lustfully has already committed adultery with her in his heart" (Mt 5:27-28). Jesus does not treat sexual lust lightly. He recognizes that lust is a rival god that may reign in the soul long before it makes its epiphany in outward actions. What is so radical about Jesus' redemptive approach is that he deals with the overt act by attacking the covert desire. Obedience is measured not in a court of law but in the sight of God. God alone can see the heart.

Jesus closes the gap between body and soul by stressing that what is harbored in the heart is as good as done in the flesh. "If your right eye causes you to sin, gouge it out and throw it away. It is better for you to lose one part of your body than for your whole body to be thrown into hell." And just to make sure that no one misses his message, he repeats it: "And if your right hand causes you to sin, cut it off and throw it away. It is better for you to lose one part of your body than for your whole body to go into hell" (Mt 5:29-30). Jesus calls for drastic measures to avoid eternal punishment. Is sex such a core issue that it is crucial to my eternal destiny? Jesus thinks so and the measures suggested for saving oneself are extreme. Can you imagine what would happen if someone sought counseling for sexual lust and was told to gouge out an eye or cut off a hand? This sounds like the ultimate behavior modification.

Note that Jesus does not suggest actual castration. Ironically some in the early church, notably Origen of Alexandria, took Jesus literally on this point and castrated themselves. Tragically, as their barbaric practice illustrates, they missed the message. Jesus was not advising self-mutilation but self-mortification. The believer is disabled, not literally but volitionally, for the sake of the gospel. It is as if the believer has no eyes to see what should not be seen or hands to do what should not be done. Jesus advocates a whole new understanding of the relationship between body and soul, one that makes seducing and being seduced unthinkable.

Don't do it! Don't go! Behave as if you have actually cut off your hands and feet and have flung them away, and are now crippled and cannot do the things or visit the places which previously caused you to sin. That is the meaning of mortification. Paul captures the difference between mortification and mutilation when he writes, "I have been crucified with Christ and I no longer live, but Christ lives in me. The life I live in the body, I live by faith in the Son of God, who loved me and gave himself for me" (Gal 2:20). Paul follows Jesus, his Lord, in uniting body and soul, the physical and the spiritual, under the will of God.

Don't look! Behave as if you have actually plucked out your eyes and flung them away, and are now blind and cannot see the objects which previously caused you to sin. Think of yourself as Samson at the end of his life, with his eyes gouged out! His lustful days were over and he could do nothing but overcome evil with the power of God.

9

CONVICTION & COMPASSION

*"For the grace of God that brings salvation has appeared to all men. It teaches
us to say 'No' to ungodliness and worldly passions,
and to live self-controlled, upright and godly lives in this present age,
while we wait for the blessed hope—
the glorious appearing of our great God and Savior, Jesus Christ,
who gave himself for us to redeem us from all wickedness
and to purify for himself a people
that are his very own, eager to do what is good."*

TITUS 2:11-14

IN SOME CIRCLES GRACE HAS BECOME SHORTHAND FOR ACCEPTANCE
and approval regardless of whether or not people are convicted of
their sin and genuinely repentant. Some who speak of the grace of
God seem reluctant to speak of the law of God. They speak of God's
love and acceptance without emphasizing sincere repentance for sin
and the radical transformation of one's moral and spiritual life. An
indication that a Christian has gone too far in accommodating to the
spirit of the age is when attention to the law of God is judged to be
legalistic. Some people react with good cause to rigid, pharisaical
parenting and rules-for-rules'-sake morality, but the majority of
Christians today are growing up in an extremely permissive society,

where everyone is doing what is right in their own eyes (see Judg 17:6).

Soulcraft distinguishes the gospel message of grace from the rhetoric of acceptance. Spiritual discernment does not reconcile or accommodate the truth of the gospel to tolerance for all types of consensual sex. We are not at liberty to remove the message of grace from the biblical context of moral pain, repentance and conversion. I am aware that many confessing Christians have come to believe that this moral conviction is not only naive but wrong, inconsistent with the style of compassion that Jesus would show. It has become popular to speak of God's grace toward those who are "different" from us and to avoid discussion of God's law. Those whom the apostle described as "having lost all sensitivity" since they gave "themselves over to sensuality so as to indulge in every kind of impurity" (Eph 4:19) are now described as victims of the Christian community.

In many Christian circles today it is rare for teenagers to consider avoiding R-rated movies because they might negatively affect their relationship with Christ. Exposure to intense profanity, violence and sexual immorality is not unusual in the lives of many young believers today. Parents seem more concerned that their children have a good time than that they cultivate moral discernment. For both parents and children, "freedom in Christ" has become an excuse for experiencing evil. Nearly all of the Christian couples who come to our church to be married are sexually active. Most had multiple sexual relationships before their engagement. Conversations with most of these couples convince me that we are far from overemphasizing a righteous life in Christ. The current trend is toward moral permissiveness, not moral rigidity; the issue is not legalism but license.

The Grace of God's "No"
There is a form of compassion advocated in the Christian community that compounds the problem of sin. It is a reactionary compassion, often derived from personal experience with moral rigidity and legalism. Its advocates do not want to appear negative and insensitive. They rightly seek to offer the gospel of grace to every-

one, no matter how sinful, but they wrongly abuse that grace when they use it to minimize the problem of sin. They forget that to be justified by the grace of Christ is not to be excused but to be forgiven and sanctified. God's grace does not condone, it atones.

The great apostle of grace, Paul, is emphatic about righteous living. One wonders if we are willing to be as bold as Paul in exposing the futility of today's thinking about premarital sex, adultery, bisexuality and homosexuality. Why are we so reticent to affirm the commands of God when it comes to holy living? Those who accuse concerned Christians of being fixated on sexual issues may need to read the apostle more receptively:

> Having lost all sensitivity, they have given themselves over to sensuality so as to indulge in every kind of impurity, with a continual lust for more. You, however, did not come to know Christ that way. Surely you heard of him and were taught in him in accordance with the truth that is in Jesus. You were taught, with regard to your former way of life, to put off your old self, which is being corrupted by its deceitful desires; to be made new in the attitude of your minds; and to put on the new self, created to be like God in true righteousness and holiness. (Eph 4:19-24)

Compassion minus God's "No" to ungodliness boils down to "I'm OK, you're OK" acceptance.

When grace overlooks the commands of God there is little appreciation for the negative impact that ongoing tolerance of sinful lifestyles has on the household of faith. Paul's warning to the Corinthians is relevant to our own day. "Your boasting is not good. Don't you know that a little yeast works through the whole batch of dough?" Or, to quote from The Message, "Your flip and callous arrogance in these things bothers me. You pass it off as a small thing, but it's anything but that. Yeast, too, is a 'small thing,' but it works its way through a whole batch of bread dough pretty fast. So get rid of this 'yeast.' Our true identity is flat and plain, not puffed up with the wrong kind of ingredient" (1 Cor 5:6-7).

It was clear in Paul's mind that there is an important distinction between the believing community and the unbelieving community.

When Paul wrote to the Corinthian believers "not to associate with sexually immoral people," he did not mean that they should not relate to avowed unbelievers. If that had been the case they would have had to cut themselves off from the world entirely. What he meant was that they should not relate to professing believers who persisted in sexual immorality or greed or idolatry or slander (1 Cor 5:9-11). The kind of soulcraft practiced by the apostle distinguished between the grace that was powerful to save people from a life of sin and the abuse of grace that used salvation as an excuse to keep on sinning.

The Power of God's Grace
My brother in the Lord stood over me with his two hands squarely on my shoulders, and earnestly prayed that I would continue to faithfully proclaim and practice the whole counsel of God. When Bob Blackford finished praying there was hardly a dry eye in the circle of sixteen men. Few in the group had expected that Bob would still be alive ten years after he contracted AIDS, and that he would still be praying and ministering so profoundly. And no one is more surprised and filled with gratitude at the fullness of God's redeeming love than Bob himself.

Bob and Joanne had completed college, had gotten married, and had followed God's call into ministry. After graduating from Fuller Theological Seminary, being married for eight years, and welcoming two daughters into their family, they had been serving the Lord in a vital ministry to young people. And then Bob had begun a long detour into darkness and deceit by giving in to his sexual confusion. Through his brokenness and poor choices, he lived a double life involving homosexual relationships. This resulted in deep shame and guilt, and his hypocrisy and sin weighed heavily on his soul.

In 1985 he learned that he was HIV positive, which shattered his marriage, his family, his ministry and, ultimately, his life. It seemed to him an utterly hopeless, impossible situation. He had thought he would make it into God's kingdom, but just barely. He had anticipated that he would experience heaven as if from the back of a darkened theater where he would be sitting with other saved perverts. Basically, he had been living to put his affairs in order and prepare to die. He felt like the prodigal son, only worse than the prodigal son, because he had squandered everything his heavenly Father had given him, not just money. He had been unfaithful and deceitful, living a lie and betraying those whom he dearly loved.

But, as Bob says, "God said, 'No!'" The Lord would not let him fold up and die. The prodigal son had returned, but unlike the original prodigal son, Bob says he had come back with "leprosy." But in spite of a diseased body and a wretched soul, Bob had discovered the wonderful love of the Father's embrace. He was experiencing the severe mercy of AIDS, which had prompted him to confess his sin and turn to the Lord for healing grace.

For years Bob walked through the valley of the shadow of death, living under a death sentence. He believed that God could never heal his secret passions and compulsions, and was convinced that change in his hidden self was utterly impossible. But over time God moved him from resignation to a vital hope in the resurrection. Now each day he is overwhelmed with an indescribable experience of God's grace. His life and marriage have been redeemed and healed through the love of Jesus Christ.

The Great Reversal

The power of sin to penetrate to the core of our being is both real and frightening. We should be neither naive nor casual in our assessment of soul-deadening strategies. The "authorities . . . [and] powers of this dark world" (Eph 6:12) influence our lives in ways that we can scarcely imagine. We may not readily admit it, but we know it is true.

> The heart is deceitful above all things
>   and beyond cure.
>   Who can understand it? (Jer 17:9)

No part of our being, biological, psychological or spiritual, is free from the insidious attacks of evil. In our moral and spiritual self we are vulnerable to disorientation so deep and profound that good becomes evil and evil becomes good. We recall Isaiah's warning:

> Woe to those who call evil good
> and good evil,
> who put darkness for light
> and light for darkness,
> who put bitter for sweet
> and sweet for bitter. (Is 5:20)

The prophet Jeremiah was well versed in the strategies of evil in a culture that presented itself as religious, sophisticated and pleasing to God. He was a prophet of God not only for his own time but for ours as well. To listen to Jeremiah today is to be soberly reminded of what we are up against both within ourselves and within culture. Jeremiah laments the impact and intensity of sin in the believing community. He accuses the prophets and priests of moral and spiritual malpractice:

> They dress the wound of my people
> as though it were not serious.
> "Peace, peace," they say,
> when there is no peace.

He asks, "Are they ashamed of their loathsome conduct?" His answer is unequivocal:

> No, they have no shame at all;
> they do not even know how to blush.
> So they will fall among the fallen;
> they will be brought down when I punish them. (Jer 6:14-15)

The perception of the truth about same-sex relationships has become gravely distorted, with the result that we are witnessing an unprecedented moral reversal. What was once widely condemned as sin is quickly becoming a cause for celebration in many religious circles. But unlike many issues, homosexuality does not lend itself to theological compromise, which has become so typical in the mainline church. The fact that a sexual issue should assume such

SOULCRAFT

importance in the church today is symptomatic of a much larger
and irreconcilable clash of theological convictions. This crisis has
been skillfully dodged for decades by those who have been unwill-
ing to look below the rhetoric at what people actually mean theolog-
ically and ethically.

The Orwellian language game has finally played itself out. Religious words have remained the same, but theological meanings
have been eviscerated. When salvation history has been reduced to
the autonomous individual's faith journey, should we not anticipate
a radical change in the recognition of the Bible's authority on sexuality? If the incarnation, atonement and resurrection are vacated of
specific historical meaning and reduced to poetic metaphors for
spiritual experience, what discourages a theologian from saying
that the writers of the Bible never meant to inhibit sexual expression? When the Bible is no longer the authoritative Word of God but
a collection of religious stories with which the reader may identify
existentially, why not discredit those texts which the reader finds
untenable?

Fundamental theological differences have been obscured under
the cover of shared religious rhetoric and generic spirituality, but the
debate on homosexuality breaks this untenable compromise. This
issue is so powerful and so personal that people can no longer pretend that they share the same biblical and theological convictions.

The Last Prejudice
There appears to be two broad categories of arguments in support of
the practice of homosexuality within the church today. Arguments
in the first category take the more benign approach in an effort to
minimize any tension over the issue. The second broad response
seeks to commend homosexuality as a gift from God to be honored
and respected.

Proponents of the arguments in the first category accept the fact
that homosexual practice is sin but contend on biblical, theological,
biological and sociological grounds that the church should take a
softer stand than it has in the past. They believe that homosexual

practice is like other sins, such as lying or cheating, which persist after conversion. They are inclined to say, "Let him who casts the first stone be without sin." They see the sin of same-sex intercourse as no different from pride or envy, and since we don't bar Christians who are often proud and envious from leadership and ordination, why prevent practicing homosexuals from playing active roles in the church?

They perceive homosexuality to be, in a theological sense, more a weakness to be compensated for than a sin to be separated from. They think that since Jesus never makes a big deal about homosexuality, we shouldn't either. Homosexual believers are encouraged to claim God's support in dealing with their trial, stressing that what God said to Paul holds true for them: "My grace is sufficient for you, for my power is made perfect in weakness" (2 Cor 12:9).

This position is bolstered by the biological argument: that homosexuals have no choice in their sexual orientation. They are genetically predetermined to be sexually attracted to people of the same sex. Finally, this softer position is defended from the sociological perspective: homosexuality is a hot topic in the culture wars, but the church should not submit itself to divisive public issues.

The anthropological argument holds that different cultures have different concerns and mores regarding sexuality. For example, we may speak of sexual orientation, but the ancient Greeks were persuaded that no man should ever assume the role of either a boy or a woman and desire to be sexually penetrated. Instead of distinguishing between homosexual and heterosexual, the Greeks distinguished between the active and the passive sexual partner. Cultural differences, it is claimed, relativize the significance of homosexuality. Proponents of this position simply conclude that it is not the big issue that many conservatives make it out to be.

Proponents of arguments in the second category support homosexuality as a God-ordained expression of sexuality. Peter Gomes, minister in The Memorial Church, and Plummer Professor of Christian Morals at Harvard College, is a winsome, articulate spokesperson for this approach. Gomes, who is gay, has been preaching at

Harvard University for two-and-a-half decades. "It's very important," says Gomes, "for anxious and paranoid heterosexuals to realize that the world is filled with perfectly capable, well-adjusted,
competent homosexuals. Homosexuality is not a deviation, it is a
variation. And people need to know that."[1]

Whatever tension Gomes may have experienced over his sexuality was resolved by his religion:

> In my religion, whose primary statement is that we are created in
> God's image, God does not make mistakes, we are children of God. I
> therefore figured it out: "OK, if God made me this way and I am in
> the image of God, this is who I am and there's nothing to be done
> about it and I better make the best of it as best I can." . . . For me it was
> my religious consciousness which ultimately redeemed the sexuality
> issues and has provided, I think, the stability with which I live and
> work today.[2]

Gomes devotes a chapter to the subject of homosexuality in his
highly acclaimed *The Good Book: Reading the Bible with Mind and
Heart*. He implies that since the term *homosexuality* was developed in
the latter half of the nineteenth century, our modern English ver-
sions of Scripture are misleading. Echoing John Boswell's argument
in *Christianity, Social Tolerance, and Homosexuality*,[3] Gomes argues
that the only reason homosexual behavior was considered an
"abomination" was that it violated ritual purity laws. Homosexual
practice was not intrinsically wrong, according to Gomes, it just
wasn't kosher because the Gentiles did it. Under the special conditions experienced by God's frontier people, wandering in the wilderness and preparing to enter the Promised Land, God prioritized
the need for procreation. Over time, however, God's people would
learn that sex is more than procreation and the stigma attached to
homosexual relationships could be lifted.

It is not the homosexual act that Paul condemns in Romans 1,
argues Gomes; it is "the worship of sexual pleasure." Paul was ignorant of homosexual nature and the only form of homosexual practice he was familiar with "was the debauched pagan expression of
it."[4] Gomes does not explain why Paul and the Jews were so unfa-

miliar with the concept of a homosexual nature if, as Gomes insists, homosexuality was a morally valid sexual expression. But Gomes contends, as Boswell does, that the whole point of Romans 1 is that Paul condemns heterosexuals for doing homosexual acts. The perversion that Paul is concerned about is the sinful tendency to violate one's own sexual nature. Paul never knew about permanent, monogamous, faithful, intimate homosexual relationships that are based on a natural orientation to homosexuality. All Paul knew, argues Gomes, was a homosexuality that consisted of prostitution, pederasty, lasciviousness and exploitation.[5]

For Gomes the homosexual issue is "the last prejudice" following on the heels of racial and gender issues. True enlightenment will serve to defend the God-given reality and God-given validity of various sexual orientations and will produce a paradigm shift in the church's understanding, even as it did for racial and gender equality. This shift in understanding can be likened to the apostle Peter's experience of overcoming his prejudice against Gentiles and discovering that Gentiles as well as Jews were meant to receive the gospel. Another popular metaphor for homosexual acceptance is Israel's exodus. Just as God's people were brought out of bondage in Egypt, homosexuals are liberated not from the sin of same-sex relationships but from the oppression and persecution fostered by puritanical, pharisaical and reactionary conservatives who have made an idol of the Bible and do not understand the love of Christ.

These two approaches advocated by major elements in the American church tend to put Christians who consider homosexual practice as an evil with grave consequences on the defensive. What for Gomes is the last prejudice has become for many believers a defining issue. Seldom do we have the luxury of choosing our defining issues; they are thrust upon us. The early church experienced this when following Jesus as Lord was inconsistent with paying homage to Caesar. Refusing to accommodate to the spirit of the age, Christians lost their lives rather than bend the knee to Caesar.

We might prefer that this defining issue had nothing to do with sexuality and personal feelings, but unfortunately it does. We might wish that it did not divide churches and families, but sadly it does. We wish we could say people are entitled to their own opinions, to their own ways, but how can we say that and recognize the Lordship of Jesus Christ and the authority of his word? We cannot.

A Defining Issue

The advocacy of same-sex relationships is divisive because it denies biblical authority, challenges God's moral order and threatens physical and emotional health. It is spiritual malpractice to pretend otherwise, but it is also a serious sin to show contempt for practicing homosexuals. There may be no more important issue in our day for which we need to heed the apostle's admonition to speak the truth in love (Eph 4:15). The sin of homosexual behavior is especially provocative when emotionally charged advocates seek to encourage it as a viable way of life for Christians. But that is no excuse for timidity on the one hand or hateful reproach on the other. True soulcraft refuses to compromise Christlike conviction and compassion.

Those who argue in favor of same-sex relationships seek to raise doubts about the ability of God to communicate his will to us. Satan's original strategy of deception remains in effect: "Did God really say . . . ?" The clear, straightforward Word of God is questioned, with the thinly veiled accusation that God is holding out on us, his creatures. "For God knows that when you eat of it your eyes will be opened, and you will be like God, knowing good and evil" (Gen 3:5).

The controversies about race and gender have caused Christians to reexamine what it means for humankind to be made in the image of God. God's created order has been reaffirmed against the impact of sin and evil that has separated races and divided men and women. But the Genesis revelation of God's will for marriage, the one-flesh union of man and woman, is perceived by advocates of homosexuality as an embarrassing oversight of the full picture of human sexuality. Doubts are raised and excuses given for this one-sided emphasis, and apologists for homosexuality argue that Genesis offers a limited, culture-bound perspective.

No amount of Scripture-twisting hermeneutics erases the clarity and force of the Word of God when it comes to same-sex relationships. Defending the practice of homosexuality on the basis of God's Word is like the executive of a tobacco company insisting that smoking does not cause cancer. The texts are well known and have often been debated. In the case of the attack on God's messengers at Sodom (Gen 19:4-8) and the tragic events at Gibeah (Judg 19:22-24), homosexual defenders at first claimed that the sin condemned in these accounts was not homosexuality but lack of hospitality. A more recent argument, however, is that homosexual gang rape is the issue, rather than homosexuality as such. This conclusion is drawn in spite of the statement in Jude 7 that the people of Sodom "gave themselves up to sexual immorality and perversion." Nowhere does the Bible even hint at a distinction between homosexual promiscuity and homosexual fidelity. Second Peter 2:7 refers to Lot being "distressed by the filthy lives of lawless men."

The appropriateness of the moral imperative in Leviticus 18:22, "Do not lie with a man as one lies with a woman; that is detestable," is discounted on the basis of one other prohibition in the chapter, namely, the command not to have sex with a woman during her menstrual period. Of all the prohibitions included in this chapter, such as incest, intrafamily sexual relations, adultery, child sacrifice and bestiality, this is the only one that causes many to be offended today when it is considered a perversion. But this was not primarily a health issue: homosexuality is classified not as a cultic issue or a health issue but as a moral issue. To negate the prohibition of homosexuality on this basis is to negate the prohibition of the rest. Unless someone wishes to argue for child sacrifice and bestiality, it would be wise to let the prohibition against homosexuality stand.

The fact that we no longer require the death penalty as the punishment for the "abomination" of homosexuality (Lev 20:13) does not disqualify homosexual behavior as sin. What the Lord commanded as punishment to preserve the integrity of the people of God, who were surrounded by pagan cultures, is not commanded today in the gospel. The Lord still desires, however, to preserve the integrity of the church, for the sake of the salvation of the world through faithful obedience to his Word.

The clarity of the New Testament leaves little doubt as to the Bible's conclusion on same-sex relationships. Paul advises the believers in Corinth, "Do not be deceived: Neither the sexually immoral nor idolaters nor adulterers nor male prostitutes nor homosexual offenders nor thieves nor the greedy nor drunkards nor slanderers nor swindlers will inherit the kingdom of God" (1 Cor 6:10).[6] The argument that Paul does not distinguish between homosexual orientation and homosexual acts is beside the point. The suggestion that genetically determined homosexuality excuses homosexual practice would be no more convincing to Paul than the argument that monogamous homosexual relationships are righteous, while pederasty, lasciviousness and exploitation are sinful. These distinctions "would simply have been seen by the Apostle as further manifestations of the power of sin to confuse and blind human thinking."[7]

Paul's description of human depravity in Romans 1 emphasizes the close relationship between sexual immorality and spiritual idolatry. From the apostle's perspective, homosexuality illustrates sexually what idolatry is spiritually. Sin is sin, but sexual sin, unlike many other sins, seems to go to the core of one's being, turning the object of one's sexual desire into an idol to be worshiped.

> Therefore God gave them over in the sinful desires of their hearts to sexual impurity for the degrading of their bodies with one another. They exchanged the truth of God for a lie, and worshiped and served created things rather than the Creator—who is forever praised. Amen.
>
> Because of this, God gave them over to shameful lusts. Even their women exchanged natural relations for unnatural ones. In the same way the men also abandoned natural relations with women and were inflamed with lust for one another. Men committed indecent acts with other men, and received in themselves the due penalty for their perversion.

Furthermore, since they did not think it worthwhile to retain the knowledge of God, he gave them over to a depraved mind, to do what ought not to be done. (Rom 1:24-28)

Everything Paul says in this passage in Romans is consistent with what we know of the negative spiritual, physical and emotional impact of homosexual practice. Thomas Schmidt writes in his excellent work *Straight & Narrow? Compassion & Clarity in the Homosexual Debate:*

> Paul wrote in Romans 1:27 that homosexuals "received in their own persons the due penalty for their error." It is not clear what he meant by "penalty" in his time, but it is hard not to make a connection between his words and the health crisis we observe in our time. Sexual liberation has brought homosexuals out of the closet into a shadow of physical affliction where a score of diseases lurk. And as if this were not gloomy enough, the more deadly specter of HIV infection deepens the shadow, not only for the ever-growing number who die but also for those who are left behind to grieve and to wonder who will die next. . . .
>
> No honest look at current scientific research allows us to view homosexual practice as peaceable and harmless. For the vast majority of homosexual men, and for a significant number of homosexual women—even apart from the deadly plague of AIDS—sexual behavior is obsessive, psychopathological and destructive to the body. If there were no specific biblical principles to guide sexual behavior, these considerations alone would constitute a compelling argument against homosexual practice. Our bodies must not be martyrs to our desires.[8]

Soulcrafters must not turn a blind eye to the moral, spiritual and physical condition produced by homosexual acts. To do so is to abdicate our calling and to threaten the care and nurture of souls as well as bodies. The most grace-filled response to ungodliness is a clear and resounding "No." We cannot afford to say, as they did in Jeremiah's day, "Peace, peace," when there was no peace. Nor should we treat serious wounds casually. As Paul says, "Encourage and rebuke with all authority. Do not let anyone despise you" (Tit 2:15). Hope and compassion are not given by those who concede the biblical position and yet endorse homosexual practice. Present and future generations depend rather on our speaking the truth in love and being willing to lay down our lives for our brothers and sisters (1 Jn 3:16).

Joanne Blackford

Bob Blackford may not have experienced God's redeeming, sanctifying love apart from the grace of God working through his wife, Joanne. Her story models the steadfast love and perseverance required of those who are committed to soulcraft. With God's help she rose above betrayal and pain. In spite of a broken heart and shattered dreams she remained committed to Bob and to their marriage. She laid her life down for her husband. In her own words, Joanne describes the power of God's abiding love in her life and marriage.

> By the early 1980s I began to feel some tension in our marriage. Things just didn't appear quite right. On one hand I was living with a man whom I knew loved the Lord and led many searching high schoolers to the arms of Christ, and on the other hand I was living with an easily frustrated, anxious, blameful man. I tried to fix it. And I soon realized that wasn't my job.
>
> In November of 1985 Bob told me that he needed to talk to me. I do believe that that was the first time in fourteen years he had said that, so I figured this was pretty serious. That Thursday night he told me that he had had a homosexual relationship and that he was also HIV positive. The relationship had ended in 1983 and he did not desire this in his life. I was naively hopeful in the beginning and then reality began to hit. That first year my heart was breaking.
>
> We did gather several friends around us immediately and they agreed to pray for us, to help us make decisions, whatever we needed. We were all pretty new at this. If I had not been able to bring my brokenness and confusion to two very dear friends, who became Jesus with skin on for me, I would have lost my mind. They were listeners without judgment and listeners with understanding. And I'm a better friend because of these two dear women.
>
> Even so the journey was a lonely one. I didn't know what this pic-

ture should look like. And only I could make decisions concerning so many difficult issues. I did not know one other person whose husband had fallen into homosexuality, was HIV positive, and still desired to follow the Lord. And if there was such a person I didn't want to meet her, at least not yet. My life had taken a 180-degree turn. My dreams were shattering. Young Life ministry was not a safe place for me anymore. I was overcome with shame and fear, and yet I respected my husband at the same time.

I constantly weighed the future and grieved my way through everything. So many losses. I knew enough psychology to understand my husband's struggles. I was not condemning. But nevertheless our wedding vows had been broken. There had been years of deception and the trust factor was difficult. Our sexual intimacy could never be the same. My husband could die from AIDS. And what about my health? What about our daughters? We waited until our girls were seventeen and twenty before we told them and in the meantime we did our best to give them great family memories and a home filled with the Spirit of the Lord. Bob and I hung on. The Lord faithfully kept him healthy.

However, Bob did struggle with some more confusion that led to some more deception. And this time my understanding came harder. Anger was bubbling within me. I never thought I would be put into such a situation again. Could I forgive as the Lord commands us in Matthew 6:14-15? "If you forgive other people their failures, your heavenly Father will forgive you. But if you don't, neither will he forgive you your failures." What kind of an option was this? I felt used and of no regard.

The walls began to build between us. I did not feel in love. I needed to withdraw to survive and search out where my faith really lay. Could I learn to love again? Choices: Should I divorce? It entered my mind for the first time. I had biblical permission, but the Holy Spirit grabbed my gut. Divorce would not be the answer. The bottom line of this story is this: Bob Blackford has been and always will be a man after God's heart. I would rather put my efforts into healing a marriage and the persons involved, than destroying a marriage and allowing bitterness a foothold.

Tearing down walls is tough and healing heart wounds is even tougher. My character is being challenged with the only scenario that would bring me to the feet of Jesus and face to face with myself. I have to choose, with faith believing that Jesus does do what I have seen and read all my life. He is carrying my grief and holding my sorrow. He has forgiven me and released me from the shame held by my seeking a proper reputation (whatever that is). The shame and fear of a damaged reputation still festers but thank the Lord recovery time is quicker each round. Jesus is in the business of healing and loving. I cannot be healed until I have been wounded. How could I really learn to love until I thought I would never love again? Jesus heals. His faithfulness is rich with loving kindness. Psalms 139:23-24 says,

> Search me, O God, and know my heart;
>   test me and know my anxious thoughts.
> See if there is any offensive way in me,
>   and lead me in the way everlasting.

And Psalm 117:2 reminds us, "Great is his love toward us, and the faithfulness of the LORD endures forever."[9]

As we read Joanne's story we catch a glimpse of the true nature of soulcraft. This is not achieved by a formula she follows but through the faithfulness she practices. Conviction and compassion are rooted together. Her biblical understanding of right and wrong is consistent with a biblical understanding of sacrificial love. Joanne uses the truth not as an excuse to reject her husband but as a motivation to embrace her husband. She chooses to forgive Bob—to love and to cherish him. She might have become bitter or defensive, but instead Joanne turned to the Lord and devoted her energies to healing their marriage. Her honest lament, personal humility and heartfelt praise remind us of the Psalms and evidence the compassion of Christ.

10
SOULMATES

"Submit to one another out of reverence for Christ."

E P H E S I A N S   5 : 2 1

T HE SHARED WORK OF MARRIAGE, A TRUE SPIRITUAL DISCIPLINE, IS not to be confused with the therapeutic exercise of working on your marriage. Soulcraft distinguishes between the features of a good marriage and the costly, vowed commitment of a Christ-centered marriage. It is one thing to discuss the day-to-day, practical issues of marriage, it is quite another to root the one-flesh relationship in a mutual "until death do us part" commitment that proclaims that Jesus is Lord. Soulcraft explores what it means to follow the Lord Jesus into marriage for a lifetime.

When you hear couples say that they are working on their marriage, they invariably mean well. They truly want a strong marriage and they are willing to work hard to get it. They read books on the subject of marriage, attend seminars and carve out special times in their busy schedules to check in with each other. They regularly take the temperature of their relationship and work at showing appreciation for each other. The modern couple is especially astute at self-analysis and paying attention to each other's felt needs. When the situation warrants, they turn to experts to help sort through issues and propose solutions. There are plenty of popular resources to help enhance the marriage relationship. The bottom line for much of this advice seems to be how to get the most out of marriage.

Focus items on the "how to build a strong marriage" check list include: communicating effectively with your spouse, balancing career and family, confronting honestly and thoughtfully, building your mate's self-esteem, experiencing good sex, sharing the household tasks, making time for one another, and so on. All of this is important and perhaps none of it should be taken for granted. I am not disparaging the how-to counsel that we all need to strengthen our marriages. What I am concerned about underscoring is the foundation and character of marriage that God intends for us to have and to hold.

There are several discernable differences between the shared work of marriage in Christ and the popular notion of working on your marriage.

Modern couples tend to see marriage as the grand experiment. Instead of the costly commitment that God intended it to be, marriage is thought of as a risky adventure destined for success or failure. For many the longevity of marriage depends on whether or not the relationship works. One would think that marriage is just another expensive commodity, only without a very good warranty. And even that is changing: marriage is now offered with a money back guarantee. The growing popularity of prenuptial agreements and contractual arrangements confirms the fact that marriage for many is a gamble. People are hedging their bets and protecting their assets in case the relationship doesn't work out.

Many people perceive the experiment as risky especially because they already have what they really want in a relationship without marriage. They fear that the pressures and demands of marriage may work against the feeling of sexual intimacy and freedom that they already enjoy with one another. Instead of marriage providing the sacred security for sexual intimacy, it becomes a dreaded burden to an otherwise spontaneous relationship.

Added to the idea that marriage is an experiment is the notion that marriage is a project. Task-oriented high achievers turn the gift of marriage into a project to be pursued for the sake of its potential. Instead of enjoying marriage as a living, organic experience of growth and maturity, they make it into an operation to be managed efficiently and productively so that they can realize the greatest amount of personal profit. The question "What's in it for me?" remains a constant concern. Much of the how-to literature on marriage tends to emphasize coping and communication strategies designed to help spouses achieve what they want out of the relationship. Marriage becomes a "giving-getting" project, guided by the motto, "You only get out of it what you put into it." It is a quid-pro-quo arrangement.

Many Christians who write books and develop videos on marriage seem to have a secular market in mind. God serves as an underlying assumed truth with little direct application. The counsel is often derived from pop psychology, common sense, motivational theory, self-help strategies and the latest news on gender differences. I have been surprised to pick up a book on marriage by a highly acclaimed Christian author only to find virtually no reference to Christ. There is plenty of entertaining practical advice and easy-reading anecdotal material but very little that expresses distinctively Christian thinking about marriage. This belies the fact that soulcraft brings a radically different perspective to marriage than is popular in our culture.

Contemporary psychology and the accumulated wisdom of multiple interpersonal relationships can be helpful in guiding a husband and wife into a more honest and caring relationship, but these insights need to find their basis and meaning in the larger context of God's will. How can we possibly speak of marriage and ignore the Christian ethic of self-denial, the biblical call of discipleship and the very real, costly challenge firmly planted in the center of our lives, called the cross? They are ignored only with great difficulty, but sad to say, we manage to do it.

The first thing that people see when they enter the sanctuary of Cherry Creek Presbyterian Church in Denver is a twelve-foot, free-standing wooden cross off to the side of the pulpit. I have always found it to be a powerful reminder of God's grace and our Lord's call to a life of discipleship. One engaged couple surprised us all by requesting that the cross be removed for their wedding. They complained that the cross was "so religious" and that it was bound to show up in some of their wedding pictures. We were happy to inform them that the cross in the sanctuary couldn't be removed; it was permanent.

First Love
Soulcraft integrates the work of the cross into the life of a marriage in three basic ways: (1) the powerful analogy between our love for the Lord and our love for the one we marry, (2) the comprehensive and costly vowed commitment of all that we are and have in an exclusive and permanent relationship, and (3) the spiritual discipline of sacrificial love in marriage.

The experience of falling in love is like no other. First love is not the fantasy feeling of infatuation but the abiding commitment to the beloved that blends excitement and understanding. People in love have an amazing ability to focus on the one they love. They think about them all the time. They write love letters and poetry. They show their love in special ways and spend as much time together as they possibly can. Lovers look into each other's eyes and listen with their hearts as well as their heads. Being in love gives a new intensity to life and a new leisure as well. Schedules are changed and efforts are made for the sake of the beloved. Hours are spent walking together, talking on the phone, holding hands, just being together. First love is spontaneous and exciting, and a little crazy. There is nothing calculated and mathematical about falling in love. Love does not try to prove something or satisfy a set of expectations. Love is not a matter of duty or requirements. Love comes naturally, beyond arguments and proofs. First love is an appreciative love, a thoughtful love, a caring love.

In the Garden of Eden, Adam and Eve's love for one another was not in competition with their fellowship with God. These two loves, marital love and love for God, work together to strengthen and enrich one another. Devotion to God and devotion to one's beloved are designed to be mutually satisfying. The meaning of first love is an immediate reminder of the vitality and intensity of two distinct, yet inseparable, devotions. As I already emphasized in chapter four, our passion for God does not depend in any way on marital love. The provision of wholeness is exclusively found in our relationship to the Lord Jesus. Apart from God there will always be a serious lack of completeness. The spiritual void will be filled with misdirected loyalties, unresolved sin and guilt, and a sentence of doom that disturbs the soul.

Devotion to God can stand alone, but devotion to the beloved cannot. When the love and forgiveness found in the grace of God are absent, a marriage endures a tremendous strain. This is why soulcraft is so insistent on emphasizing one's relationship to God and its impact on marriage. The best way to keep alive the vitality of first love between a husband and wife is to have an abiding relationship with God. This is why soulcraft encourages the rhythms of grace at the center of marriage, not in a rigid pietistic and legalistic way but in a sincere and personal way. Christ-centered worship, witness, service and sacrifice are not religious components attached to a relationship; in a real sense they are the very essence of a husband and wife's life together.

Marriage

The photographer's bill alone for a recent wedding in our church was three thousand dollars. When the father of the bride told me, I could hardly believe it. An amount equaling a year's tithe for some people was spent on wedding pictures. It's hard not to wonder if we've lost something of the meaning of marriage in the immoderation of weddings. Author Maggie Gallagher observes in *The Abolition of Marriage*, "Weddings have gotten more extravagant as marriage has become more fragile. . . . The diamonds and the receptions grow bigger as the thing they symbolize, a permanent union of lovers, grows increasingly elusive."[1] The same culture that has made marriages exceedingly difficult because of casual sex, easy cohabitation, easy divorce and gender wars has made weddings very expensive.

Robert Farrar Capon, an Episcopal priest, writes:

> All I want to say is that I don't like weddings, and I do like the marriage rite, and I feel very funny about doing what I have to do. We sit down, they and I, for a couple of sessions of what the canon law blithely refers to as 'instructing the parties as to the nature of matrimony.' But being in the same room is about as close as we ever get to each other. I talk marriage; they think wedding. I tell them that the average wedding is a kind of irrelevant fling with no connections before or after—a preoccupation with the details of thirty minutes at the expense of the commitments of a lifetime. They listen with glazed, enraptured eyes. I urge them to steep themselves in the words of the rite, to eat, drink and breathe its atmosphere. I expound it, line by glorious line. Then I invite them to dialogue—to pursue the richness together. Do you know what questions, what comments, they have? Do you know what they ask me? They want to know if they can have the rehearsal an hour earlier, because his cousin Frances who is one of the bridesmaids has a hairdresser's appointment at eight.[2]

In this same vein Eugene Peterson writes,

> Weddings are easy; marriages are difficult. The couple wants to plan a wedding; I want to plan a marriage. They want to know where the bridesmaids will stand; I want to develop a plan for forgiveness. They want to discuss the music of the wedding; I want to talk about the emotions of the marriage. I can do a wedding in twenty minutes with my eyes shut; a marriage takes year after year of alert, wide-eyed attention. Weddings are important. They are beautiful; they are impressive; they are emotional; sometimes they are expensive. We weep at weddings and we laugh at weddings. We take care to be at the right place at the right time and say the right words. Where people stand is important. The way people dress is significant. Every detail—this flower, that candle—is memorable. All the same, weddings are easy.

But marriages are complex and difficult. In marriage we work out in every detail of life the promises and commitments spoken at the wedding. In marriage we develop the long and rich life of faithful love that the wedding announces. The event of the wedding without the life of marriage doesn't amount to much.[3]

By design, soulcraft aims for a wedding to serve the marriage, not a marriage to become an excuse for the wedding. Ginny and I are coming up to our twenty-fifth wedding anniversary, but I have to admit that twenty-five minutes after our wedding the memory was a blur. I'm afraid I was one of those grooms who becomes over-whelmed by the event and appears lost in space, while my bride was completely aware of every detail.

What I do remember is waiting three long years to walk down the aisle! I became convinced early in our relationship that Ginny was the one. It took her quite a bit longer to be sure that the feeling was mutual. Before we were engaged, I spent a year teaching Bible in Taiwan. It was by far the longest year of my life. I really wanted to be married to Ginny, and the sooner the better as far as I was concerned. But the wait prepared us for marriage by building self-discipline into our lives and by almost forcing us to honor commitments and consider others, which we might not otherwise have done. In so many ways we were already soulmates before our wedding.

By the time that June date finally arrived we were truly ready to be husband and wife and get on with life together. The cover of our wedding invitation read: "If you have any encouragement from being united with Christ, if any comfort from his love, if any fellow-ship with the Spirit, if any tenderness and compassion, then make my joy complete by being like-minded, having the same love, being one in spirit and purpose" (Phil 2:1-2).

Making marriage the thing that matters in a wedding is a spiritual discipline worth every ounce of energy a couple can give. Colossians 3:12-17 is an especially meaningful wedding text. It begins, "Therefore, as God's chosen people, holy and dearly loved." This opening affirmation reminds the wedding party and invited guests that this marriage issues out of a couple's abiding relationship with God. They are "chosen, . . . holy and dearly loved." We affirm at the outset that this marriage is shaped by God's providence and gracious redemption. Their life together depends not on the couple's human potential and dreams but on what God has done and will do. Their identity is derived from having been chosen by God; their purity is a result of the holiness of God and their security is founded on the love of God. They begin their marriage with God's great salvation remaking and transforming them into his image. Our confidence lies in Christ, who has begun a good work in them and has promised to carry it on to completion until the day of Christ Jesus (see Phil 1:6).

This understanding spares a couple from foolish vows that idolize love itself as a spiritual abstraction ("Our love extends beyond sea, wind, earth and flame: it is greater than who we are and meaningless without us. Our love is the essence of our lives"). Humanistic vows focus marriage on the self. Past sins and griefs are dismissed ("We bring to this union no regrets for the past and no fears for the future"). The only will and purpose that matters is the couple's will ("We come here today secure in the knowledge that we have chosen each other"). The vows are designed to protect the self ("I ask you to be no one other than who you are. My aim is not to change you but to grow with you").

On the surface what appears to be an expression of humility may actually be a burden of selfish expectations imposed on the relationship ("I needed the strength of a companion who could understand me and accept me for who I was. I needed a special friend with whom I could share both laughter and tears. I needed a confidant who would always be ready to share hopes, dreams and secrets. I needed you. Finding and loving you has become the central event of my life").

Such vows tend to equate a pledge to fidelity with the promise to be fun-loving. There is little appreciation for concerns outside of their relationship, and there is often no reference to God or to their extended family. God's purpose for their lives is a nonissue.

The contrast between a marriage shaped by the realities of God's choosing, purifying and loving, and a marriage that is a self-made relational arrangement, are profound. It is not just a matter of words but of radically different commitments and expectations. Salvation brings a married couple into a large world of immense realities that are completely unknown to a self-centered couple. Consider the differences between a couple shaped by God's gracious forgiveness and a couple shaped by expectations of self-fulfillment, between a couple who chooses the hymn "Great Is Thy Faithfulness" for their wedding to express their deep gratitude to God and a couple who chooses Shania Twain's "Still the One."

While there may be romantic hints at self-denial, for all practical purposes the secular relationship is founded on "what is in it for me." Giving up your life and laying it down for your beloved is not the tenor of the modern wedding.

A Wedding's Worship Service

Soulcraft intends for the wedding itself to be a worship service with Christ as the focus of the prayers, the subject of the preached Word, and the witness of the vowed commitment.

The pastor stands before God's "chosen, . . . holy and dearly loved" couple and says something like this:

> Marriage depends upon your personal relationship with God and your covenant commitment to one another. Today you pledge yourselves to one another, and the language of your vows is grandly inclusive of all you are and will be. This comprehensive commitment is also a timeless commitment; "as long as our lives shall last" is the bottom line of a costly vow. Though all things change and there is uncertainty in the world, this commitment before God and between yourselves shall persist to comfort you. Your God and this vow shall be a stay against the confusion and uncertainties of life. In the words of Jonathan to David you pledge to one another: "Let the Lord be between you and me for all generations."

The apostle's admonition is then read from Colossians 3:12-17:

> "Clothe yourselves with compassion, kindness, humility, gentleness and patience."

Your vowed commitment will lead you into the work of marriage, which is a putting on of "compassion, kindness, humility, gentleness and patience." We are properly attentive to what we wear for a wedding, so give attention, and I know you will, to what you put on for your marriage. The clothes you have on fit perfectly. But you will have to grow into the clothing that God is giving you. Through these qualities you will build respect for each other's dignity and worth. Dressed in compassion and patience you will put off selfishness. Clothed in kindness and humility you will put off pride and a harsh spirit. Sin will be disrobed and exposed for what it is.

"Bear with each other and forgive whatever grievances you may have against one another. Forgive as the Lord forgave you."

The work of marriage requires that you give yourselves to the work of forgiveness. Communication is so important; your marriage will be a burden without it. But not just any communication will do. Let the thing communicated be forgiveness. This is the single most significant tool you have for meeting and for healing the troubles which marriage shall surely breed between you.

"Over all these virtues put on love, which binds them all together in perfect unity."

Marriage may be based on genuine forgiveness but it aspires for perfect unity. Such a goal is not too optimistic nor is it overly idealistic. In the same paragraph in which Paul speaks of grievances, he also addresses the promise of perfect unity. Christians should not sell marriage short. The vows you offer are vows of love, and the life you share together has not only the promise but the power of a great unity. You have every prospect of developing the habits of the soul that will nurture everyday love expressed in "compassion, kindness, humility, gentleness and patience."

Your vows are a burden, perhaps an impossible one to carry apart from the Word of Christ and the peace of Christ! The mystery of a mature and loving marriage is not a secret. It is a revelation! Paul offers this two-fold exhortation: "Let the peace of Christ rule in your hearts, since as members of one body you were called to peace. And be thankful. Let the word of Christ dwell in you richly."

This unique challenge calls you to pay special attention to the One who preserves your life, your love and your relationship together. There is so much that threatens to rule our hearts: anxiety, insecurity and pride.

But the mystery of a beautiful marriage is found in the peace of Christ ruling our hearts and the word of Christ dwelling in us abundantly.

Spiritual discipline and Christian community are necessary for your marriage. You will need the challenge and the growth that other Christians offer. And the result of such a marriage founded in Christ and sustained by Christ is ministry: the ministry of teaching yourselves and others, the ministry of praise and gratitude in your heart and before others, and the ministry of service to one another as well as to others in need.

The marriage union is signified publicly in several ways—the wedding ceremony, the pledge of vows, the exchange of rings, and the giving and receiving of a name. "A man will leave his father and mother and be united to his wife" (Gen 2:24). He offers a name, she receives a name and the two become united under a new name. This is great, but there is another name I want you to think about. Another name more powerful and more enduring that you want to be known by.

"And whatever you do, whether in word or deed, do it all in the name of the Lord Jesus, giving thanks to God the Father through him." Amen.

The pastor continues, "As an expression of your willingness to engage in these obligations and as a seal of the holy vows you are about to make, will you face one another and join your hands." And then the pastor asks the groom:

> Bruce, do you take Lisa to be your wife, and to live together after God's command in holy marriage? Do you promise to be her considerate, faithful and loving husband and to submit your life to the authority of God's Word? Do you covenant to love her, support and serve her, guide and cherish her in prosperity and in adversity; in sorrow and in happiness; in sickness and in health; and forsaking all others, be united to her so long as you both shall live?

The groom replies,

> Lisa, I take you to be my wife. I love you and give myself and all I am to you. With deepest joy I join my life with yours. I promise to cherish and uphold you from this day forward as long as our lives shall last. And as a symbol of my promise I give you this ring, a celebration of our union in Christ, in the name of the Father, and the Son and the Holy Spirit. Amen.

The pastor asks the bride,

> Lisa, do you take Bruce to be your husband and to live together after
> God's command in holy marriage? Do you promise to be his consid-
> erate, faithful and loving wife, and to submit your life to the authority
> of God's Word? Do you covenant to love him, support and serve him,
> guide and cherish him in prosperity and in adversity; in sorrow and
> in happiness; in sickness and in health; and forsaking all others, be
> united to him so long as you both shall live?

The bride replies,

> Bruce, I take you to be my husband. I love you and give myself and
> all I am to you. With deepest joy I join my life with yours. I promise to
> cherish and uphold you from this day forward as long as our lives
> shall last. And as a symbol of my promise I give you this ring, a cele-
> bration of our union in Christ, in the name of the Father, and the Son
> and the Holy Spirit. Amen.

The couple and the congregation are then led in prayer by the
pastor:

> God of love and faithfulness, you have witnessed this vow of com-
> mitment. May you give Bruce and Lisa the grace they need to fulfill
> their vows. May they know your wisdom and insight. May the
> strength and endurance of your Holy Spirit guard and protect them
> and give to them all that is required in their daily pursuit of love,
> faithfulness and service.
>
> Holy Father, help them surrender to the authority of your Word.
> Grant to them the qualities of compassion, kindness, humility, gentle-
> ness, patience and love in their relationships with each other and with
> all others.
>
> May the home they establish be blessed with peace and spiritual
> understanding. May your grace, mercy and peace be on their mar-
> riage from this day forward, through Jesus Christ our Lord. Amen."

The wedding service ends with a declaration and a benediction:

> We acknowledge, Bruce and Lisa, that you have given your marriage
> vows in the presence of God and before this company. Therefore, I
> declare you to be husband and wife, in the name of the Father, Son

and Holy Spirit. Those whom God has joined together, let no one separate. Amen.

May the Lord bless and protect you, may the peace of Christ rule in
your hearts, and may the Word of Christ dwell in you richly. And
through the power of the Holy Spirit, may whatever you do, whether
in word or deed, be done in the name of the Lord Jesus Christ, giving
thanks to God the Father through Him. Amen.

Shared Work

The shared work of marriage is soulcraft at its best. Before the presence of God and by his grace a man and a woman fulfill their holy
vows to live together after God's command in holy marriage. The
language of their vows is grandly inclusive of all they are and will
be. Their comprehensive commitment is a covenant, not a contract.
Don't be fooled—marriage is real work, but it's the kind of work we
are called to do. "Continue to work out your salvation with fear and
trembling," declares the apostle, "for it is God who works in you to
will and to act according to his good purpose" (Phil 2:12-13). There
is no assurance against heartbreak, but if one's heart gets broken it is
better for it to be broken out of self-sacrifice than out of selfishness.
Mike Mason observes:

> Marriage comes with a built-in abhorrence of self-centeredness. . . .
> amidst all our pleasant little fantasies of omnipotence and blameless-
> ness and self-sufficiency, marriage explodes like a bomb. It runs an
> aggravating interference pattern, an unrelenting guerrilla warfare
> against selfishness. It attacks people's vanity and lonely pride in a
> way that few other things can, tirelessly exposing the necessity of giv-
> ing and sharing, the absurdity of blame.[4]

It would be a shame if our understanding of the work of marriage degenerated into a hot debate about gender differences. What
I would prefer to do is to set the practical theological context in
which husbands and wives may apply the principle of the cross,
"my life for yours," in every facet of their life together.

Let me say this up front. I believe the Lord would be disappointed with me if I felt cleaning the toilets or washing the dishes or

putting in a load of wash was beneath me. How else will my sons learn to clean bathrooms and wash the kitchen floor if their father doesn't set the example? In our household Ginny oversees the finances. She keeps the budget, pays the bills and works on taxes. Routinely she fills my billfold with cash. Incidentally, this is the same way my parents operated, and my father was a math professor. When it comes to a division of labor, I would rather mow the grass, maintain the cars and take out the garbage than write checks.

The clear division between wives doing housework and husbands doing office work is a thing of the past. Our current culture may be more sympathetic to the work ethic of the farm than to the suburban model of the 1950s. There are much bigger issues at stake in a marriage that help to determine how the mundane tasks and chores of family life are processed. What is needed is a division of labor that reflects both mutuality and flexibility.

Paul expounds on the principle of the cross in Ephesians 5. His specific counsel to husbands and wives is proceeded by a call to moral purity and spiritual diligence. "Be very careful how you live—not as unwise but as wise, making the most of every opportunity, because the days are evil" (vv. 15-16). Paul warns us of the dangers of spiritual sloth, of filling our time with little indulgences, distracting pleasures and mind-numbing busyness. Eugene Peterson reminds us:

> Sloth is doing nothing of what we were created to do as beings made in the image of God and saved by the Cross of Christ.
>
> Sloth is laziness at the center, while the periphery is adazzle with a torrent of activity and talk. . . . It is the sin that unobtrusively avoids Creator-attentiveness and creature-awareness, and then noisily and busily diverts attention from the great avoidance with a smoke screen of activity.[5]

The apostle opposes any self-indulgent escape from the real work we are called to do. "Do not get drunk on wine, which leads to debauchery. Instead, be filled with the Spirit" (Eph 5:18). Many things compete against the Spirit and tempt us with an intoxicating allure. It may be career success or playing golf or shopping.

Paul mentions alcohol, but there are plenty of other addicting pursuits that captivate the soul and work against "being self-aware as
a creature of God."[6]

To be filled with the Spirit, Paul admonishes, means encouraging
one another in the Lord, worshiping the Lord, expressing gratitude
to God for everything and submitting to one another out of reverence for Christ (Eph 5:18-21). This is absolutely vital to the shared
work of marriage. Precisely because love can be romanticized, senti-
mentalized or spiritualized, Paul uses the verb *submit*. Marital love
depends not on romantic feelings or pious feelings but on covenant
and commitment. Fidelity does not depend upon feelings, but feelings depend upon fidelity. Romance does not create love; it is love
that creates romance. Mutual submission "out of reverence for
Christ" applies the principle of the cross to the marriage relationship in a million ways. "A man and a woman schooled in pride cannot simply sit down together and start caring," writes Robert
Capon. "It takes humility to look wide-eyed at somebody else, to
praise, to cherish, to honor."[7]

The reason Paul's spiritual direction in Ephesians has caused
such debate is because of our sinful tendency to confuse humility
with humiliation. Whenever we can turn humility into humiliation
and loudly complain of injustice, we do so. Some may be quick to
dismiss Paul's counsel as cultural convention, while others may try
to interpret *submission* in such a way as to give themselves the
upper hand in marriage. For Paul the issue is not who is superior
but who should surpass the other in sacrifice. And if anyone is to lay
his life down for the other it is to be the husband. The humility Paul
has in mind has nothing to do with passivity or subservience, but
rather with obedience and faithfulness. A wife's life is not subject to
the whim of her husband but is defined in Christ, even as a husband's love is patterned after Christ's love for the church.

"The husband is the head of the wife just in so far as he is to her
what Christ is to the Church," writes C. S. Lewis. "He is to love her
as Christ loved the Church—read on—'and gave his life for her'
(Eph 5:25)." Lewis rightly observes that what the apostle had in

mind was hardly a husband's superiority but rather his Christlike sacrifice:

> This headship, then, is most fully embodied not in the husband we should all wish to be but in him whose marriage is most like a crucifixion; whose wife receives most and gives least, is most unworthy of him, is—in her own mere nature—least lovable. For the Church has no beauty but what the Bride-groom gives her; he does not find, but makes her, lovely. The chrism of this terrible coronation is to be seen not in the joys of any man's marriage but in its sorrows, in the sickness and sufferings of a good wife or the faults of a bad one, in his unwearying (never paraded) care or his inexhaustible forgiveness: forgiveness, not acquiescence. As Christ sees in the flawed, proud, fanatical or lukewarm Church on earth that Bride who will one day be without spot or wrinkle, and labors to produce the latter, so the husband whose headship is Christ-like (and he is allowed no other sort) never despairs.[8]

The apostle Paul gives husbands two high-impact images to shape their understanding of how they should relate to their wives. The first image, Christ's love for the church, calls a husband to love his wife sacrificially, to strengthen and support her. The second image Paul uses is as personal as the first image is exalted: "Husbands ought to love their wives as their own bodies. He who loves his wife loves himself. After all, no one ever hated his own body, but he feeds and cares for it, just as Christ does the church" (Eph 5:28-29).

The "oneness" Paul envisions for the marriage relationship is more radical and intimate than any of the advice we hear today from secular counselors. Paul's advice depends on redemption and creation. He draws on the principle of the cross, "my life for yours" and the principle of creation, "and the two will become one flesh." We don't find such radical wisdom in popular culture or in modern therapeutic literature. Paul's advice is not inventive, but it is original. His Spirit-inspired analogies depended on the One who made us and saved us.

Becoming true soulmates is not achieved through clever insights into the feminine psyche or building up the male ego. A happy marriage doesn't depend on expensive get-away vacations or placating a spouse's selfishness. The shared work of marriage has to do with truthfulness, self-control, forgiveness and compassion. It involves speaking the truth in love and knowing when "to keep one's mouth shut and one's heart open."[9] Soulcraft offers to a husband and wife wisdom that is both more original and more radical than the world can understand. The apostle says it well, "We have not received the spirit of the world but the Spirit who is from God, that we may understand what God has freely given us" (1 Cor 2:12).

11

A LITTLE SEMINARY

*"Fathers, do not exasperate your children; instead, bring them
up in the training and instruction of the Lord."*

E P H E S I A N S   6 : 4

ALL THAT WE HAVE SAID ABOUT THE SOULFUL SELF AND WHOLE-
ness in Christ relates to parenting. Rather than a few lines of Scripture pertaining to parenting, we have the whole counsel of God
shaping our understanding of what it is to be a father or a mother.
Soulcraft connects being a parent to knowing God in a personal,
down-to-earth, real relationship. To know God in this way is to
encourage an in-depth, person-to-person knowing of one another in
the family. Knowing God and being known by God is the key to
relationships in the family. Soulcraft frees us from the burden of
turning parenting into a special performance. The qualities
well-suited to being a father or a mother are the same qualities that
prepare a person for living life: "compassion, kindness, humility,
gentleness and patience" (Col 3:12).

At first glance the Bible seems to say very little about being a parent. One is hard pressed to find much more than a paragraph in
Paul's letters on the subject. The apostle's one-line exhortations

seem almost too concise: "Children, obey your parents in the Lord, for this is right" (Eph 6:1). Or, "Encourage the young men to be self-controlled" (Tit 2:6). We want strategies of implementation, but Paul only gives blunt imperatives.

The well-known text in Deuteronomy 6, which instructs parents on how to impress their children with the commands of God, is very important, but it is only a small didactic passage. We expect much more on the subject of family than the Bible appears to provide. Parental instruction and filial obedience are emphasized in the book of Proverbs and clearly assumed in the New Testament, but this spiritual direction is always woven into the larger picture of the people of God. For many parents the famous line in Proverbs represents not a promise but pressure. "Train a child in the way he should go, and when he is old he will not turn from it" (Prov 22:6). Their immediate response is "Yes, I've heard that before, but how? How am I suppose to train my child?"

A full chapter on the role of parents is simply not found in the Bible. But of all the subjects on today's agenda, parenting has to rank near the top. People have a genuine hunger for insight and information on building strong families. Our eagerness to know more is an indication of our felt need. We want to be better parents. Typically, if a church offers a seminar or a Sunday school class on family issues, it is the most popular class. Judging from book and video sales, believers long for any idea, suggestion or strategy that will help them to be more effective parents. Soulcraft seeks to take advantage of this yearning for wisdom and aims to guide parents in the whole counsel of God. Soulcraft is different, however, from run-of-the-mill cultural approaches to family life. Instead of concentrating on relatively minor issues, it focuses attention where it counts.

Eugene Peterson writes:

> When I observe the families where parents seem to be doing a good job of living the Christian faith in relation to their children, it is readily apparent that actual practices vary widely. Particular rules, techniques of discipline, variations in strictness and permissiveness—

they run the gamut. One thing stands out: These parents seriously, honestly, joyfully follow the way of Christ themselves.[1]

Faith-Filled Parenting

Parenting is not defined by matching skills and duties, nor is it a task-oriented job like that of computer programmer or a surgeon. There is no instruction manual that can make parents effective, no technical guide for expert parenting. "A parent's main job is not to be a parent, but to be a person."[2] The moment we understand this we realize that everything the Bible says about being a man or woman of God applies to being a parent. Today's step-by-step analysis and emphasis on technical know-how is great for computers, but it doesn't work for families.

Modern adults imagine that they lack the relational proficiency to do a good job as parents. They assume that kids are like computers, amazingly complex systems that require some know-how in order to maximize their potential. Too many of today's parents are looking for the right relational software to run their "how to be a good parent" programs. They think of parenting as a project requiring the application of skills and the mastery of techniques in order to be successful.

Soulcraft's orientation is different. Parental pragmatism is a temptation to be resisted, and the ever popular how-to approach is to be avoided in favor of a more personal, Christ-centered relationship between parent and child. It is not what parents know about the human psyche that counts; it is whom they know that matters. Growing up in the grace and knowledge of the Lord Jesus Christ will do more for parents than all the seminars and self-help books they can get their hands on. Learning to pray the Psalms will be far better preparation for the day-to-day rough and tumble of the real world than courses and seminars on the latest trends in parenting.

On the subject of family, my father's words were as succinct as the Scriptures. I don't ever recall him addressing his role as a father. I doubt if he distinguished between being a father and being himself. Neither he nor my mother thought of parenting as a task in competition with other responsibilities. They gave my brother and me constant companionship, love, direction, protection and support.

According to Jerry Sittser, good parents don't just attend to their children's needs, they carry them in their heart. That's what my parents did for us. Mature parents learn what Sittser experienced: "I once *performed* as a parent; now I *am* a parent."[3] Being a father or a mother ought to be the most highly integrative calling that we can possibly fulfill. God doesn't ask us to be specialists; God calls us to be real. "The parent's main task," writes Eugene Peterson, "is to be vulnerable in a living demonstration that adulthood is full, alive and Christian."[4] This is what I saw in my mother and father: two people devoted to the Lord, to one another and to their sons. There was no doubt in my mind that my parents would lay down their lives for us in a heartbeat; neither was there any wavering in their insistence on respect and obedience from us.

When I wrote to my father from college on his forty-seventh birthday, I had no idea that it would be my last birthday card to him, that he would die within the year. The cancer at work in his body had not yet been detected.

> Happy Birthday! I hope this gets there on the day. I'm sorry there is no gift with it. There is just nothing here at all that you would want. I enjoyed talking with you on the phone last night. You sounded real good and rested which you hadn't for quite awhile. So glad that you were able to sing in the evening service with Jon accompanying you. The Lord is good and has seen fit to use all three of you in many different ways.
>
> Thanks for being such a good Dad. The Lord has really worked through you to be the example I've needed. It is great to know that my parents are strong for the Lord and want the Lord's will accomplished in their sons' lives. I know this isn't a recent desire on your part, for it has been manifested since my early years. This may sound more like a Father's Day card than a birthday card, but it's something I rejoice in continually. It makes me think of the great responsibility Jon and I have because of our upbringing. "To those who have received much, much is expected." Thanks again for being the Dad

you are. I'm looking forward to seeing you and Mom and Jon in a couple of weeks. Love, Doug.

I like to think that Abraham and my father had something in common. They shared a quiet fortitude and a no-nonsense faithfulness. For both Father Abraham and my father, the pattern of their lives proved more instructive than their temperaments. It was never a question of being an ideal dad but rather one of being a faithful father. Holiness counted more than hobbies. Character was more important than achievements. It was not the little subjective features of my parents' lives that mattered but the fundamental commitments worked out over time.

Father Abraham and Mother Sarah

Soulcraft explores the biblical pattern of being a faithful parent. Abraham and Sarah serve as our first in-depth examples. About all we learn from Adam and Eve is that ideal parents never existed and that two very different sons can be raised under the same roof. Noah and his family offer similar lessons. The Bible appears to be nonjudgmental when it comes to parents of wayward children. The Bible says that there is no excuse for faithless parents, but it also affirms that sons and daughters are fully responsible for their own actions (see Mt 21:28-31; Lk 15:11).

The reason Abraham and Sarah are prime examples of soulcraft is that they illustrate what it means for Christian parents to be counter-cultural, sacrificially faithful and humbly consistent. It is fitting that the story of their family should coincide with salvation history.

When you think of how the story of Abraham and Sarah begins, John the Baptist's retort to those who trust in their Abrahamic lineage is ironic. "Do not begin to say to yourselves," cries John, " 'We have Abraham as our father.' For I tell you that out of these stones God can raise up children for Abraham" (Lk 3:8). In a manner of speaking, making a nation out of nothing is exactly what God did. God took a man from nowhere, the son of no one in particular, and decided to make him into a great nation. Out of the blue, God promised to bless all peoples on earth through Abraham. There is no explanation for this apart from the grace of God. Just as God took that which was formless, empty and dark and shaped it into rhythms of grace, the Lord God took Abraham and made a great nation. Furthermore, "the leaving and the uniting" so fundamental in God's plan for marriage was applied to Abraham and became strategic in God's plan for his people. The Lord said to Abram, "Leave your country, your people and your father's household and go to the land I will show you" (Gen 12:1).

Abraham and Sarah did what God told them to do. They left their home culture, obeyed God's command, and in the process assumed a distinctive identity that was both counter-cultural and dangerous. They left the familiar and lived by faith. Abraham and Sarah became resident aliens, carving out a new existence in a wilderness filled with idolatries and threatening forces.

Abraham is not remembered for his wisdom or his poetry or his leadership qualities. He is remembered best simply as a man of God who, although prone to weakness, lived by faith. As Hebrews 11:8 says, "By faith Abraham, when called to go to a place he would later receive as his inheritance, obeyed and went, even though he did not know where he was going." One of the most distinctive acts Abraham performed was to build altars in the wilderness and worship the Lord God. Wherever he went, he built an altar to the Lord and called on his name. Other people built idols, Abraham built an altar. The altar consisted of a pile of rocks, a slain lamb, a consuming fire, and the prayer of a man of faith making his way through the wilderness. The altar was not a monument but a symbol of holy communion.

Abraham learned what it was like to be God's dependent. Salvation was not a doctrine or an idea for the future; it was the whole experience—from day to day to everlasting, from a faith journey to a family of faith. Long before God blessed Abraham and Sarah with a son, their character was forged in the crucible of trust and faith, worship and prayer. They knew that they belonged only to God.

The well-crafted, true story of Abraham and Sarah offers a model to Christian parents of what it means to be in the world but not of the world. The one thing, above all else, that Abraham and Sarah had was a relationship to God. This was foundational to everything about them. God's grace brought this couple out of their small world of inconsequential pleasures and achievements into the large world of his salvation history. Here too is where Christian families begin. We are no longer alienated from God, but we are

> fellow citizens with God's people and members of God's household, built on the foundation of the apostles and prophets, with Christ Jesus himself as the chief cornerstone. In him the whole building is joined together and rises to become a holy temple in the Lord. And in him you too are being built together to become a dwelling in which God lives by his Spirit. (Eph 2:19-22)

Cultural Pressures
Many of today's Christian parents are uncertain about what to hope for in their children, because they have lost this distinctive *in-Christ* identity. Their lack of confidence and insecurity stems from their conformity to the world. They are reduced to organizing and managing their children's activities rather than nurturing and shaping their souls. The net effect is a superficial replication of parental preferences and social style in their children. Beliefs and convictions are minimized or pushed aside by the pressures of materialism, consumerism, self-promotion and image. Today's child is not so much mentored, as manufactured. The elementary-school-age child is entertained, chauffeured, clothed and equipped with the best that parents can afford. In high school, peer identification and youth culture combine to conform teenagers to a market-driven generational image.

Parents often feel disabled by these social forces. Feeling powerless to mentor their child into maturity, parents helplessly stand by and watch as a highly manipulative, consumer-oriented culture dictates the mood and image of their son or daughter. The teen's resulting re-imagined self has only a borrowed identity, plagiarized from external influences such as music, sports, fashion and movies. The reason stereotyping the generations (baby boom, baby bust, generation X, millennial generation) has become so popular is that the power of conformity in everything from fashion to feeling is at an all time high. Identity is no longer a matter of soul but of style. Identity turns out to be but a thin veneer over a lost soul.

In *Reviving Ophelia: Saving the Selves of Adolescent Girls*, Mary Pipher describes the destructive forces that affect young women in American culture. She writes:

> America today is a girl-destroying place. Everywhere girls are encouraged to sacrifice their true selves. Their parents may fight to protect them, but their parents have limited power. Many girls lose contact with their true selves, and when they do, they become extraordinarily vulnerable to a culture that is all too happy to use them for its purposes.[5]

Young girls are pressured to evaluate themselves on the basis of appearance. Many scorn their bodies and punish themselves in a desperate attempt to remake themselves so they will match the image of beauty demanded by the culture. They are under immense pressure to abandon their family identity, buy into McSex junk values and starve themselves into perfection.

Instead of the weight of glory shaping a girl's self-worth, her weight in pounds controls her self-image. Identity is subverted by "a national cult of thinness." Since the strength and support of primary relationships are replaced by superficial secondary relationships, people (especially young women) are judged by their appearance, not their character.[6] The defining values shaping who they are and how they think about themselves are skin deep and weighed on a scale.

The power of beauty to threaten the believer's identity was not foreign to Abraham and Sarah's situation. When famine forced them to search for food in Egypt, Abraham coached Sarah to lie. "I know what a beautiful woman you are. When the Egyptians see you, they will say, 'This is his wife.' Then they will kill me but will let you live. Say you are my sister, so that I will be treated well for your sake and my life will be spared because of you" (Gen 12:11-13).

This emphasis on beauty endangered Abraham and Sarah and nearly cost them everything. Abraham's method of coping left much to be desired. His plotting and deceiving may have spared his life, but he came close to losing his wife. If the Lord had not intervened by punishing Pharaoh for taking Sarah into his harem, the identity and destiny of this family could have died right there in Egypt. So God not only had set Abraham and Sarah apart from the surrounding culture, but God preserved them when the culture might have overwhelmed them. Too many of us come off looking like Abraham trying to live off Pharaoh while we put our families at risk.

The vulnerability of Christian girls to these cultural dynamics is painfully evident in the church today. We can only conclude that our parenting has been too superficial and cosmetic. We have not gone deep enough with our children to present them with an identity in Christ that helps them resist conformity to the world's dehumanizing, accountability resistant strategies. We have been unwitting accomplices in the "lookism" and consumerism of a self-indulgent, affluent culture. Instead of helping them grow up in Christ we have timidly hoped that our daughters will grow out of the "phase" they are going through. But it isn't that easy. The massive influence of the world is not like a virus that runs its course and then leaves us alone. It is more like a malignancy that grows and intensifies over time.

At a time when many of our sons and daughters not only feel but truly are vulnerable, insecure and directionless, parents need to "get out of Egypt," so to speak, and establish priorities and strategies that reflect their identity in Christ. The world's cynicism and unbelief make even a quiet, humble, honest stand for Christ extraordinary! Ordinary people like you and me can stand out as adventuresome and courageous to our teenagers by being true followers of Jesus in the Monday-morning marketplace and in the most real world of worship and faithfulness. As William Willimon says, "An unbelieving world can make a saint out of almost anybody who dares to be faithful."[7] Abraham and Sarah model for us what it means to live by faith in a world that is not our home. They came to rely on the Lord God to give their lives significance and to shape their destiny.

The Principle of the Cross

The second important dimension in Abraham and Sarah's parental paradigm is sacrifice. Twenty-five of their years of married life must have felt like a contradiction. God had promised to make them into a great nation and they didn't even have a child to claim as God's blessing. Most parents can identify with Abraham and Sarah's coping strategies; I know I certainly can. We feel it is necessary to do something, to make life work out according to plan. Our anxiety and inability to wait pressures us to preempt God and take matters into our own hands.

Sarah felt it was her responsibility to act. She said to her husband, "The LORD has kept me from having children. Go sleep with my maidservant; perhaps I can build a family through her" (Gen 16:2). Instead of exercising willed passivity and waiting patiently on God to act, Abraham complied with Sarah's suggestion and impregnated Hagar. The strategy backfired and threatened the marriage. Hagar despised Sarah, Sarah blamed Abraham, and Abraham just wanted the problem to go away. In spite of the Hagar-Ishmael fiasco, God stayed with Abraham and Sarah. And even though there were grave consequences for their actions, God remained faithful to his promises. Abraham and Sarah were not model parents, but they are used by God to model for us God's patience and steadfast love in spite of poor human decisions and selfish motives.

After years of waiting and trusting and depending upon the promises of God, Sarah finally gave birth to a son, and they named him *Isaac*, which means "he laughs." How thrilled they must have been to receive this child—this confirmation of God's will. And then some time later, years later, God said to Abraham, as clearly as he had spoken his promises, "Take your son, your only son, Isaac, whom you love, and go to the region of Moriah. Sacrifice him there as a burnt offering." (Gen 22:2). How could God tell Father Abraham to sacrifice his one and only son, Isaac? Only idol worshiping pagans appeased their imaginary gods with child sacrifices. How could God, the Author of life, ask Abraham to give up his "pride and joy" and sacrifice the promise?

We have no insight into Abraham's agony of soul; we have only a moving picture of his faithfulness. "Early the next morning Abraham got up" and headed out (Gen 22:3). For three days Abraham suffered his Gethsemane ("Not my will, but your will be done"). For three days he tried to understand the ways of God. Why was a sacrificial lamb unacceptable and their only son required? After three days of soul-searching one thing was certain in Abraham's mind. His obedience to the living God would not result in the destruction of his son. He left the two servants who had accompanied them with this promise, which was for Abraham a heartfelt conviction, "We will worship and then we will come back to you" (Gen 22:5). The book of Hebrews says, "Abraham reasoned that God could raise the dead." (11:19).

We receive our sons and daughters as gifts from God. They are from God and belong to God, and God is quite capable of dramatically bringing this truth home to us at critical stages in our children's lives. We know that the lesson God had in mind was not primarily for Isaac, although it must have had a profound impact on him. The lesson was for Abraham. Was there a danger that Abraham might turn God's gift of a son into an idol? Was Abraham's devotion focused on his family or his Lord? God knew Abraham's heart. Did Abraham know his own heart? We don't know, but God did require of Abraham tangible, physical evidence of his single-minded devotion to God.

It is easy to think of children as a gift of God when they are cute, cuddly, cooing infants, but our perspective often changes as they get older. Eugene Peterson writes, "It never occurs to me to think of sullen adolescents—door-slamming fifteen-year-old daughters or defiantly argumentative sixteen-year-old sons" as a gift from God.

Infants are manifestly God's gifts. . . . [They are given to us at a time in life] when it is most easy to suppose that *we* are in control, that the world owes us a living, that through our education and training we have reduced our environment to something manageable—at this time God gives us a child to restore our sense of creaturehood, our own sense of being a *child* of God, so we may experience a renewal of the prerequisite condition for entering the kingdom of God (Mt 18:1-3).

But the adolescent is no less a gift of God. As the infant is God's gift to the young adult, so the adolescent is a gift to the middle-aged. The adolescent is 'born' into our lives during our middle decades (when we are in our thirties, forties, and fifties). In these middle decades of life we are prone to stagnation and depression—the wonders of life reduce to banalities and the juices of life dry up. . . . And then God's gift: In the rather awkward packaging of the adolescent God brings into our lives a challenge to grow, testing our love, chastening our hope, pushing our faith to the edge of the abyss.[8]

Our children's adolescence is not a problem to be solved but an experience to be embraced as a means for growing up in Christ.

As God used Isaac in Abraham's life, God uses our teenagers to challenge the character and vitality of our faith. The testing of Abraham's faith is a reminder to us of the passion that God expects from us. Abraham's faith was tested to the limit not for God's sake but for Abraham's sake. Abraham proved that he would not allow his only son, Isaac, God's blessing, to become an object of idolatry. Abraham's parental paradigm challenges us to let nothing substitute in our family life for God himself. No one was dearer to Abraham than God himself.

This dramatic episode in Abraham's life reminds us of an even greater truth. Abraham not only modeled what it means for parents to be faithful to God; he illustrated what it means for God to be faithful to us. The passion God expects from us is transcended by God's passion for us. Abraham is a picture of God giving up his one and only Son that we might live.

Legacy of Love
To be good parents, Abraham and Sarah embraced their God-shaped

identity. They evidenced the meaning of sacrificial devotion to God through their willingness to obey the Lord no matter what. To these two dimensions (identity and sacrifice), we add a third, Abraham's legacy of love. It is found in the beautiful story of Isaac and Rebekah (Gen 24). Grieving the loss of Sarah, Abraham focused his attention on Isaac's future and prayerfully sought a wife for his son. Far from dismissing this as an arranged marriage, we should view Abraham's earnest efforts as a demonstration not only of his love for Isaac but also of how we ought to love our children by preparing them for the future.

Abraham modeled a parental approach that neither dominated nor abdicated responsibility for Isaac's future. He would have been the last person to say that he chose a wife for his son. What he did was to act in accordance with God's will to preserve the distinctive identity of his family. Parents can learn from Abraham's example to pray for their children's future spouses. They should encourage them to seek husbands and wives who are committed to Christ. In meaningful and loving ways parents and children can overcome generational segregation and individual autonomy. Home should be a place where all generations gather together to strengthen each other in their identity in Christ.

Abraham charged his trusted servant with the task of seeking a wife for Isaac from among his relatives. Abraham insisted on two things: "You will not get a wife for my son from the daughters of the Canaanites, among whom I am living" (Gen 24:3), and "make sure that you do not take my son back there [to Abraham's original home]" (Gen 24:6). Abraham was convinced that God would find a wife for Isaac, and he felt led by God to take this practical initiative. He wanted to protect Isaac from compromising his future with a Canaanite wife or disobeying God by leaving the promised land. The prayer of Abraham's servant is a beautiful expression of humility and dependence upon God:

> O LORD, God of my master Abraham, give me success today, and show kindness to my master Abraham. See, I am standing beside this spring, and the daughters of the townspeople are coming out to draw

water. May it be that when I say to a girl, "Please let down your jar that I may have a drink," and she says, "Drink, and I'll water your camels too"—let her be the one you have chosen for your servant Isaac. By this I will know that you have shown kindness to my master. (Gen 24:12-14)

God's answer to this prayer is recounted in great detail, clearly showing that the people of God enjoyed a good love story. The whole episode is filled with worship, prayer and testimony. No one can miss the point that Rebekah is God's choice for Isaac. Abraham's servant is a faithful ambassador for God, as well as for his master, serving as a bridge between two families and bringing two people together in marriage through the testimony of answered prayer. To use Rebekah's father's words, "This is from the LORD" (Gen 24:50).

When they returned to Canaan, Isaac was there to greet them. Rebekah saw him from a distance before he saw her. We are told that the servant then informed Isaac of all that had happened. No mention was made of Abraham, who apparently remained in the background. Even the conclusion of the story is meant to remind us of the effectiveness of Abraham and Sarah as parents. "Isaac brought her into the tent of his mother Sarah, and he married Rebekah. So she became his wife, and he loved her; and Isaac was comforted after his mother's death" (Gen 24:67).

Long before Mount Sinai and the giving of the commandments, God offered Abraham and Sarah as a soulcraft model to inspire the Christian home. Their family story woven into salvation history helps us to understand more fully what it means to be an effective and faithful parent whose identity, priorities and legacy are in Christ.

Table Fellowship

There are many metaphors that help us to conceptualize the soulcraft meaning of family life. Unlike religious tourists who sample the faith from a safe and impersonal distance, Abraham and Sarah were true sojourners. Their family story was a pilgrimage in faith and trust in the living God. Other important metaphors also come to mind. The early church referred to the home as a "little monastery." The Puritans spoke of the family as a "seminary." They believed that the Christian home was where life made up its mind, where the basic skills of worship and prayer, comfort and caring were modeled and taught. As Edith Schaeffer says, "The family is the place where loyalty, dependability, trustworthiness, compassion, sensitivity to others, thoughtfulness, and unselfishness are supposed to have their roots. Someone must take the initiative and use imagination to intentionally teach these things."[9]

The well-known counsel given by Moses describes just how simple, good and solid parental soulcraft can be. According to him there is no "secret" to becoming an effective mother or father. It doesn't take much to figure out what to do, but it does take humility, integrity, patience and love to be the kind of parent Moses pictured:

> Love the LORD your God with all your heart and with all your soul and with all your strength. These commandments that I give you today are to be upon your hearts. Impress them on your children. Talk about them when you sit at home and when you walk along the road, when you lie down and when you get up. Tie them as symbols on your hands and bind them on your foreheads. Write them on the doorframes of your houses and on your gates. (Deut 6:5-9)

Literalists have had trouble grasping the meaning of Moses' metaphors. Religious people in Jesus' day took this passage so literally that they made small receptacles containing verses of Scripture and bound them to the forehead and left arm. Today's literalists feel they need to have a scriptural proof text for every occasion, but their "know it all" answers are too glib, too pat. Their tendency to moralize and spiritualize indicates their lack of authenticity. The kind of home life encouraged by Moses requires integrity and authenticity. Parents are to be real with their children and not afraid to engage them in serious discussion.

If we want to relay the truth from one generation to another, we should begin not with the pulpit but with the kitchen table. Our table talk is the test of orthodoxy. The command to impress our children is not optional. God intends that we present a running commentary both in our actions and in our words because children need both example and dialogue. God's truth is expressed conversationally. The subject matter ranges from the meaning of the cross to what to look for in a vocation; from how to deal with a difficult teacher or a tough class to the meaning of heaven; from how to spend a vacation to how to minister to the poor. We don't need to wait, nor should we want to wait for a religious setting to discuss God's truth. It's not a Sunday subject alone. Our most lively dialogue about the things of God may come on Monday night. Talk about it! Get into it! Use the daily routine of life to shape the souls of those called by God into your household. Know the Word of God like the back of your hand. Consider it your duty and privilege to think Christianly about the totality of life.

Table fellowship has always been a key element in family life. It is a window into the soul of a family. In her novel *Dinner at the Homesick Restaurant*, Anne Tyler describes a family that is never able to finish a meal together. Something always goes wrong. The family members always have their own agendas and manage to get in their cutting comments and their put-downs. Selfishness crowds out sensitivity, and criticism overshadows concern for each other. They learn that finding out what a person has to say does not always improve relationships. Tempers flair. Egos compete. Someone invariably leaves in a huff or in tears, and dinner ends in disaster—every time. Perhaps for some dysfunctional families it would be better if they didn't sit down together, but that would signal the defeat of the family.

Table fellowship has always been important in our family; in fact, I like to think of our kitchen table as the table of the Lord. This is where we meet for most of our discussion, debate, humor, prayer and sharing of God's Word. We probably do more arguing and more affirming around the kitchen table than we do anywhere else. Dining well as a family is a skill. It takes preparation and planning, scheduling and prioritizing. Around the family table we are equal. We may not be equally mature or equally gifted or even equally accountable for the well-being of the family, but we are all equal members of the family. No one has more of a right to sit at the table than another.

Family meals are always intentional. Someone goes to a lot of work to put on a meal. Others may just have to show up with clean hands and a clean shirt. Somebody has to plan the menu, purchase the food, prepare the meal, set the table and insist on attendance. Someone else cleans up (and if possible it should be somebody other than the person who planned and prepared the meal). It's a lot of work, yet it is good work. Those involved in preparing the food should not limit their expectations to food. After all, food was made for the family meal, not the family meal for food. Being together is more important than nourishment, and nourishment is more important than good taste, although each has its place.

Someone has to set the tone, establish order and encourage dialogue. We not only bring an appetite to supper, we bring an attitude. At times, maybe most of the time, the food is secondary to the fellowship and listening is far more important than eating. And sometimes the best part of the meal is when the food is finished and we stay at the table talking.

We always begin our meals with prayer, not because we are pious but because we are thankful. I pity people who feel too sophisticated or too self-conscious to bow before God in gratitude and acknowledge their dependence upon the Lord. We like to end our family meals with Bible reading and prayer because it seems fitting to gather up what has been talked about and present it to Christ.

The family meal has fallen on hard times in our culture. People have their own agendas and seem too preoccupied with themselves or too distracted to sit down together. Dinner becomes a casualty of conflicting schedules and busyness. Eating in front of the television has replaced breaking bread together, with commercials giving just enough time to grab a second helping. Fast food is not only a convenience, it is a culture. Most people understand that food not only is necessary for physical well-being but is also an occasion for social well-being. Nevertheless, in our culture eating has become more a matter of consumption than community.

Permit me to encourage a very practical soulcraft resolution: Break bread together. Make meal time an opportunity for fellowship in the Lord, for a meeting of the minds, for sharing each other's lives. Remind yourselves through prayer at the beginning and Bible reading and prayer at the end of each meal that you are the people of God. Center your time on Christ and make your table fellowship into the Lord's table.

Loving God and Loving Our Children

Children are impressionable, and parents are given the opportunity to impress them. A make-or-break starting point for effective, faithful parenting is a humble acceptance of the Word of God. The courage of true convictions begins with a humble acceptance of God's authority. Good parents are not self-made men and women, making up the rules of life as they go. There is no proud boast: "I did it my way!" Good parents are humble parents, knowing that "the fear of the LORD is the beginning of wisdom" (Prov 9:10). As Robert Capon observes, "The moral laws are not just a collection of arbitrary parking regulations invented by God to make life complicated; they are the only way for human nature to be natural."[10] True impact-parenting wholeheartedly agrees with Joshua's affirmation, "As for me and my household, we will serve the LORD" (Josh 24:15).

When the apostle Paul wrote to Timothy, he acknowledged the legacy of faithfulness founded upon the Word of God that had shaped Timothy's commitment. "I have been reminded of your sincere faith, which first lived in your grandmother Lois and in your mother Eunice and, I am persuaded, now lives in you also" (2 Tim 1:5). Humility before God and the courage of our convictions go hand in hand. Together they lead to a parental confidence that does not moralize or spiritualize the truth of God. Furthermore the law of love and the love of the law are inseparable. Law and gospel cannot be divorced. God's love is a definable, substantive and sacrificial love (Phil 1:9-11). Before we can impress our children or our grandchildren with the Word of God, we have to have been impressed with the Word of God ourselves. A pastor once was asked when parents should begin thinking about teaching their children the Bible. The pastor replied, "About twenty years before they're born."

Loving God wholeheartedly means that we grasp the commands, decrees and laws of the Lord by heart. Our commitment to the Lord must not be compartmentalized. The whole self and all of life is under the lordship of Christ. This includes the intellectual as well as the emotional, the physical and the spiritual. True learning takes place when the Word of God is integrated into every dimension of living.

Loving God wholeheartedly means that we look at ourselves and our children in a new way. When we hold our children as tiny infants, helpless and dependent, we are reminded that we, too, are children of our heavenly Father. When we see them struggling with their identity and with the meaning of life, we share their struggle. As they work through the questions of the faith, we work through the questions of the faith. As they form their worldview, we form our worldview. God has called us all, parents and children, heavenward in Christ Jesus. When we see our children growing "in wisdom and stature, and in favor with God and men" (Lk 2:52), we sense the dawning of our new relationship with them as brothers or sisters in Christ.

Loving God wholeheartedly means that our identity is in Christ—which frees us to become better parents. Our identity is not wrapped up in our job or our performance, nor is our identity fulfilled through our children. Our children don't have to prove themselves. They don't have to make a name for themselves. They don't have to become something just to please their parents. Our children are not our alter egos.

Loving God wholeheartedly means that we lay aside the image of "Father knows best" or "Mother is always right." For we don't have all the answers. We are not the Lord. The Lord our God is one, and there is only one God. And I bow before the same Lord God that my children do. Parents are not sovereign, God is. I need to pray and direct, but I don't need to pontificate and dictate.

Loving God wholeheartedly means that I will not let my children bully me or intimidate me. I am not a perfect parent, but I am their parent, and with this calling comes a responsibility, an accountability before God. Conviction and compassion, law and gospel, go together. I cannot lay aside my role as spiritual director and mentor. I don't want to impose upon them choices and decisions that they are not prepared to make, but I will insist on cooperation, obedience and respect. As long as my children live in my home and sit at my table I am responsible for their safety, protection, guidance, discipline and provision, and most importantly, I am responsible to love them wholeheartedly and show them Christ.

When my friend Bob Parrish graduated from high school, his father wrote out his thoughts in a letter:

Dear Bob,

I wanted to talk to you about some of the changes your life will be taking as you graduate from high school. . . . I am proud of you and your life. Not just the grades in school, but your attitude toward life, and your belief in Jesus Christ. The most important thing in your life will not be your education or intelligence; what you achieve or your sparkling personality. It will be your dedication to living your life for Christ. In anything you do, or whatever direction HE leads you.

Even though you're still a teenager, beginning today you're a man, with all the responsibilities that come with growing up. The world is more difficult to live in now then when I was growing up. There is a lot more dishonesty . . . more drugs . . . more free and easy sex. If you are strong in your faith and trust in God, you will have happiness that money or things cannot bring you. You can not begin to know the happiness I've had through you, your sister, and mother, all brought about by God's love for me and my trust in Him. . . . May God bless you and bring you happiness that only he can bring to you the rest of your life.

Yours,

Dad

Chuck Parrish wrote that letter to Bob three months before he was diagnosed with a brain tumor and eleven months before he died. Even though his days on earth were numbered, his impact as a loving father was great. His down-to-earth, God-fearing soulcraft mentored his son and shaped future generations in Christ.

What will be the soul-shaping effect of our parenting on our children? Will our sons and daughters perceive that we are wholeheartedly committed to the Lord God? Will our humility before God be evident to them and will they see the joy of the Lord in our lives?

Moses affirms our parental responsibility to be our children's primary mentors (Deut 6:5-9). We certainly need the support of the household of faith, but it is up to us as parents to proclaim Christ, admonishing and teaching our children with all wisdom, so that we may present them grown up in Christ. To this end we labor, struggling with all his energy, which so powerfully works in us (see Col 1:28-29).

12

BROKENNESS

"The sacrifices of God are a broken spirit;
a broken and contrite heart,
O God, you will not despise."

PSALM 51:17

T HE WISDOM OF GOD'S LOVE TO CONFRONT AND COMFORT, TO CON-
vict and console is precisely what is needed when we deal with the
brokenness of divorce. Those who have broken faith with their
beloved and violated their vowed commitment need to encounter
the convicting power of God's discerning love. Those who have suffered the trauma of divorce and felt the pain of adultery, abandonment or abuse need to be embraced by the comforting power of
God's discerning love. The quality most sought after in the apostle
Paul's prayer for love was discernment: may "your love . . . abound
more and more in knowledge and depth of insight, so that you may
discern what is best and may be pure and blameless until the day of
Christ Jesus" (Phil 1:9-11). Paul's soulcraft prayer reminds us that
the love of Jesus is shaped and empowered by the law of God and
the gospel of grace. Love is not pitted against the law, nor is the
power of grace experienced minus the commands of God. To love is

to obey and to obey is to love. Soulcraft unites what the world separates.

When soulcraft is practiced skillfully, it is both convicting and compassionate. For those who have been disobedient, the work of soulcraft produces shame and conviction of sin; for those who have been sinned against, soulcraft produces strength and comfort. Soulcraft convicts those who have treated others shamefully and consoles those who have been treated shamefully. The double-impact work of the Spirit of God leads sinners to repentance and sufferers to relief. At times the counsel of God humiliates us in order to humble us and shames us to restore us. Soulcraft reminds us that what we need is not affirmation and a pat on the back but true deliverance from the power of sin. A physician of the soul is often in a position of treating people who are confused about the source and seriousness of their condition. They don't know how sick their sin has made them. Their adulterous and abusive ways are terminal illnesses if not treated by the radical surgery of God's sanctifying grace.

Jesus on Divorce

Jesus is not silent on divorce, but he is brief. The Pharisees raised the subject in order to test Jesus. Apparently they had heard that he was unrealistically conservative when it came to divorce. Some time earlier he had mentioned divorce in the Sermon on the Mount in an illustration of a new kind of righteousness. Instead of teaching that righteousness is based on compliance with the law, Jesus teaches that righteousness is based on a heartfelt commitment to the Lord. Jesus' inside-out righteousness surpasses the outwardly conforming righteousness of the teachers of the law. Therefore, instead of approving divorce as a legal procedure to be completed decently and in order, Jesus views divorce as a violation of God's will: "It has been said, 'Anyone who divorces his wife must give her a certificate of divorce.' But I tell you that anyone who divorces his wife, except for marital unfaithfulness, causes her to become an adulteress, and anyone who marries the divorced woman commits adultery" (Mt 5:31-32).

Jesus had been branded an extremist by the scribes, and his perspective on divorce was one more indication to them that Jesus' ethic didn't work well in the real world. The religious parties were debating the legal grounds for divorce. The more conservative school of Rabbi Shammi strengthened the position of women because it discouraged divorce when there were insignificant grounds, such as when the wife was a poor cook or a sloppy housekeeper. The school of Rabbi Hillel, on the other hand, promoted a more lenient, no-fault approach, which gave men the freedom to divorce their wives for just about any reason they wanted. The Message, a contemporary-language version of the Bible, offers a fresh hearing of this controversial discussion:

> One day the Pharisees were badgering [Jesus]: "Is it legal for a man to divorce his wife for any reason?" He answered, "Haven't you read in your Bible that the Creator originally made man and woman for each other, male and female? And because of this, a man leaves father and mother and is firmly bonded to his wife, becoming one flesh—no longer two bodies but one. Because God created this organic union of the two sexes, no one should desecrate his art by cutting them apart."
>
> They shot back in rebuttal, "If that's so, why did Moses give instructions for divorce papers and divorce procedures?"
>
> Jesus said, "Moses provided for divorce as a concession to your hardheartedness, but it is not part of God's original plan. I'm holding you to the original plan, and holding you liable for adultery if you divorce your faithful wife and then marry someone else. I make an exception in cases where the spouse has committed adultery."
>
> Jesus' disciples objected, "If those are the terms of marriage, we're stuck. Why get married?"
>
> But Jesus said, "Not everyone is mature enough to live a married life. It requires a certain aptitude and grace. Marriage isn't for everyone. Some, from birth seemingly, never give marriage a thought. Others never get asked—or accepted. And some decide not to get married for kingdom reasons. But if you're capable of growing into the largeness of marriage, do it." (Mt 19:3-12)

Soulcraft takes its cue from Jesus, who skillfully removes the issue of divorce from the hands of the lawyers, eliminates the gender bias and emphasizes the positive meaning of marriage. Jesus refuses to make divorce a legal matter. He insists on treating it as a tragedy of the heart. When Jesus links divorce with adultery he takes away the prerogative of the husband. He rejects the gender bias by making the man who divorces his wife and marries another guilty of adultery and the woman who divorces her husband and marries another guilty of adultery. The emphasis in Jesus' day on male prerogative was nullified immediately if it meant the husband who divorced would be guilty of adultery.

Jesus does not ignore marital unfaithfulness and the hardness of the human heart. He gives permission for divorce, but the grounds for divorce don't assume primary significance in Jesus' mind, and he never handles them in a legalistic way. The word Jesus uses for adultery, *porneia*, has a range of meanings; the meaning of his exceptive clause depends not on a precise legal interpretation but on a theological understanding of marriage (Gen 2:24). Some today would define *adultery* too narrowly, as in the case of a person who contends that performing oral sex with someone other than one's spouse does not amount to an adulterous relationship. This is where the range of meanings for *porneia* proves helpful in exposing the false and deceptive nature of such defenseless arguments. Addictive patterns of illicit sex, including so-called Internet sex and other forms of pornography can constitute *porneia* and rob a marriage of fidelity.

Other than violation of the one-flesh marriage relationship, Jesus insists that there are no grounds for divorce. As far as he is concerned the bottom line remains as it was from the beginning, "Therefore what God has joined together, let no one separate" (Mk 10:9 NRSV).

Our soulcraft strategy has sought to reflect Jesus' positive emphasis on marriage. It is for this reason that chapters on God's created order (chap. 2), the soulful self (chap. 3), the sanctity of human sexuality (chap. 7) and soulmates (chap. 10) have preceded our discussion on the causes and consequences of divorce. My hope is that a biblical perspective on singleness (chap. 4) and parenting (chap. 11) will contribute to our understanding of a healthy and holy marriage and will serve to prevent divorce. It is important to understand and affirm the true nature of a Christ-centered marriage relationship before dealing specifically with the trauma of divorce. Jesus responds to the controversial issue of divorce with positive teaching about marriage. Based on his example, our best response to a culture of divorce is to mentor and model mature marriages.

It is worth noting that in Matthew and Mark the divorce debate between Jesus and the Pharisees is followed by an account of people bringing their children to Jesus for his blessing. The positioning of these two incidents back-to-back focuses our attention on the issue of acceptance and responsibility in the kingdom of God. The disciples questioned whether Jesus' view of marriage was practical enough. You can almost hear them say, "Jesus, you may be right, but does it work?" They were decidedly pessimistic: "If this is the situation between a husband and wife, it is better not to marry" (Mt 19:10). Ironically, their next recorded action was to prevent parents from bringing their children to Jesus. Picture this: they couldn't accept Jesus' teaching on marriage and they couldn't accept children running up to Jesus for a blessing! The two reactions are not unrelated. Their reticence to accept Jesus' view of marriage corresponded with their rebuke of parents, most likely mothers, who were bringing little children to Jesus for prayer.

Spiritually speaking, the most human response would have been for them to affirm Jesus' teaching on marriage and to warmly receive the parents and little children who sought Jesus' blessing. Instead their bias toward the husband's advantage in divorce and their slanted, male-conditioned indifference toward children influenced their reaction. Mark tells us that Jesus was indignant: "He said to them, 'Let the little children come to me, and do not hinder them, for the kingdom of God belongs to such as these. I tell you the truth, anyone who will not receive the kingdom of God like a little child will never enter it'" (Mk 10:14-15). It is quite possible that Jesus had in mind a far more significant form of hindering little children from entering the kingdom than sternly sending them away from a prayer service. That is bad enough, but putting them through the trauma of divorce is horrendous. The price children pay because their parents cannot accept God's will for marriage is incalculable. The disciples were wrong and deserved Jesus' rebuke, and so do parents who defiantly subject their children to divorce.

Jesus sides with the young mothers and the children. He took these children in his arms, put his hands on them and blessed them. It is not surprising to find that Jesus and children share the same expectations when it comes to marriage and family. Children expect a family to remain intact; they expect family members to be committed to each other in enduring, loving relationship. Children expect their parents to sacrifice for them, even as Jesus calls parents to a life of self-denial. The principle of the cross is planted squarely at the heart of Jesus' theology of marriage, and it should be in ours as well. Jesus sees divorce as an accommodation to the hardness of the human heart. He doesn't exalt the permission to divorce over the principle of marriage.

Unfortunately, children usually see divorce as a hardness of heart against them. For most children divorce is not the liberation a parent might claim but instead an awful tragedy. That is how Jesus sees it too. Children normally hold out for reconciliation. They keep hope alive, thinking that somehow their parents will get back together. The basis for Jesus' teaching on marriage are forgiveness and reconciliation. God's creation ideal is possible because of redemption and loving discernment. Neither Jesus nor children agree with a culture of divorce.

A Culture of Divorce

John Stott wisely observes that the higher our view of marriage the more painful is the experience of divorce.

> The higher our concept of God's original ideal for marriage and the family, the more devastating the experience of divorce is bound to be. A marriage which began with tender love and rich expectations now lies in ruins. Marital breakdown is always a tragedy. It contradicts God's will, frustrates his purpose, brings to husband and wife the

acute pains of alienation, disillusion, recrimination and guilt, and precipitates in any children of the marriage a crisis of bewilderment, insecurity and often anger.[1]

Stott's perspective may raise the notion that if we lower our view of marriage we will soften the impact of divorce. If we begin to think of marriage as a temporary experience rather than a permanent bond, will it ease the pain of divorce?

In recent decades society has attempted to put a positive spin on the tragedy of divorce. Evolutionary psychologists claim that it is natural for men and women to lose interest in their mate and become sexually attracted to someone else. Adultery, they say, is simply consistent with how we are genetically wired. Lust is nature's ingenious way to motivate the human animal to reproduce more. The more powerful the male the greater the drive to acquire more sexual partners. Without embarrassment some modern scholarship draws its conclusions about infidelity from animals. For example, scientists rate the sexual activity of male baboons in relationship to their social standing to help explain why powerful men tend to have busier sex lives and more sex partners. It is claimed that exalted social status and extramarital affairs are naturally connected. But when business tycoon J. Paul Getty said, "A lasting relationship with a woman is only possible if you are a business failure," he may not have had the social hierarchy of baboons in mind.[2]

Psychologists sympathetic to evolutionary theory claim that the impulse for males to proliferate their genes through "sexual variety" and for females to acquire more resources is natural and normal, and not necessarily right or wrong. The modern conclusion is ambiguous: perhaps these impulses need to be inhibited for the sake of marriage, or perhaps not. What our culture does imply is that biblical sexual morality is not normal. Robert Wright concludes, "We are potentially moral animals—which is more than any other animal can say—but we are not naturally moral animals. The first step to being moral is to realize how thoroughly we aren't."[3]

According to anthropologist Helen Fisher, humans are better

suited to serial monogamy. She reasons that the agrarian ideal of pairing-for-life is giving way to the modern ideal of personal gratification and autonomy. As we become more nomadic in our double-income urban jungle, "we are returning to traditions of love and marriage that are compatible with our ancient human spirit."[4] She expects the number of divorces and remarriages to boom as people cycle through relationships. "The human animal," writes Fisher, "seems built to court, to fall in love, and to marry one person at a time; then, at the height of our reproductive years, often with a single child, we divorce; then, a few years later, we remarry again."[5]

Psychologists and anthropologists who base their opinions on evolutionary theory are not the only ones urging us to believe that divorce is normal. In a variety of ways, from television sitcoms to the human potential movement, society sends the message that divorce, while emotionally difficult and messy, may be the best thing for personal fulfillment. It is popularly argued that staying in a difficult marriage is not worth the trouble. Barbara Dafoe Whitehead coined the phrase "expressive divorce" to describe society's changing attitudes. What used to be considered a social ill is now looked upon as a civil liberty with a psychological benefit. Divorce is considered by many to be "an instrument for self-development, self-actualization, self-expression . . . a way to be a new and better me."[6] Whitehead laments this new development and points to evidence that shows that divorce causes long-lasting damage to the relationship between parent and child.

In spite of the trauma that divorce causes to everyone involved, Whitehead observes that divorce has become a kind of ethical imperative. "That is, one is obligated to pursue divorce if it seems to promise greater personal happiness, and that obligation comes before other obligations in the marital commitment."[7] The weight of expert opinion has shifted and now divorce has become the therapy of choice for dealing with marital unhappiness. As Maggie Gallagher writes, "Where once we feared becoming the kind of person who could abandon a husband or wife, we now fear becoming the kind of person who needs a husband or wife or, worse, stays with a spouse even after our need has passed."[8]

When divorce is viewed as a rite of passage, people look down on marriage for life as unrealistic and naive. Those who remain married to the same person for twenty-five or fifty years are considered odd. They are suspected of lacking the courage to make changes that would enhance their lives. Fear, it is said, holds them back from pursuing what, in the end, would be best for all concerned. Proponents of divorce argue that people in their thirties are not the same as when they were in their twenties. Time has changed them; new priorities and new experiences require new relationships and new spouses. Reimagining life and the pursuit of happiness calls for at least the possibility of serial monogamy.

Marriage "has been ruthlessly dismantled, piece by piece, under the influence of those who . . . believed that the abolition of marriage was necessary to advance human freedom."[9] But has this dismantling made divorce any easier to accept? Columnist John Leo writes:

> The therapeutic custodians of marriage don't believe in it anymore and seem determined not to bolster, promote, or even talk about it much. The "M" word seems to have disappeared from the American Association for Marriage and Family Therapy's basic vocabulary. Why? Probably because the group is committed to a non-judgmental culture in which all relationships are equally valuable, endlessly negotiable and disposable. So talk about marriage as a long-term, serious commitment that must be shored up or preferred over other lifestyles becomes dicey and embarrassing. . . . The point is that wide-open, anything-goes, no-fault divorce has unexpectedly created its own accelerating culture of noncommitment.[10]

Has this culture of noncommitment made life more meaningful and enjoyable, or has it progressively robbed us of the peace and joy found in lasting primary relationships?

The effort to transform public opinion about divorce has not changed the human heart. It is unlikely that the theories of evolutionary psychologists are responsible for the disintegration of the family. Nor is it very probable that the preaching of the benefits of divorce explains why so many people are getting divorced. Those who make such arguments are attempting to interpret a phenomenon that many know goes far deeper than biology and the latest expert opinion. Divorce is a soul issue. It flows out of a sinful human heart. It happens when the commands of God are disobeyed, when selfishness rules and me-first attitudes prevail. It happens when hearts become so hard that all they can do is break the hearts of those around them. Theory aside, the reality of divorce is painful and the consequences are tragic. Defending divorce only seems to prove the hardness of the human heart.

The pressure is on to accept divorce as a way of life, but our soulful instincts instruct us otherwise. I remember one man in a church that I served as pastor who seemed oblivious to the consequences of divorce. He had divorced his wife of more than fifteen years because he had fallen in love with another woman. But by the time the divorce was finalized he had met and fallen in love with a third woman. After a few years he divorced again and remarried his first wife. His third marriage didn't last long either, and in spite of his appeals for forgiveness and promises of fidelity, he left his first wife again to marry a much younger woman.

All the while this man tried to maintain a high profile of respectability in the church. He sat in the church service with his new wife, seemingly oblivious to the fact that his now twice-divorced first wife tried to worship in the same service. He couldn't understand why the church leadership refused to consider him for the position of Bible study leader or elder, even though the reasons were clearly expressed to him. He also couldn't understand why his first wife refused to attend parties that he hosted for their children. He thought, *Why can't we just remain good friends? It isn't my fault that I fell in love with another woman.*

To this day I marvel at his inability to grasp how deeply he had hurt his first wife and how unrepentant he was for all the pain and suffering he caused her and others. His quickness to claim the grace of God was one aspect of his arrogant air of denial. He believed in the myth of the romantic divorce with everyone living happily ever after, when in fact he had consumed his spouse and then discarded her. Mike Mason writes, "The popular modern notion that partners can separate amicably, and even be 'better friends apart than when they were living together,' is a preposterous myth."[11] In time the man left our church and the Lord graciously provided a very loving, Christ-centered husband for his first wife.

The trauma of divorce has a huge impact on children. They suffer the breakdown of the one relationship that was supposed to endure for their protection, nurture and accountability. At a critical point one or both of their parents place a premium on personal happiness over their welfare. For her book *Second Chances*, Judith Wallerstein studied the effect of divorce on families in a white, middle-class community. She reasoned that these families were less likely to suffer the stresses of poverty, racism and poor education, factors that could obscure the impact of divorce. What she found was that children of divorce who do not have to face war, racism, hunger, violence or grinding poverty still live in fear. Even five years after their parents' divorce, many children were intensely angry with their parents for giving priority to adult needs rather than to their needs. Few children understood why their parents divorced even though the parents thought the reasons were obvious. Wallerstein observes:

> In most crisis situations, such as earthquake, flood, or fire, parents instinctively reach and grab hold of their children, bringing them to safety first. In the crisis of divorce, however, mothers and fathers put children on hold, attending to adult problems first. Divorce is associated with a diminished capacity to parent in almost all dimensions.[12]

Universal exposure to the impact of divorce has been as devastating to our moral and relational selves as nuclear fallout would be to our physical selves. Spiritual carcinogens have penetrated the soul of our culture, and society seems intent on putting a positive face on a tragic situation. Ironically, children grow up blaming not biology or the human potential movement for their parents divorce but God. In moments of desperation these abandoned children cried out to God to heal the awful brokenness between their parents. And because God apparently didn't respond, they find it terribly difficult to trust in him. Today's situation is a poignant reminder of Jesus'

SOULCRAFT

exhortation, "Let the children come to me, and do not hinder them, for the kingdom of heaven belongs to such as these" (Mt 19:14).

Adultery

Jesus emphasizes that marriage is meant to be an enduring, exclusive, permanent union, but as a provision of last resort he gives permission for divorce on grounds of marital unfaithfulness. Refusing to deal with divorce the way the scribes did, as a legal issue to be decided on technical grounds, it is unlikely that Jesus means for us to wrangle about definitions of marital unfaithfulness. Jesus acknowledges that the one-flesh relationship between husband and wife can be violated to such an extent as to permit divorce and the possibility of remarriage. According to Jesus, divorcing one's spouse on any other grounds than marital unfaithfulness reduces the second marriage to an adulterous affair. If sex between a husband and wife symbolize the oneness of the marital union, then sex outside marriage can become grounds for marital collapse. We must be clear, however: Jesus never commands divorce. Divorce is never required as a consequence of a spouse's actions. Jesus permits divorce because of the hardness of the human heart.

The unique power of illicit sex to destroy marriage as well as the soul is discussed by the apostle Paul. He claims that sexual immorality violates not only the marriage relationship but the believer's relationship with the Lord. Paul insists, "The body is not meant for sexual immorality, but for the Lord, and the Lord for the body. . . . Do you not know that your bodies are members of Christ himself?" he asks. "Shall I then take the members of Christ and unite them with a prostitute?" The apostle's response is emphatic, "Never! Do you not know that he who unites himself with a prostitute is one with her in body? For it is said, 'The two will become one flesh.' But he who unites himself with the Lord is one with him in spirit" (1 Cor 6:13, 15-17).

Sin is sin, but the power of sexual immorality to destroy marital intimacy and true spirituality is especially potent because it goes to the core of our being and threatens our soul like few other sins can.

That is why Paul is so emphatic: "Flee from sexual immorality. All other sins a man commits are outside his body, but he who sins sexually sins against his own body" (1 Cor 6:18). As Brendan Byrne explains:

> The immoral person perverts precisely that faculty within himself that is meant to be the instrument of the most intimate bodily communication between persons. He sins against his unique power of bodily communication and in this sense sins in a particular way "against his own body." All other sins are in this respect by comparison "outside" the body—with "body" having in this verse the strong sexual overtones that appear to cling to it throughout the passage as a whole. No other sin engages one's power of bodily personal communication in precisely so intimate a way.[13]

Marital unfaithfulness has become so widespread that every precaution should be taken to assure personal faithfulness and sexual purity. If a person of King David's spiritual stature, "a man after God's own heart," could commit adultery, deception and murder, who are we to think that we are above temptation? (2 Sam 11—12). The apostle's warning, "If you think you are standing firm, be careful that you don't fall!" is surely relevant for us today (1 Cor 10:12).

As in the case of David, optimal conditions for adultery surround many of us. A Near Eastern potentate's exercise of his sovereignty to obtain sexual gratification from any desired source was about as accepted in David's culture as sex on campus is in ours. The sovereignty of the self and the sensuality of the situation are strikingly familiar. Leisure and luxury afforded David the opportunity to gratify his fantasies. It cannot be said that the circumstances of life conspired against him, but we can see how his circumstances and ours may weaken the resolve to remain faithful to the Lord. His advantageous circumstances became a snare to him, even as our personal freedom may become a trap to us. As M. Scott Peck says, "We are not forced to be trapped by evil. We set up the trap ourselves."[14]

"Adultery is never a sudden, spontaneous, and totally unexpected act," writes Walter Wangerin. "It is always preceded by a longer drama, at the beginning of which we are not helpless."[15]

Something of the horror of being unfaithful and the tragedy of the spiritual and relational consequences should weigh on our minds. A healthy and holy fear of the Lord should impress our hearts. "Let no one seriously insist of his adultery, 'I couldn't help it. I don't know what came over me.'" Wangerin is right. "No adultery is sudden. Every adultery has its lingering history. Only the willfully blind are taken by surprise."[16]

Soulcraft strengthens the bond of marriage not only for the sake of pleasure but for the protection of the marriage. Marital partners are aware of the dangers that threaten their relationship and they work to protect one another from the seduction of the soul. They don't allow secret sectors or closeted compartments of life to develop between them. Resources are not drained off into private accounts. Life is shared completely and unreservedly. There is sensitivity between husband and wife in the way they relate to others. Flirtatious behavior and passes are identified. "They sound the warning at the 'maybe' moments. Moderate jealousy is an alarm bell to be heeded—and only those who are self-centered in their love think all jealousy purely suspicious and evil."[17]

Marriage partners who practice soulcraft have a fearful respect for the power of evil and cultivate a responsive moral sensitivity. When they read warnings in God's Word such as, "Each one is tempted when, by his own evil desire, he is dragged away and enticed," they don't dismiss it or make light of it. They know that the Holy Spirit's warning is as real for them as it is for anyone: "Then, after desire has conceived, it gives birth to sin; and sin, when it is full-grown, gives birth to death" (Jas 1:14-15). We would do well to share Billy Graham's fear of the Lord: "I have run scared for nearly 40 years. I stay scared, afraid that I may do something or say something that might bring disrepute to the name of Christ or hurt the Gospel. I have prayed that God would take me to heaven before I would do something that would hurt the cause of Christ."[18]

Abandonment

If marital unfaithfulness was limited to adultery alone, the grounds for divorce would be simple. But as the apostle Paul indicated to the believers at Corinth, divorce and remarriage are more complicated than illicit sex. The hardness of the human heart does not lend itself to simple black and white solutions. One of the issues facing the Corinthian church was whether or not a believer should remain married to an unbelieving spouse. It was not an issue of believers marrying unbelievers. Paul's response to that particular issue can be safely assumed. "Do not be yoked together with unbelievers," applies to many aspects of life, not the least of which is marriage (2 Cor 6:14). It would have been inconceivable to Paul that a believer would willingly marry an unbeliever. "What does a believer have in common with an unbeliever?" (6:15). The situation Paul had in mind was that one marriage partner might come to Christ whereas the other did not. Paul's counsel is clear, "If any brother has a wife who is not a believer and she is willing to live with him, he must not divorce her. And if a woman has a husband who is not a believer and he is willing to live with her, she must not divorce him" (1 Cor 7:12-13).

Paul follows the spiritual direction of Jesus by respecting the permanency of the marriage union and by treating each gender equally. Initiating a divorce is the prerogative of the unbeliever, not the believer. If the unbeliever desires to remain married to the Christian spouse, they should remain married. Paul sees great redemptive advantage to this for the sake of the unbelieving spouse and their children. He assumes that the believing spouse will have a powerful impact for Christ on the entire family (1 Cor 7:14). But if the unbelieving spouse wants out of the marriage, Paul advises the believing spouse to allow it. "A believing man or woman is not bound in such circumstances; God has called us to live in peace" (7:15).

We can only imagine how much false guilt the apostle Paul dismisses by offering this spiritual direction. He frees the believing spouse from feeling forced to remain in a marriage where the unbelieving spouse despises the faith and wants a divorce. I agree with biblical scholars who conclude that Paul's "marital release" establishes the freedom to remarry.

It is obviously not Paul's purpose to teach a more casual approach to divorce and remarriage. On the contrary, he emphasizes that the initiative in the divorce is the burden of the unbeliever, and that to remain married offers the potential of eternal redemption. "How do you know, wife, whether you will save your husband? Or, how do you know, husband, whether you will save your wife?" (1 Cor 7:16). Nevertheless, Paul's encouragement, "God has called us to live in peace," is important spiritual direction to consider when counseling couples whose marital crisis has led to irreconcilable differences. Paul clearly develops the teaching of Jesus to make provision for divorce and remarriage on grounds other than extramarital sex. He addresses the phenomenon confronting the Corinthian church by applying the teaching of Jesus in a new way. He expands the notion of marital unfaithfulness to include an unbelieving spouse's insistence on a divorce.

Abuse

What if the unbelieving spouse doesn't insist on a divorce but constantly abuses spouse or children? From what we know of human nature we would expect that some husbands might seek to punish their wives for their faith rather than initiate a divorce. Or what if a wife says she is a believer but acts like she hates her husband? What would Jesus say about the bond of marriage that has become bondage, even though there is no hint of sexual immorality? Is there relief from a marriage that has become a living hell for all involved?

Emotional and physical abuse may destroy a marriage as profoundly as adultery. Violence in the home is a form of marital unfaithfulness that we dare not ignore or refuse to address. Both husbands and wives may be abusers; however it is usually the husband who victimizes the wife and children. James and Phyllis Alsdurf in their book *Battered into Submission* describe the profile of the wife abuser. Usually his very legalistic, highly traditional worldview supports an exaggerated need to dominate his wife and children. He is often a victim of abuse himself and may have witnessed his father abusing his mother. Typically he has poor verbal skills and difficulty understanding his own emotions. He has a negative self-image and fears intimacy. His dual personality can be charming and cruel, selfish and generous. He is extraordinarily possessive and extremely jealous.

The profile of the abused wife reveals a woman who is warm, sensitive, empathetic and forgiving. According to Dr. Constance Doran, founding director of Fuller Theological Seminary's SAFE (Stop Abusive Family Environments) program, she "sees herself as entirely responsible for her husband's emotional and spiritual well-being."[19] She doesn't want to admit to herself that her marriage is awful and that she is living with a cruel abuser. She hopes each violent outburst will be the last as she prays for her husband to change. Yet she reaffirms her resolve to endure her husband's torture. As the Alsdurfs observe, "Out of guilt, fear, a sense of religious duty, helplessness or just a lack of options, battered women generally stay with their abusive husbands long after it is safe or responsible to assume that change will come."[20]

Instead of admitting that wife and child abuse exists and is a very real problem in Christian homes, the church often ignores abusive husbands and compounds the guilt and fear of the abused wife and children. The myth is fostered that wives drive their husbands to beat them. Abused wives allegedly needle and nag and frustrate their nonverbal, passive husbands until they finally explode in rage and strike back. Paul Meier and Frank Minirth have the nerve to imply that women bring on the abuse by provoking their husbands. It is hard to imagine that the following could be said to a woman seeking help because of an abusive husband: "Whenever a battered wife comes seeking advice and consolation because her husband beats her up twice a week, our usual response is, 'Oh, really! How do you get him to do that?'"[21]

The tragedy of wife abuse reveals the false standard that many conservative Christians assert unbiblically and accept uncritically. In the words of Rev. Marvin De Haan, "The primary responsibility for a good relationship in marriage lies with the wife. If the wife is submissive to her husband, they'll have a good relationship."[22] The apostle Paul tells husbands to love their wives just as Christ loves the church and gave himself for her (Eph 5:25), but some conservative Christians seem bent on condoning the behavior of husbands who turn to violence to work out their frustrations and self-esteem problems.

More than ten years ago I received the following letter after preaching a message on wife abuse:

> Thank you for such a beautiful sermon yesterday. I am sure that there were women sitting in church who needed to hear many of the things you shared.
>
> In all the years I have been attending church, you are the only minister I have heard make positive and definite statements in defense of women on this subject. Why is this? Could it be that deep down a lot of pastors really believe that the biggest responsibility for a good marriage rests with the woman?
>
> I remember sitting in church one Sunday and hearing a pastor say that he had advised a woman to go back to her husband, even though he had threatened to kill her. I sat there very angry inside, and wondering how he could possibly know what that woman had to endure. I felt that the attitude he had was a dangerous one. That scares me when a minister thinks that way. Why do people expect women to endure things they would never expect of a man?
>
> I also want to say that there are many difficult women who make things very hard for men to have a good relationship.
>
> I think an important thing you brought out was that it might be necessary for a woman to leave her husband. I am sure that you will get some disagreement there! Nevertheless it needed to be said, and we thank you for having the courage to say it!

In addition to identifying and addressing the tragedy of marital abuse, the church ought to encourage responsible action. No one should feel consigned to an abusive marriage or trapped in a life-threatening situation. In cases of chronic abuse, permission to divorce is as valid as if the abuser is an adulterer or an unbeliever who insists on a divorce. Adultery, abandonment and abuse qualify as acts of marital unfaithfulness. They are hardhearted attacks against marriage that lead to brokenness.

The prophet Malachi draws an analogy between apostasy and divorce. The spiritual strength of the people of God is reflected in the strength of their marriages. He claims there is an inevitable connection between spiritual fidelity and sexual fidelity. Wherever there is idolatry there is adultery and wherever there is adultery there is idolatry. The two were linked in Malachi's day and they are linked today. When a husband abandons the wife of his youth, he abandons the God of his people. Malachi asks, "Did not one God create us? Why do we profane the covenant of our fathers by breaking faith with one another?" (Mal 2:10). God's concern for spiritual integrity is matched by God's concern for marital integrity. "So guard yourself in your spirit, and do not break faith with the wife of your youth. 'I hate divorce,' says the LORD God of Israel, 'and I hate a man's covering himself with violence as well as with his garment,' says the LORD Almighty" (Mal 2:15-16). For a believer to strike his wife is tantamount to demanding a divorce. In such a case, actions speak louder than words, and the victim, after considerable prayer and wise counsel, may follow through with granting the divorce. Such a situation is comparable to an unbelieving spouse insisting on a divorce from the believing partner.

Agape Love

In a no-fault world where everything is gray, soulcraft lovingly discerns the difference between real guilt and false guilt. Faithful exposition of the Word of God convicts the sinner and comforts the brokenhearted. It "penetrates even to dividing soul and spirit, joints and marrow; it judges the thoughts and attitudes of the heart" (Heb 4:12). We are all sinners, but we are not all adulterers, deserters or abusers. For the sake of repentance and redemption, evil deserves to be named, confessed and forsaken. We do the sinner no favor when we obscure sin with excuses and rationalizations.

The 1995 Hollywood-movie version of Nathaniel Hawthorne's famous *The Scarlet Letter* concludes with a rhetorical question, "Who is to say what sin is in God's eyes?" For the sake of love, soulcraft answers that question with authority and clarity. Instead of echoing the satanic question "Did God really say . . . ?" soulcraft seeks to discern the difference between the abuser and the abused, fidelity and infidelity, desertion and devotion, because, as even a child knows, they are radically different.

Soulcraft insists that it is for the good of the sinner that evil is identified and dealt with. Denial forces the sin to work like a cancer eating away at the soul. King David says it well:

When I kept silent,
   my bones wasted away
   through my groaning all day long.
For day and night
   your hand was heavy upon me;
my strength was sapped
   as in the heat of summer. (Ps 32:3-4)

If we cover up and conceal a specific sin through complex strategies of self-deception, then we refuse the power of God's forgiveness to set us free from "the sin that so easily entangles" (Heb 12:1). Soulcraft insists that there is no unpardonable sin except the refusal to repent and turn to God for mercy. God's mercy is graciously available to the worst adulterer on the face of the earth. Agape love is able to redeem the vilest abuser. No sin is too powerful to be redeemed by the work of Christ's atoning sacrifice on the cross. Repentance, forgiveness and transformation can only be accomplished through the power of God's love. Paul reminds us: "where sin increased, grace increased all the more" (Rom 5:20). To pray as David prayed, out of the brokenness of the heart, is to experience the restoration that only God can provide:

For I know my transgressions,
   and my sin is always before me.
Against you, you only, have I sinned
   and done what is evil in your sight,
so that you are proved right when you speak
   and justified when you judge. . . .

Hide your face from my sins
   and blot out all my iniquity.

Create in me a pure heart, O God,
   and renew a steadfast spirit within me.
Do not cast me from your presence
   or take your Holy Spirit from me.
Restore to me the joy of your salvation
   and grant me a willing spirit, to sustain me. (Ps 51:3-4, 9-12)

Soulcraft insists that God's gracious provision of redemption is for even the worst sinner. Remember the Samaritan woman whom Jesus met at the well (Jn 4). She had been married five times and the man she was living with was not her husband. Jesus talked with her about living water and introduced himself as the Messiah. She became convinced that Jesus was the Savior and eagerly reported to the townspeople that he "told me everything I ever did" (Jn 4:29). Jesus had sought her out and, knowing everything about her sexual past, had carried on one of the most important dialogues reported in the Gospel of John. She was just the kind of woman Jesus came to save. Do you think if Jesus had been asked to preside over yet another wedding for this saved woman that he would have? I believe he would have done so joyfully.

True soulcraft understands that there are those like the Samaritan woman who need to be convicted of their sin, and there are also those who need to be comforted because they have been sinned against. Their hearts are broken not because of what they have done but because of what has been done to them. Those who have been betrayed, abandoned and abused are in urgent need of God's consolation and comfort. The power of God's love to heal and restore a broken marriage should not be underestimated. A marriage nearly destroyed by sin can be restored. Where eros love has all but died, agape love can bring it back to life. The redemptive possibilities are great, provided there is real repentance and transformation.

God is fully able to generate forgiveness and healing in the spouse who has been sinned against. In the midst of persistent sin and abuse, suffering spouses must be released from false feelings of guilt and shame. Someone needs to declare convincingly that the suffering is not their fault. We should underscore the apostle Paul's spiritual direction: "A believing man or woman is not bound in such circumstances; God has called us to live in peace" (1 Cor 7:15). When the bond of marriage has been broken against their will, they are no longer in bondage but are free to fulfill God's will for their lives. This may mean remaining single or it may mean remarriage.

My prayer is that those who have weathered the awful storm of adultery, abuse or abandonment by an unrepentant spouse will know in the depth of their soul that God dearly loves them. Soulcraft applies the promises of God in the midst of heartache and painful memories. The ancient promise of God through Jeremiah the prophet still holds true today for those who turn to the Lord:

> "For I know the plans I have for you," declares the LORD, "plans to prosper you and not to harm you, plans to give you hope and a future. Then you will call upon me and come and pray to me, and I will listen to you. You will seek me and find me when you seek me with all your heart. I will be found by you," declares the LORD, "and will bring you back from captivity" (Jer 29:11-14).

The only way out of the relational nightmare that many people have experienced is through a primary relationship with their Lord. In the face of unspeakable humiliations there is true power in practicing humility before God. "Humble yourselves before the Lord, and he will lift you up" (Jas 4:10).

13

FROM EVERLASTING TO EVERLASTING

"From everlasting to everlasting
the LORD's love is with those who fear him,
and his righteousness with their children's children—
with those who keep his covenant
and remember to obey his precepts."

PSALM 103:17-18

F AR FROM ENABLING US TO ESCAPE THE PAINFUL EXPERIENCES OF life, soulcraft embraces the intensity of grief. Bereavement can be a soul-stretching experience. Working through grief's agony, despair, pain and exhaustion is a major task of soulcraft. To love and to be loved is to open ourselves up to the inevitable anguish of suffering and death. We cannot ignore this vital dimension of soulcraft. All that we have said about soulcraft as it pertains to sexuality and spirituality, singleness and wholeness, marital love and parental faithfulness leads us to a final, unavoidable subject, namely, grief and death. And just as there is a discernible difference between the nonbeliever and the believer on sexuality, singleness, marriage and parenting, there is a marked contrast between how the world manages grief and how Christians sanctify grief.

A Labor of Love

Soulcraft is a labor of love: God-centered love at work at the heart of our relationships. Such love abounds in practical wisdom, holy living and real hope. Soulcraft offers a vision for singleness, marriage and family life that is "filled with the fruit of righteousness" (Phil 1:11). Soulcraft's energy comes from the Spirit of Christ, who causes us to grow in the grace and knowledge of our Lord and Savior. Soulcraft is not easy in the sense of being convenient or user-friendly, and it refuses shortcuts and stopgap measures that might provide quick-fix solutions while causing long-term damage.

But it is the only thing that is truly easy, as offered by Jesus when he invites us to take his yoke upon us and learn from him, "for I am gentle and humble in heart" (Mt 11:29). Soulcraft looks to Jesus and what Jesus would do to find rest for our souls. The yoke is easy and the burden is light when the truth we accept and practice is of Jesus. Soulcraft is motivated out of the fear of God, shaped by the Word of God and energized by the Spirit of God.

Soulcraft's loving discernment is careful to distinguish between hubris and humiliation on the one hand and true humanity and humility on the other. Soulcrafters do quality work because the standard of excellence has been set by the Master. They are not making up life's solutions as they go and learning by trial and error. The tools of the trade may not be popular, but they are priceless. They may not be acceptable to many, but they are irreplaceable to those who know they are working with people made in the image of God. Soulcraft is a work of prayer, a cultivation of our mind in Christ, and a ministry of grace.

What farming is to an agricultural society, soulcraft is to a God-centered community. The family farm involves everyone in the farming experience, just as soulcraft involves everyone in the household of faith, for the craftsmanship of the soul belongs not solely to experts or specialists but to each and every follower of Jesus who desires to grow up in Christ. This is down-to-earth, back-to-the-basics, every-believer spiritual direction. Soulcraft is a labor for the sake of God that sits at the center of our relationships. It would be

tragic if we forsook this primary work for some prefabricated inferior product that promotes the self at the expense of the soul. Soulcrafters reject mass-produced conformity to the world in favor of
the slow, sometimes painstaking but often passion-filled work of
conforming to Christ.

Soulcraft's labor of love leads not only to in-depth insights but to
transformed lives. Its purpose is that we might be "pure and blameless until the day of Christ" (Phil 1:10). Clearly the aim of soulcraft is
not modest, but that in no way indicates any lack of humility on the
part of the soulcrafter. As C. S. Lewis writes, "Perfect humility dis-
penses with modesty."[1] To settle for an imperfect humility would be
out of character for the true soulcrafter, who refuses to accept moral
mediocrity and spiritual sloth. The goal of purity and blamelessness
must not be quietly put aside because there are self-righteous pre-
tenders who define and defend an inferior "purity" of their own
design. Soulcraft's high calling is determined by the Master, not by
personal desire or popular demand. In this sense it is like landing a
state-of-the-art fighter jet on an aircraft carrier or performing heart
surgery. Mediocrity is unacceptable in either the pilot or the surgeon, because lives are at stake. This is true of soulcraft as well.

When it comes to the soul, there are eternal consequences for a
sloppy, halfhearted effort. We don't set the standard, God does, and
by his grace and wisdom he transforms us "into his likeness with
ever-increasing glory, which comes from the Lord, who is the Spirit"
(2 Cor 3:18). Humility causes us to welcome this high calling with
gratitude and to accept the Lord's standard as our own. We have all
the advantages of working under the Master's supervision and all
the motivation of working at what we like to do best.

Soulcraft is a lifetime investment with an eternal reward. "Until
the day of Christ" (Phil 1:10) reminds us that the work of soulcraft
has an end in view like no other enterprise. It is so much larger and
greater than ourselves. It is an eternal work right at the heart of
everyday, ordinary life. It restores the rhythms of grace to the rou-
tines of life and inspires us to live today in the light of eternity. This
is not pie-in-the-sky religious myth but bold, practical, Christ-hon-

oring, cross-bearing living. God has set eternity not only in our hearts but at the center of every relationship, every commitment, every ambition and every grief.

The Pain of Death

I have no intention of spiritualizing grief as if to pretend that Christians somehow experience less of it. In fact, to the contrary, I am inclined to believe that Christians often suffer greater pain because the bond between loved ones is so much deeper in Christ. The grief is truly great when we lose someone dear to us whose life was in tune with God's rhythms of grace, whose sense of self-worth was rooted in Christ, and whose self-sacrifice and joy were real. The hole left by the absence of such a person, whether close friend or spouse, parent or child, leaves us gasping for air, swallowing hard and wondering whether we are going to make it. The tears come suddenly, without warning, the chest grows heavy as if weighed down with a load of bricks, and the mind alternates between dull ache and acute anguish.

Soulcrafters do not grieve less, but we do grieve differently from the world. It is not the amount of pain but the meaning of pain that distinguishes Christian grief. As the apostle Paul writes, "Brothers, we do not want you to be ignorant about those who fall asleep, or to grieve like the rest of men, who have no hope" (1 Thess 4:13). The difference between those who grieve with hope and those who grieve without hope is the difference between judgment and salvation; it is the difference between eternal death and eternal life. The secularist says that death ends all, but the soulcrafter believes that death is overcome by Christ's resurrection power. Grief without hope ends with resignation; grief with hope begins with resurrection.

The power of loss to shape the soul is something that all mature believers learn to accept. One of the best descriptions I have read of how the soul grows through loss is found in Jerry Sittser's *A Grace Disguised*. As they were driving home from a visit to an Indian reservation in rural Idaho, the Sittsers' minivan was struck head-on by a car whose driver was drunk and traveling eighty-five miles per hour. Jerry watched, panic stricken, as his wife, Lynda, his mother, and his young daughter Diana Jane all died before his eyes. His three other children survived. John, his youngest, suffered a broken femur. It is hard to imagine how his loss could have been greater. He writes, "The woman to whom I had been married for two decades was dead; my beloved Diana Jane, our third born, was dead; my mother, who had given birth to me and raised me, was dead. Three generations—gone in an instant!"[2]

What strikes me in reading Jerry's account of his experience of heart-wrenching, catastrophic loss is the depth of worship, maturity and character that God's grace had worked in his life. He describes the importance of soulcraft decisions,

> Many people are destroyed by loss because, learning what they could have been but failed to be, they choose to wallow in guilt and regret, to become bitter in spirit, or to fall into despair. While nothing they can do will reverse the loss, it is not true that there is nothing they can do to change. The difference between despair and hope, bitterness and forgiveness, hatred and love, and stagnation and vitality lies in the decisions we make about what to do in the face of regrets over an unchangeable and painful past. We cannot change the situation, but can allow the situation to change us.[3]

Through loss we face "the frightening truth of our mortality. We are creatures, made of dust. Life on earth can be and often is wonderful. But in the end all of us die."[4] The frailty of human life and the sovereignty of God are back-to-back truths which serve to anchor soulcraft in God-shaped reality.

I was twenty years old and a sophomore at Wheaton College when my father was dying from stomach cancer. I still remember the phone conversation I had with Mom as she tried to gently break the news to me that it would be good if I came home, because it didn't look like Dad was going to survive. Up to that moment the idea that my father might not live through this disease had not occurred to me. I just assumed he would get better. He was, after all, only forty-eight years old. I hung up the phone and the awful impact of what my mother was trying to tell me hit me with full force.

Ever since the death of my father I have not been able to shake the immediacy of mortality. Three years before my father's illness I had had extensive surgery for lymphoma, but that experience didn't affect my teenage expectation of immortality one bit. It wasn't until I stood beside my father as he was dying that grief and loss became real to me. As I approach the age that my father was when he died I can't help but be mindful of the brevity of life. The idea of dying from old age is a foreign concept to me. I understand what the psalmist meant when he wrote,

> As a father has compassion on his children,
>   so the LORD has compassion on those who fear him;
> for he knows how we are formed,
>   he remembers that we are dust.
> As for man, his days are like grass,
>   he flourishes like a flower of the field;
> the wind blows over it and it is gone,
>   and its place remembers it no more. (Ps 103:13-16)

To grasp the brevity of life does not mean we accept the futility of life. On the contrary, soulcrafters know that this short life span is framed by God's sovereign purposes and infused with God's eternal meaning. We pray to the Lord, "Teach us to number our days aright, that we may gain a heart of wisdom" (Ps 90:12). Joy and sorrow are closely linked in the life of the believer. To love well is to experience great loss. I have known people who felt relief over the death of their father. The relationship they had with their father was so strained and painful that they were thankful to have that chapter of their life over. But such an experience is even more tragic than death itself. The inevitable pain of loss does not cause Christians to shy away from a deep and abiding commitment to one another. We give ourselves to one another knowing that this life counts for eternity.

Choosing to Trust
The practice of soulcraft involves some very difficult choices that

require a strength and skill beyond our ability. Apart from the Master we cannot begin to sanctify grief, but with the Lord's help we can walk through the valley of the shadow of death. We are not helpless, passive creatures who sit idly by and watch the loss of a loved one slowly destroy our life. "We can run from the darkness, or we can enter into the darkness and face the pain of loss," writes Jerry Sittser.

> We can indulge ourselves in self-pity, or we can empathize with others and embrace their pain as our own. We can run away from sorrow and drown in addictions, or we can learn to live with sorrow. We can nurse wounds of having been cheated in life, or we can be grateful and joyful, even though there seems to be little reason for it. We can return evil for evil, or we can overcome evil with good. It is the power to choose that adds dignity to our humanity and gives us the ability to transcend our circumstances, thus releasing us from living as mere victims. These choices are *never easy*. Though we can and must make them, we will make them more often than not only after much agony and struggle.[5]

The convictions that guide these choices are more easily stated than practiced, but we have to know them to act on them. Soulcraft stresses the importance of learning and praying through these fundamental truths before catastrophic loss overtakes us. We will be far stronger in the day of grief if we have become personally convinced of the first conviction: that God is truly sovereign over our lives.

I remember the counsel of my wife's uncle George Long on this particular truth before he married us. He shared that on the night of their wedding his wife, Catherine, had an overwhelming dread that something terrible was about to happen to them. She feared the worst and felt paralyzed by that fear. They talked it through and reminded themselves of the Lord's sovereign care and providential purpose in their lives. They knelt and prayed on their wedding night and entrusted their lives to God's control and care, confident that nothing could happen to them apart from God's plan and purpose. Over the years George and Catherine have reminded themselves of that experience and renewed their trust in facing the future with God's peace.

Our choices are also shaped by our determination to act on a second conviction: that we must submit to God. There was a period of time when everything seemed to go wrong for our family. It began with my cancer surgery, peaked with my father's death and continued with my mother's hospitalization due to a serious heart condition. My brother wondered what was going to happen to him, and who could blame him? This sequence of events was immediately followed by the failing health and death of my grandparents and great aunt.

As I think back on it now, I marvel at the endurance and perseverance of my mother, who was the principle care giver for me, her husband, her in-laws and a distant relative who had nobody left to care for her. My mother was the one who gave the most emotional comfort and spiritual encouragement to each of us. Besides handling the myriad of details relating to doctors and insurance, she made most of the arrangements for four burials. Yet I never thought of my mother as a victim. When I think about it now—I was too young to appreciate all that she was doing for us then—she faced her life in much the same way that Jesus faced the cross. Without bitterness or self-pity, she determined to trust in God and face each day renewing her dependence upon her Lord. I don't think she ever contemplated any other way to live in the midst of this extended period of grief and loss.

The ministry of Robertson McQuilkin to his wife, Muriel, is another wonderful example of soulcraft worked out in loving ways. When he was fifty-seven years old and was president of Columbia Bible College and Seminary, Robertson McQuilkin faced the difficult question of which should be sacrificed: his formal seminary ministry or caring for Muriel. Muriel was suffering in the advanced stages of Alzheimer's. She experienced severe memory deterioration and disorientation. "It did not seem painful for her," writes Robertson, "but it was a slow dying for me to watch the vibrant, creative, articulate person I knew and loved gradually dimming out." Trusted lifelong friends urged him to arrange for institutionalization. Others handled the dilemma lightly as if the decision was obvious, "God first, family second, ministry third." But sorting out the call of God is not always easy. Robertson writes:

> When the time came, the decision was firm. It took no great calcula-
> tion. It was a matter of integrity. Had I not promised, 42 years before,
> "in sickness and in health . . . till death do us part"? This was no grim
> duty to which I stoically resigned, however. It was only fair. She had,
> after all, cared for me for almost four decades with marvelous devo-
> tion; now it was my turn. . . . As I watch her brave descent into obliv-
> ion, Muriel is the joy of my life. Daily I discern new manifestations of
> the kind of person she is,—the wife I always loved. I also see fresh man-
> ifestations of God's love—the God I long to love more fully.[6]

The third foundational conviction that guides our choices in facing grief and loss is that the salvation of God comes through the
risen Lord Jesus. Wisdom encourages us to trust in the sovereign
care of God, even though our world seems to be falling into chaos
and we join Job on the ash heap. Soulcraft calls us to submit to the
will of God, even when he leads us through Gethsemane to the
cross. Faithfulness guides us to look to God's great salvation for
peace and for joy and for life itself.

Two weeks after Tim Brewer, pastor of Central Presbyterian
Church in St. Louis, took his own life, Beth Brewer gave one of the
most powerful salvation testimonies I have ever heard. The courage, conviction and hope of this remarkable soulcrafter reminds
me of the huge difference between managing grief and sanctifying
grief. Four months before his death, Tim was seriously injured in a
train accident. Even though his leg had to be amputated and his
body was racked with pain, he returned to Central's pulpit to
powerfully preach the gospel of Christ. In retrospect it is clear that
he came back to ministry too fast. No one realized the stress he
was under until it was too late. The emotional and spiritual pressures of pastoring a large church, the demands of a young family
with three children, two of whom were severely handicapped,
together with the physical trauma and emotional despair triggered
by his disability, all added up to an overwhelming crisis. Beth
shared,

Here was a man who had suffered more than any other man I had
ever met in my life. At the time of his death, his depression was
aggravated by drugs he never should have been on, confusing the
messages he was receiving in his brain so that life no longer made
sense. He knew enough that what he was going to do was horrible,
yet he was too weak. He knew he couldn't stop himself from doing it.
In the darkest hour, terrified, alone, Tim took his life and died before
the sun rose the next morning.

The question that we all ask is "Why? Why God? Why did a man
have to suffer so much? Why didn't you just let him die in that train
accident in that tunnel? Why did you put him through those four
months of torture that you put him through?"

Beth turned to the twelfth chapter of the book of Revelation to
explain the depth of evil and the power and immensity of God's
grace that brings salvation. She then said in a voice firm and unaf-
fected,

So where does it leave us as a church? Well, first of all, I know the
psychologists have been giving us the seven steps of grieving and the
first is "Well, it's okay to be angry at God." Psychology can give us
insight in how to relate to one another in our human relationships. It
dare not dictate to us how our response to God should be. After Job
had been horribly afflicted, his wife looking at him said, "Are you still
holding on to your integrity? Curse God and die." Go ahead, Job, let
him know how angry you are. Job replied, " 'You are talking like a
foolish woman—shall we accept good from God and not trouble?' In
all this Job did not sin in what he said." What are we saying when we
say it's okay to be angry with God? We're saying to God, "We don't
trust you, you're unjust, you're unfair! How could you do this?" We
attribute horrible characteristics to God that are blasphemy.

God gets our attention. In the death of a man who was so loved and
so faithfully proclaimed the gospel of truth God disciplined his
church. Had Tim died in that train wreck we would have mourned
the loss of a godly man, but God allowed Tim to run the most gruel-
ing leg of the race and suffer the most intensely so the church would
have to look at itself and say, "What happened? What was my part in
this?" We take our anger and we look at ourselves and the Holy Spirit
enlightens the darkness that's there. We repent and fall before God

and we realize that it is impossible to obey the greatest command-
ment, which is to love God with all of our heart, mind and soul, and
we cannot love our neighbor as ourselves—as he commands us to do.
We repent. Our hearts are changed.

Tim's last words to Beth were written in his letter to her:

> As for myself I am certainly not proud of my life. I wish that I might
> have had the strength to repent one last time like Samson and glorify
> God in my death even more than in my life. Obviously I have not.
> May God have mercy upon my soul for the damage which I have
> caused to his church, his name, and worst of all to you and our
> beloved family. It has always been true, but now more than ever, I
> know that my only hope is in the blood of Christ.
>
> Yours forever,
>
> Tim

Beth closed her testimony with these words:

> My beloved husband, Samson's last words were for vengeance. It was
> God who glorified himself in Samson's death. Your last words were
> for mercy. How much more will he glorify himself in your death.[7]

Who can measure the intensity of such suffering? Both Tim and
Beth experienced the depth of grief and loss, but God's salvation is
deeper than death itself. As tragic as their situation was, the tri-
umph of God is greater! "When the perishable has been clothed
with the imperishable, and the mortal with immortality, then the
saying that is written will come true: 'Death has been swallowed up
in victory'" (1 Cor 15:54).

Gratitude

Soulcraft insists that life is not framed by loss, nor is grief the
essence of life. The overarching reality that envelopes all pain and
suffering is the grace and goodness of God. Heaven awaits saved
sinners, those who have turned to Christ for their salvation. Hell
awaits unsaved sinners, those who have refused to turn to Christ for
salvation. Life in the middle, between creation's good beginning
and redemption's everlasting new beginning, can be filled with pain

and suffering. But God's goodness and love is greater than evil. God's light outshines the darkness.

Henri Nouwen wisely warns against dividing the past into "good things to remember with gratitude and painful things to accept or forget."[8] There is a tendency to keep a running account of those things that we thank God for in our lives and those things that we wish were not in our lives. While this may seem natural, it "prevents us from truly allowing our whole past to be the source from which we live our future." Nouwen observes, "Gratitude embraces all of life: the good and the bad, the joyful and the painful, the holy and the not so holy."[9] Everything is bracketed by God's grace. Even the dark night of the soul awaits the dawn of God's renewing grace. As Betsy ten Boom neared death in a Nazi prison camp she assured Corrie of this truth, "There is no pit so deep that he [God] is not deeper still."[10] And Job, after suffering loss upon loss, firmly declared: "I know that You can do all things; no plan of yours can be thwarted" (Job 42:2).

Nouwen asks if gratitude for everything is "possible in a society where gladness and sadness, joy and sorrow, peace and conflict, remain radically separated."

> Is it truly possible to embrace with gratitude all of our life and not just the good things that we like to remember? Jesus calls us to recognize that gladness and sadness are never separate, that joy and sorrow really belong together, and that mourning and dancing are part of the same movement. That is why Jesus calls us to be grateful for every moment that we have lived and to claim our unique journey as God's way to mold our hearts to greater conformity with God's own.[11]

At my dad's memorial service I may have spoken better than I knew. I welcomed the people who packed the sanctuary, my father's colleagues, students, neighbors and church family, with the apostle Paul's words, "Rejoice in the Lord always. I will say it again: Rejoice!" (Phil 4:4). I am sure that some people attending the service thought we were in denial; several made comments to that effect in the days and weeks that followed. But looking back I don't believe we were in denial—we were far from it, especially my mother. I remember her quiet determination to see both the loss and the hope as real and to trust in Christ for both.

Jerry Sittser movingly writes:

> The grief I feel is sweet as well as bitter. I still have a sorrowful soul; yet I wake up every morning joyful, eager for what the new day will bring. Never have I felt as much pain as I have in the last three years; yet never have I experienced as much pleasure in simply being alive and living an ordinary life. Never have I felt so broken; yet never have I been so whole. Never have I been so aware of my weakness and vulnerability; yet never have I been so content and felt so strong. Never has my soul been more dead; yet never has my soul been more alive. What I once considered mutually exclusive—sorrow and joy, pain and pleasure, death and life—have become parts of a greater whole. My soul has been stretched.
>
> Above all, I have become aware of the power of God's grace and my need for it. My soul has grown because it has been awakened to the goodness and love of God. God has been present in my life these past three years, even mysteriously in the accident. God will continue to be present to the end of my life and through all eternity. God is growing my soul, making it bigger, and filling it with himself. My life is being transformed. Though I endured pain, I believe that the outcome is going to be wonderful.[12]

Gratitude causes us to acknowledge that those who are most precious to us are a gift from the Lord. The people God brings into our lives are an evidence of his grace, not our merit. An honest way to diffuse the anger that we might feel toward God because of the loss of a loved one is to remind ourselves that everything about that loved one that caused us joy came directly from God. We don't deserve the gift of a son or daughter; we don't possess our friends; we can't proudly stamp "mine" on our relationships. When that painful, heart-wrenching loss comes, as surely it will, we must be prepared to say with Job, "The LORD gave and the LORD has taken away; may the name of the LORD be praised" (Job 1:21).

After the memorial service for my dad, my grandfather Haumersen gave my mother a letter he had received from my dad dated three weeks before his death. In the midst of his suffering he made a point of expressing his gratitude:

March 1, 1972

Dear Dad,

It is not often that I pen a note, in fact I would be hard pressed to remember the last time. I am writing this *unknown* to Louise and so I would rather you not make reference to the letter. You will receive the message and that is the important part. Ever since my operation in July I have not felt A-1 as I continued to receive 500 mg of SFU (chemotherapy) every week. It will be nine months this March and that is the time limit one generally gets the medication. This medication does have some side effects though they didn't catch up with me until the last few weeks and I have felt very sick as a result. My reason for writing is not to tell you about myself and how sick I have been. I can praise the Lord and trust that now I am over the medication he will heal me completely and will feel like swinging a hammer again soon, etc.

My real reason for writing is to let you know what a wonderful daughter you have, what a wonderful wife and mother she has been to us. Her patience, care, love and nursing has helped me through these difficult times. There were times when I was weak, somewhat scared, though I never felt the Lord let go of me, still Louise with her steadfast faith that the Lord would see us through not only in my case but also Douglas, was a momentous testimony to her faith as a rock, unmovable. I wanted to share this with you. Please take care of yourself and watch out for the ice. Stick around the house until the sun is out.

Love, Don

If soulcraft involves gratitude, and God's grace permeates everything—even pain and suffering, grief and loss—then what the apostle writes is true: "In all things God works for the good of those who love him, who have been called according to his purpose" (Rom 8:28). Then those whose hope is in God can "consider it pure joy" when they face "trials of many kinds, because [they] know that the testing of [their] faith develops perseverance" (Jas 1:2). They can

agree with Paul that "our present sufferings are not worth compar-
ing with the glory that will be revealed in us" (Rom 8:18). Soulcraft
enables us to bracket the brevity of life, with its pain and sorrow,
with the words "Praise the LORD, O my soul; all my inmost being,
praise his holy name" (Ps 103:1). Worship is both the first word and
the last word for those who have put their confidence in Christ. For
"we have this hope as an anchor for the soul, firm and secure" (Heb
6:19).

Eternity

Do we dare to live all of life from the viewpoint of eternity? This
radical soulcraft distinctive underscores the true nature of our relational experience: we can, as it were, take it with us! Soulcraft is
either delusional from start to finish or truly perceptive of the most
real world. "If for this life only we have hoped in Christ, we are of
all people most to be pitied. But in fact Christ has been raised from
the dead" (1 Cor 15:19-20 NRSV). Life's true vantage point allows us
to look beyond the brevity of life to eternity and inspires faithfulness, not fatalism. "From everlasting to everlasting the LORD's love
is with those who fear him" (Ps 103:17).

In response to the Sadducees, who were trying to put him on the
spot, Jesus said that marriage is a temporary provision for life on
this side of eternity. They had posed the most complicated relational
scenario they could think of: A woman had been married in turn to
seven brothers. Each time a brother died, the next brother in line
married his widow according to Old Testament law. Their question
was simple: "Now, then, at the resurrection, whose wife shall she be
of the seven, since all of them were married to her?" (Mt 22:28).

"You are in error," Jesus replied, "because you do not know the
Scriptures or the power of God. At the resurrection people will neither marry nor be given in marriage; they will be like the angels in
heaven" (Mt 22:29). In other words, "If you think you're going to
take your broken, sin-damaged relationships into heaven, forget it!"

The simplicity on the other side of our complex world will be
characterized not by our mixed motives and hardness of heart but

by the truth and power of God. Eternity with God opens up a whole new realm of relational fulfillment, which is only hinted at in the best of human friendships and loving marriages. On this side of eternity, at times, we can hardly imagine a love deeper and more fulfilling than that of our beloved. We feel like the couple in the Song of Songs who are passionately in love. Who could possibly imagine anything better than this? But the answer comes back: God can. Our expectations are too low. We mustn't underestimate the power of God. As the apostle says, "'No eye has seen, no ear has heard, no mind has conceived what God has prepared for those who love him,' but God has revealed it to us by his Spirit" (1 Cor 2:9-10).

We must take care not to imagine heaven as a place that is in any way less satisfying relationally than friendships and marriages on this side of eternity. I am confident that we will one day laugh about such thoughts, wondering how we could have possibly been skeptical about heaven's fulfillment. What if in eternity all of our friendships are like the best friendship we ever experienced—only better? What if heaven is not so much minus marriage but all marriage? I expect that the intimacy, companionship and fidelity that we desire in a good marriage is but a prototype of all relationships in heaven. The very imagery God's Word uses to describe the day of Christ, the marriage supper of the Lamb, anticipates a day when all loves will be empowered by the wisdom, purity and holiness of our beloved Lord. Soulcraft anticipates that day with earnest expectation.

Notes

Chapter 1: Soulcraft
[1]"Carpentry," in *The Compact Edition of the Oxford English Dictionary* (Oxford: Oxford University Press, 1971), 1:342.
[2]John Stott, *Christian Mission in the Modern World* (Downers Grove, Ill.: InterVarsity Press, 1975), p. 29.
[3]Donald Lake, "Soul," in *Zondervan Pictorial Encyclopedia of the Bible*, ed. Merrill C. Tenney (Grand Rapids, Mich.: Zondervan, 1975), p. 496.
[4]Garrison Keillor, *Wobegon Boy* (New York: Viking, 1997), p. 16.
[5]G. K. Chesterton, *Orthodoxy* (New York: Image, 1959), p. 31.
[6]Stephen R. Covey, *The 7 Habits of Highly Effective Families* (New York: Golden, 1997), pp. 160-62.

Chapter 2: Rhythms of Grace
[1]Ronald Dahl, "Burned Out and Bored," *Newsweek*, December 15, 1997, p. 18.
[2]Søren Kierkegaard, "Either/Or," in *A Kierkegaard Anthology*, ed. Robert Bretall (Princeton, N.J.: Princeton University Press, 1946), p. 24.
[3]Ibid., p. 30.
[4]Ibid., p. 31.
[5]Ibid.
[6]Wiley Miller, Washington Post Writers Group, February 1994.
[7]Kierkegaard, "Either/Or," p. 32.
[8]Walter Brueggemann, *Genesis* (Atlanta: John Knox Press, 1982), p. 35.
[9]John Greenleaf Whittier, "Dear Lord and Father of Mankind."
[10]Derek Kidner, *Psalms 1—72* (Downers Grove, Ill.: InterVarsity Press, 1973), p. 99.
[11]Ibid.
[12]C. S. Lewis, *Miracles* (New York: Macmillan, 1947), pp. 137, 141.

Chapter 3: The Soulful Self
[1]Carl Sagan, *A Pale Blue Dot* (New York: Random House, 1994), p. 405.
[2]Loren Eiseley, "The Cosmic Orphan," in *Encyclopaedia Britannica, Propaedia* (Chicago: Encyclopaedia Britannica, 1998), p. 139.
[3]Tom Wolfe, "Sorry, but Your Soul Just Died," *Forbes*, December 2, 1996, pp. 220-22.
[4]C. Stephen Evans, *Preserving the Person* (Downers Grove, Ill.: InterVarsity Press, 1977), p. 14.
[5]Sheila Larson, quoted in Robert N. Bellah, *Habits of the Heart* (New York: Harper & Row, 1985), p. 221.
[6]Daniel Yankelovich, *New Rules: Searching for Self-Fulfillment in a World Turned Upside*

Down (New York: Bantam, 1981), p. 8.
[7]Ibid., p. 187.
[8]Jack Miles, "God Decentralized," *New York Times Magazine*, December 7, 1997, p. 55.
[9]Yankelovich, *New Rules*, p. 239.
[10]C. S. Lewis, *Surprised by Joy* (London: Fontana, 1959), pp. 176, 182.
[11]Sigmund Freud, *The Future of an Illusion* (New York: W. W. Norton, 1989), p. 24.
[12]J. I. Packer, "Decadence," *Christianity Today*, October 2, 1987, p. 13.
[13]John Calvin, *Institutes of the Christian Religion* 1, bk. 1, trans. Henry Beveridge (Grand Rapids, Mich.: Eerdmans, 1981), pp. 37-39.

Chapter 4: Wholeness
[1]Michael Cavanaugh, *God's Call to the Single Adult* (New Kensington, Penn.: Whitaker, 1986), pp. 67-68.
[2]Dr. and Mrs. Hudson Taylor, *God's Man in China* (Chicago: Moody Press, 1965), pp. 17-18.
[3]Ibid., p. 28.
[4]Ibid., p. 129.
[5]Ibid., p. 132.
[6]Ibid., p. 144.
[7]Corrie ten Boom with John and Elizabeth Sherrill, *The Hiding Place* (Chappaqua, N.Y.: Chosen, 1971), p. 31.
[8]Ibid., pp. 44-45.
[9]Joni Eareckson Tada, *Joni* (Grand Rapids, Mich.: Zondervan, 1976), p. 7.

Chapter 5: Friendship
[1]C. S. Lewis, *The Weight of Glory* (New York: Macmillan, 1949), p. 19.
[2]C. S. Lewis, *The Four Loves* (New York: Harcourt Brace, 1960), pp. 66-67.
[3]Eugene H. Peterson, *The Wisdom of Each Other* (Grand Rapids, Mich.: Zondervan, 1998), p. 17.
[4]Lewis, *Four Loves*, p. 89.

Chapter 6: Two Loves
[1]Garrison Keillor, *Wobegon Boy* (New York: Viking, 1997), p. 36.
[2]Ibid., p. 58.
[3]Ibid., p. 61.
[4]C. S. Lewis, *The Four Loves* (New Hork: Harcourt Brace, 1960), p. 125.
[5]Helen E. Fisher, *Anatomy of Love: The Natural History of Monogamy, Adultery, and Divorce* (New York: W. W. Norton, 1992), p. 61.
[6]Ibid., p. 93.
[7]Ibid., p. 109.
[8]Ibid., pp. 116-17.
[9]Henri Blocher, *In the Beginning* (Downers Grove, Ill.: InterVarsity Press, 1984), p. 100.
[10]Ibid., p. 101.
[11]Ibid., p. 96.
[12]Walter Brueggemann, *Genesis* (Atlanta: John Knox Press, 1982), p. 33.
[13]Dietrich Bonhoeffer, *Creation and Fall* (New York: Macmillan, 1959), p. 62.
[14]Mike Mason, *The Mystery of Marriage* (Portland, Ore.: Multnomah Press, 1985), p. 35.

[15]Ibid.

[16]Augustine *Confessions*, in *Nicene and Post-Nicene Fathers*, ed. Philip Schaff (Peabody, Mass.: Hendrickson, 1994), 1:45.

Chapter 7: Body & Soul

[1]Peter Brown, *The Body and Society: Men, Women, and Sexual Renunciation in Early Christianity* (New York: Columbia University Press, 1988), p. 10.

[2]Ibid., p. 17.

[3]Ibid., p. 56 (emphasis added).

[4]Ibid., p. 77.

[5]Ibid., p. 78.

[6]Ibid., p. 86.

[7]Ibid., p. 96.

[8]Ibid., p. 274.

[9]Augustine *The City of God* 14.6, in *Nicene and Post-Nicene Fathers*, ed. Philip Schaff (Peabody, Mass.: Hendrickson, 1994), 2:276.

[10]Ibid., 14.18.

[11]Ibid., 14.26.

[12]Augustine *Confessions* 8.11, in *Nicene and Post-Nicene Fathers*, ed. Philip Schaff (Peabody, Mass.: Hendrickson, 1994), 1:126 .

[13]Ibid., 8.12.

[14]Brown, *Body and Society*, p. 424.

[15]Ibid., p. 427.

[16]Robert Farrar Capon, *Bed and Board: Plain Talk About Marriage* (New York: Simon & Schuster, 1965), p. 111.

[17]Bernard of Clairvaux, *The Love of God* (Portland, Ore.: Multnomah Press, 1983), p. 172.

[18]Ibid., p. 239.

[19]Ibid., p. 105.

[20]Tom Gledhill, *The Message of the Song of Songs* (Downers Grove, Ill.: InterVarsity Press, 1994), p. 13.

[21]Brown, *Body and Society*, pp. 103-4.

[22]Mike Mason, *The Mystery of Marriage* (Portland, Ore.: Multnomah Press, 1985), p. 113.

[23]Gledhill, *Message of the Song of Songs*, p. 128.

Chapter 8: East of Eden

[1]Dietrich Bonhoeffer, *Creation and Fall* (New York: Macmillan, 1959), p. 63.

[2]Paul Mickey, "Get Rid of the Lust in Your Life," *TSF Bulletin*, March-April 1986, p. 11.

[3]Tim Stafford, *The Sexual Christian* (Wheaton, Ill.: Victor, 1989), p. 59.

[4]Tom Wolfe, *The Bonfire of the Vanities* (New York: Farrar, Straus & Giroux, 1987), p. 54.

[5]Allan Bloom, *The Closing of the American Mind* (New York: Simon & Schuster, 1987), p. 99.

[6]Ibid., p. 106.

[7]C. S. Lewis, *The Four Loves* (New York: Harcourt Brace, 1960), p. 121.

[8]Michael Wilcock, *The Message of Judges* (Downers Grove, Ill.: InterVarsity Press, 1992), p. 130.

[9]Walter Wangerin Jr., *As for Me and My House* (Nashville: Thomas Nelson, 1987), p. 195.

[10]Ibid., p. 196.

[11]Name Withheld, "The War Within: An Anatomy of Lust," *Leadership,* fall 1982, pp. 30-48.

[12]Ibid., p. 31.

[13]Ibid.

[14]Ibid., p. 33.

[15]Ibid., p. 40.

[16]Ibid., p. 43.

[17]Ibid., p. 45.

Chapter 9: Conviction & Compassion

[1]Andrew Tobias, "Gay Like Me," *Harvard Magazine,* January-February 1998, p. 102.

[2]Ibid., p. 103.

[3]John Boswell, *Christianity, Social Tolerance, and Homosexuality: Gay People in Western Europe from the Beginning of the Christian Era to the Fourteenth Century* (Chicago: University of Chicago Press, 1980).

[4]Peter J. Gomes, *The Good Book* (New York: Morrow, 1996), p. 158.

[5]Ibid., p. 162.

[6]The Authorized Version of Scripture uses "effeminate" *(malakoi)* and "abusers of themselves with mankind" *(arsenokoitai)* to refer "to the more passive and the more active partners, respectively, in any male homosexual act" (Craig L. Blomberg, *The NIV Application Commentary: 1 Corinthians* [Grand Rapids, Mich.: Zondervan, 1995], p. 118). In Paul's language, *arsenokoitai* appears to come from two words, *arsenos koiten,* in Leviticus 20:13 (Septuagint), the strongest prohibition of homosexuality in the Old Testament (see D. Malick, "The Condemnation of Homosexuality in 1 Corinthians 6:9," *Bibliotheca Sacra* 150 [1993]: 479-92). There is no evidence in the text that what Paul had in mind was limited to the Greek practice of pederasty. The plain reading of the text "must be seen as an all-encompassing condemnation of homosexuality (as in Leviticus 20:13), including consenting adult homosexual relationships" (James R. Edwards, "The Bible and the Practice of Homosexuality," *Theology Matters,* May-June 1995, p. 4).

[7]Edwards, "Bible and the Practice of Homosexuality," p. 5.

[8]Thomas E. Schmidt, *Straight & Narrow? Compassion & Clarity in the Homosexual Debate* (Downers Grove, Ill.: InterVarsity Press, 1995), pp. 122, 130.

[9]Joanne Blackford, personal testimony, Vineyard Christian Fellowship of Goleta, Goleta, Calif., September 1996.

Chapter 10: Soulmates

[1]Maggie Gallagher, *The Abolition of Marriage: How We Destroy Lasting Love* (Washington, D.C.: Regnery, 1996), p. 8.

[2]Robert Farrar Capon, *Bed and Board: Plain Talk About Marriage* (New York: Simon & Schuster, 1965), p. 22.

[3]Eugene H. Peterson, *Run with the Horses* (Downers Grove, Ill.: InterVarsity Press,

1983), p. 68.

[4]Mike Mason, *The Mystery of Marriage* (Portland, Ore.: Multnomah Press, 1985), p. 45.

[5]Eugene H. Peterson, "Should We Pay More Attention to the Lord's Day?" in *Tough Questions Christians Ask*, ed. David Neff (Wheaton, Ill.: Victor, 1989), pp. 13-14.

[6]Ibid., p. 13.

[7]Capon, *Bed and Board*, pp. 46-47.

[8]C. S. Lewis, *The Four Loves* (New York: Harcourt Brace, 1960), p. 105.

[9]Capon, *Bed and Board*, p. 47.

Chapter 11: A Little Seminary

[1]Eugene H. Peterson, *Growing Up with Your Teenager* (Old Tappan, N.J.: Revell, 1976), p. 17.

[2]Ibid., p. 18.

[3]Gerald L. Sittser, *A Grace Disguised* (Grand Rapids, Mich.: Zondervan, 1996), p. 90.

[4]Peterson, *Growing Up*, p. 18.

[5]Mary Pipher, *Reviving Ophelia: Saving the Selves of Adolescent Girls* (New York: Ballantine, 1994), p. 44.

[6]Ibid., pp. 183-84.

[7]William Willimon and Stanley Hauerwas, *Resident Aliens* (Nashville: Abingdon, 1989), p. 58.

[8]Peterson, *Growing Up*, pp. 10-13.

[9]Edith Schaeffer, *What Is a Family?* (Old Tappan, N.J.: Revell, 1975), p. 83.

[10]Robert Farrar Capon, *Bed and Board: Plain Talk About Marriage* (New York: Simon & Schuster, 1965), p. 46.

Chapter 12: Brokenness

[1]John Stott, *Issues Facing Christians Today* (Hants, England: Marshalls, 1984), p. 259.

[2]Robert Wright, "Our Cheating Hearts," *Time*, August 15, 1994, p. 50.

[3]Ibid., p. 52.

[4]Helen E. Fisher, *Anatomy of Love: The Natural History of Monogamy, Adultery, and Divorce* (New York: W. W. Norton, 1992), p. 311.

[5]Ibid., p. 115.

[6]Barbara Dafoe Whitehead, "Ending the Church's Silence on Divorce," *Christianity Today*, November 17, 1997, p. 51.

[7]Ibid.

[8]Maggie Gallagher, *The Abolition of Marriage: How We Destroy Lasting Love* (Washington, D.C.: Regnery, 1996), p. 214.

[9]Ibid., p. 7.

[10]John Leo, "Where Marriage Is a Scary Word," *U. S. News & World Report*, February 5, 1996, p. 22.

[11]Mike Mason, *The Mystery of Marriage* (Portland, Ore.: Multnomah Press, 1985), p. 59.

[12]Judith S. Wallerstein and Sandra Blakeslee, *Second Chances: Men, Women and Children a Decade after Divorce* (New York: Ticknor & Fields, 1989), p. 7.

[13]Brendan Byrne, "Sinning Against One's Own Body: Paul's Understanding of the Sexual Relationship in 1 Corinthians 6:18," *Catholic Biblical Quarterly* 45 (1983): 613, quoted in Craig L. Blomberg, *The NIV Application Commentary: 1 Corinthians* (Grand Rapids, Mich.: Zondervan, 1995), p. 127.

[14]M. Scott Peck, *People of the Lie* (New York: Simon & Schuster, 1983), p. 118.

[15]Walter Wangerin, *As for Me and My House* (Nashville: Thomas Nelson, 1987), p. 196.

[16]Ibid., p. 197.

[17]Ibid., p. 198.

[18]"Interview with Billy Graham," *United Brethren*, September 1987.

[19]James Alsdurf and Phyllis Alsdurf, *Battered into Submission* (Downers Grove, Ill.: InterVarsity Press, 1989), p. 36.

[20]Ibid., p. 34.

[21]Paul Meier and Frank Minirth, *Happiness Is a Choice* (Grand Rapids, Mich.: Baker, 1978), pp. 96-97.

[22]Marvin De Haan, "Have You Excommunicated Your Spouse?" *Good News Broadcaster*, March 1982, p. 47.

Chapter 13: From Everlasting to Everlasting

[1]C. S. Lewis, *The Weight of Glory* (New York: Macmillan, 1949), p. 13.

[2]Gerald Sittser, *A Grace Disguised* (Grand Rapids, Mich.: Zondervan, 1996), pp. 18-19.

[3]Ibid., p. 86.

[4]Ibid., p. 54.

[5]Ibid., pp. 37-38.

[6]Robertson McQuilkin, "Living by Vows," *Christianity Today*, October 8, 1990, pp. 38-40.

[7]Beth Brewer, personal testimony, Central Presbyterian Church, St. Louis, Mo., July 1995.

[8]Henri J. M. Nouwen, "All Is Grace," *Weavings*, November-December 1992, p. 39.

[9]Ibid.

[10]Corrie ten Boom with John and Elizabeth Sherrill, *The Hiding Place* (Chappaqua, N.Y.: Chosen, 1971), p. 217.

[11]Ibid., p. 40.

[12]Gerald Sittser, *Grace Disguised*, p. 180.